Truth and History

Truth and History

Murray G. Murphey

SUNY PRESS

Published by
State University of New York Press, Albany

Printed in the United States of America

For information, contact State University of New York Press, Albany, NY
www.sunypress.edu

Production by Eileen Meehan
Marketing by Anne M. Valentine

Library of Congress Cataloging-in-Publication Data

Murphey, Murray G.
    Truth and history / Murray G. Murphey.
        p. cm.
    Includes bibliographical references and index.
    ISBN 978-0-7914-7623-9 (hbk. : alk. paper)
    ISBN 978-0-7914-7624-6 (pbk. : alk. paper)
    1. History—Philosophy. I. Title.

D16.8.M884 2009
901—dc22   2008003128

10 9 8 7 6 5 4 3 2 1

For Michael Zuckerman

Contents

Preface

I started working on this book when I was a child. My mother used to read to us at night, and our favorite book was the *Iliad*. Naturally enough, my brother and I played at refighting the Trojan War. Since he was older and bigger than I was, he was Achilles and I was Hector, and I got dragged three times around the house on a number of occasions. I never got to be Achilles.

It did not occur to me to question the reality of Achilles and Hector until one day my brother told me that they were made-up characters. I did not believe him until my mother confirmed what he had said. But how could anyone know whether or not they were real? I could understand that one could know about things one remembered, but how could one know about the past before that? That problem never left me, until years later I found what I think is the answer.

When I went to college, I studied American history and read the standard manuals on historiography, such as Charles Langlois and M. J. C. Seignobos,[1] These only confused me more. But I had the good fortune to live next door to my classmate Burt Dreben, even then a protégé of W. V. Quine's. I used to have long arguments about these issues with Burt. He convinced me that most of what I thought I knew was wrong, but he provided no answers—at least none that I could accept He did, however, make me a devout empiricist.

When I began to write serious history myself, it struck me that what I was doing was constructing a theory about the past that would explain currently observable data. If that was so, then historical "interpretations" were really theories, and the observations on which they were based were of presently observable objects. I was confirmed in this belief by reading R. G. Collingwood. Once I realized that, I saw that the idea of history as copying the past could not be right since the past was gone, so the standard correspondence theory of truth made no sense applied to history.

I spent a lot of time puzzling over the skeptical writing of Charles Beard, who was then regarded as the great American historian, and the standard manuals, until one day I heard Carl Hempel tell the story of how Kekule discovered the benzene ring. Going home after that class, it dawned on me that all of the skeptical arguments about history being subjective and perspectival and biased were the result of looking at the process from the wrong end. All of those arguments dealt only with the process of creating a historical account, but if one looked instead at the process by which historical theories were tested, then the role of subjectivity in the creation of the theory was irrelevant. It did not matter if your theory was suggested to you in a dream, as Kekule's was; all that mattered was whether or not it was true, and that was a question of how well the theory did when it was tested *after* it was created.

The hardest nut for me to crack was the question of historical explanation. Having been a student of Hempel's, I found his arguments for the covering law thesis irrefutable. It took me a long time to free myself from that doctrine, and what finally did it was reading Nancy Cartwright's work. Historical explanations, I belatedly discovered, do not need covering laws—well, many of them do not. What a relief that discovery was!

The last piece that fit into the puzzle was the status of narrative. I found all sorts of crazy doctrines being put forward by the so-called postmodernists, such as Paul de Man's claim that Marcel Proust was really writing about writing when it was perfectly obvious he was doing no such thing.[2] But historians do write narratives, so the question was, why is the narrative form so useful to them? It seemed to me that there are three reasons: narratives are ideal for presenting chronological sequences, and since the direction of causation is from past to future, they are excellent vehicles for presenting causal models, and they provide an effective way to describe change. But the narrative form itself is not limited to such uses, as its use in fiction makes obvious.

This book owes a great deal to a great many people. Somewhere in heaven Burt Dreben is probably arguing with Bertrand Russell about some point in logic; I hope he will have time to accept a thank-you from me. I am grateful to Bruce Kuklick and Michael Zuckerman for their criticisms of this work, without which it would be sorely lacking. And I am grateful to all of the students who endured my attempts to make my ideas clear, even though I often failed to do so.

Chapter 1

Metaphysics and Epistemology

This chapter deals with the nature of historical knowledge. It is generally agreed that history does yield some form of knowledge, and that historians believe that their works tell the truth. In view of the fact that the past persons and events that history deals with no longer exist, the question of how historical knowledge is possible requires an answer. I discuss here several proposed answers to that question: those of Representative Realism, Constructionism, AntiRealism, and Justificationism. The position I will defend is that of Constructionist Realism.

⊂⊳◇⊲⊃

History, understood as a form of knowledge, is an account of what existed and happened in the past and why it happened. This is not the only meaning of the term *history*, which sometimes refers to past events themselves rather than our knowledge of them, but it is the appropriate one if our interest is in the knowledge of the past and how we acquire it. So conceived, history seems to assume that there is a past to be known. The metaphysical question is whether or not that past is real; the epistemological question is how we know the past and its contents. These two questions are not independent, but they are conceptually distinct.

The commonsense view—the view embraced by most historians—is that obviously the past is real; even the question will strike most historians as ridiculous. But what is obvious often turns out to be obscure. Where does our notion of the past come from? The answer, again obviously, is from our own memories. It is just a fact that we do remember what has happened in our own pasts. Even young children remember what happened yesterday, or last week. No doubt for the child the most compelling evidence of the past is its personal memory, but that is soon extended by the memories of others. The child hears its elders talk about times before it can remember and learns that events occurred even before the child's birth. And in due course, the child comes to

1

share in a vast stock of memories held by members of its community. That there is a real past is thus for all of us undeniable. But, still, there are problems about the past that are not thus solved.

One is the limited character of the past known from memory. The memories of one's neighbors go back only a short time; what happened before that? There are, of course, traditions, myths, legends, and memory chains, where what one generation has told to the next is passed on to its progeny, and so on. These sources can be useful, particularly when they are institutionalized in social structures designed to ensure their accuracy. But they still take us only a short way. Anthropologists tell us of societies where there is little knowledge of or interest in what lies beyond living memory; the deep past is referred to as a "dream time" or "the time before," but little is known about it.[1] But Western cultures are interested in the deep past, and it is quite clear that our knowledge of the Roman Empire or Periclean Athens or the Old Kingdom of Egypt is not based on memory alone. Perhaps the clearest case of all is Sumer; even the existence of Sumerian civilization had been completely forgotten until archaeologists began to unearth Sumerian artifacts.

The second problem is that our memories are not always true. We discover that what we think happened did not happen or did not happen as we remember it. Others disagree with our accounts; their memories contradict ours, or we find that our own memories contradict each other, or we find a record that shows our memory is wrong. We are thus forced to recognize that memory, even our own, is not infallible. How, then, do we sort out which memories are true and which are false?

We cannot in this case go back and compare what we remember with what actually happened. The past event is forever gone; there is nothing to compare our memories to. We can require that our own memories be consistent. C. I. Lewis proposed that we should require them to be "congruent," meaning that the probability of any one memory is increased if the others are taken as premises. But, as Lewis noted, this is not enough. There are consistent formal systems, such as Lobachevsky's geometry, that are not true. Lewis's answer is that we must give prima facie credibility to our own memories; just the fact that we remember something gives that memory an initial, if a small, probability. This will allow any particular memory to be impeached, but not all of our memories at once, and, together with the requirement of congruence, it is enough to guarantee credibility to our memorial knowledge. But it must be emphasized that credibility is not certainty. The initial credibility of memories, just because they are memories, is small. Any given memory, or set of memories, may well turn out to be false. Granting initial credibility to our own memories gives us a place to start in assessing our memorial knowledge; it is no more, but no less, than that.[2]

Why should we grant such initial credibility to our memories? Lewis's answer is Kantian; without veridical memory, we can have no knowledge at all. Even to recognize that something is, for example, a tree assumes that our present sensory image can be compared to past experiences of trees and their likenesses noted. If I had no veridical memory, then I would have no basis for classifying my immediate experience; I would be faced with a shifting phantasmagoria of light and sound of which I could make no sense. The choice is therefore between initial credibility for memory or total skepticism of the moment.[3]

But the initial credibility I grant my own memories does not extend to the memories of others, nor do they extend a like courtesy to me. I remember seeing Franklin Roosevelt; for me that memory is indelible. But to anyone else, it is just what I say—my testimony as to what happened long ago. They do not remember it, and they need not believe me. Similarly, what others remember is for me simply their testimony, and like any testimonial evidence, it must be evaluated in terms of the competence of the witness, an opportunity to observe the events reported, motives, and bias, and all of the usual factors that go into the evaluation of testimonial evidence. I must give my own memories initial credibility, or I can know nothing, but I need not give such credibility to the memory reports of others.

Memory, therefore, can give us assurance that some past events and persons are real, but it does not carry us back very far. What about the reality of the deep past—the past beyond the reach of living memory? What most historians do is accept the reality of the deep past as a metaphysical postulate and go on from there. Little in the way of justification is ever given for this postulate beyond what seems to them to be common sense. After all, if memory assures us of the reality of the recent past, then why should we not assume the reality of the deep past too? But this position, reasonable as it may seem, involves serious problems. First, it should be noted that ideas about the extent of the deep past have varied wildly over time. Until 1859, almost all educated Americans believed that the world was created as the Bible says it was, and so that human history was only a few thousand years old, and a great many people in this country, and others, still believe that. Only after James Hutton did geologists begin to push the age of the earth farther and farther back, and it was Charles Darwin's incomparable achievement to have shown that human history was far deeper than anyone had previously believed possible. Only in the twentieth century, with Edwin Hubble's discovery that the universe was expanding, did astronomers begin to grasp how long ago the universe began. We still do not know just when Homo Sapiens first walked the earth, and the tale of his ancestry is still confused. The extent of the deep past, human and cosmological, has proven very difficult to determine.

But the most complex problems raised by this metaphysical view are epistemological. If we begin with the assumption of a real deep past, then how do we know that our ideas about it are true? The usual answer to this question is Representative Realism. In its standard form, Representative Realism holds that

1. there is a real world,

2. we have access to that world through sensory experience,

3. on the basis of such experience, we can construct a theory about the real world,

4. our theory about the real world is approximately true as far as it goes, though it may be incomplete, and

5. alternative theories are possible, but further data can be found that will decide among them.

This leaves us with a correspondence theory of truth and no way to prove that the correspondence actually obtains. Restating this position in terms of the past, consider the following:

1. There is a real deep past, with real people and events.

2. We can access that past through sensory experiences of documents and artifacts that survive to us.

3. From these data, if they are adequate, we can reconstruct what happened in the past.

4. Our reconstructions may be incomplete, but given adequate data, they are approximately true.

5. Alternative interpretations of the data will be possible.

The last point calls for a particular comment. Most historians regard alternative interpretations of the data as simply a fact of life. This conviction rests upon the fact that the body of data regarding any historical question is limited, and that unlike natural scientists, historians cannot expand their database at will. Given any fixed, finite body of data, it is always possible to invent alternative theories that can explain the data. But it does not follow that those alternative theories will be equally good at explaining new data as they are discovered.

The other propositions raise problems as well. Historical events and actions no longer exist; we have no sensory access to them. Can we in fact access these past factors through surviving remains? And, if so, just how is that done? Most critical of all, how do we know our "reconstructions" are true about the real people and events of long ago? We have again a correspondence theory of truth with no way to prove that the correspondence obtains. It is not surprising that under these conditions history became a favorite subject for Idealists, who believed that—somehow—we could share the thoughts of people of long ago.

If the Metaphysical (i.e., Representational) Realist position described earlier is unsatisfactory, then what are the alternatives? The two that will require discussion are Constructivism and AntiRealism. The former is also a realist position, while the latter is not. We will look first at Constructivism, which is the position I wish to defend, and then at two versions of AntiRealism—van Fraassen's and Dummett's.

Whatever are to serve as historical data must be objects that are observable to us now.[4] We cannot observe historical events directly, as they no longer exist. Even in the case of memory, we have only our present memories of what once occurred. For reasons already discussed, we must grant our own memories initial credibility, but no such requirement holds for other data, including the testimony of others. What we actually confront are various objects, which may be documentary or nondocumentary, about which we pose such questions as: Where did this come from? Why is it here? What is it for? These objects are all that remains to us from the past and are our only contact with the deep past. Whatever we can know about that past must be based on the observation of these currently existing objects.

Viewed in these terms, our historical accounts are hypotheses to account for present data. If we wonder why a particular building is so hideous, then we construct an account of when, why, and by whom it was designed and built that will explain why it looks the way it does. Such an account is an explanatory hypothesis to account for our observations. Again, if in Aunt Tilly's attic we find a letter dated June 3, 1840, and signed "Henry Livingston," and we want an explanation of it, then we try to construct an account of who Henry Livingston was and why this letter should have been in that attic. The function of such accounts is explanatory; the accounts tell us why what we now observe is as it is.

Historians usually think of their accounts as both descriptive and explanatory; What constitutes an adequate description of an event includes a description of what they take to be the chief causal factors involved. Thus an account of Burgoyne's defeat at Saratoga will emphasize Howe's abandonment of the original plan that called for him to drive up the Hudson to meet Burgoyne and his attack on Philadelphia instead, Burgoyne's problems of supply, the mobilization of the colonial forces, and so on. A historian writing about a particular event wants his readers to understand what happened, and part of understanding what happened is understanding why it happened.

Historians usually think of themselves as explaining historical "facts": Why did the French Revolution occur? Why did McKinley win the 1896 election? Why did Burr shoot Hamilton? Historians are not wrong about what they do, but what needs to be noted is that historical "facts" are themselves constructs to account for present data. We cannot observe the French Revolution or the election of 1896 or the duel. That these events ever occurred are hypotheses to explain data that we have now. The electoral records, newspaper accounts, journal accounts, campaign literature, campaign buttons, and so on that remain today from the 1896 election are the data on the basis of which we say that the election took place and that McKinley won; that claim explains the data that we have. We will of course ask why McKinley won over Bryan, which is a question about how matters relate within our hypothetical account, but whatever the answer we give, it must also rest on and account for present data. Historical knowledge is a theoretical construct to account for presently observable data.

This point requires some elaboration. When a historian embarks upon an investigation, he rarely thinks of himself as explaining the existence or the characteristics of a datum. Such studies do occur—witness the controversy over the Vinland map—but usually the historian seeks to explain such things as why the Civil War occurred, why the French Revolution occurred, or why Woodrow Wilson won in 1912. That is, the historian usually undertakes to explain facts in terms of other facts, but doing so obviously takes the existence of these facts for granted. Yet as we have seen, none of those "facts" are observables; that there was a Civil War in 1861 or a Revolution in France we only know on the basis of certain presently observable data. We account for that data by hypothesizing that the Civil War occurred and the French Revolution occurred; only then does it make sense to ask about why they occurred. Thus if one views our historical knowledge as a whole, it is a complex structure. At the base are our observations of the data themselves, and upon that base rests the claims of what persons and facts existed.

Then we have the questions of how past facts and persons relate. An explanation of why the Civil War occurred is also an explanation of a mass of data from which the facts are inferred. One can see why the classical historiography should have thought the facts were established first and then interpreted. But the classical historiography was wrong. Facts are part of the theory; they are as much postulates to account for the observable data as are the relations among them that classical historiography considered to belong to the "interpretation," that is, to the theory. Even the distinction between fact and theory is unclear. That the Civil War occurred is a fact. But how do we know that? We know it because we have masses of data—documents, legends, artifacts, myths—the existence of which is best accounted for by postulating that the Civil War occurred. If the data were sparser, then we would be less certain of the fact. Did Samson really thrash the Philistines in the Le Hi Valley? We are less certain that this is a fact because we have only one documentary source for it. Or consider the following case. In eastern Nebraska there is a stream called the Weeping Water. The name translates an equivalent Indian name that was established before Lewis and Clark reached the area and comes from an Indian legend that two Indian tribes fought a battle at what is now the headwater of the stream in which all of the warriors on one side were killed. When their widows and daughters reached the battlefield, they wept over the fallen, and from their tears came the stream.[5] Is it a fact that such a battle took place? The occurrence of the battle would explain why the stream was given the name it bears. Yet although the legend exists in several forms, all of which agree on the occurrence of the battle, I think no historian would consider the evidence (data) sufficient to assert that the occurrence of the battle is a fact.

It may seem odd to refer to historical accounts as theories, but here I follow Quine in holding that one's theory about something is the set of sentences about that thing one holds for true.[6] In an obvious sense, historical accounts have to be theoretical, since they postulate the existence of objects and events that are not observable and so must be indirectly confirmed. But does it really make sense to say that the existence of Abraham Lincoln is a theoretical postulate? In such a case, the amount of data is so overwhelming that it seems absurd to question Lincoln's existence. But to get a sense of what is involved, consider cases where the amount of data is not overwhelming. Take, for example, Samson, Abraham, and Moses. We do have data to support the hypotheses of their existence, namely, the Bible. Yet I think only biblical literalists believe that Samson was a real person. The question of Abraham is more difficult. The Bible is the *only* evidence that supports the claim for his reality, just as it is for Samson's, and it is unlikely that any other evidence will ever come to light. Whether or not he ever existed remains an open question. The case of Moses is the most complicated. With Abraham, the nature of the biblical story, if true, makes it unlikely that there is any other source but the Bible. This is not true of Moses. Given the Egyptian captivity of the Jews, the events the Bible describes concerning Moses, the Exodus, and so forth, one might predict that there would be both Egyptian records and archaeological data supporting the biblical account. None of these have been found. The events described in the Bible involved the highest levels of the Egyptian state, yet no Egyptian record mentions any of them. Worse, according to the Bible, a large population of Jews resided in Egypt for an extended period of time. One would think that there would be some archaeological evidence of such a community, yet the search for such evidence has thus far been fruitless. Given the centrality of Moses and the Exodus to Jewish history, one hesitates to say that Moses never existed, and that the Exodus never occurred, but we have only the biblical evidence to support that claim, and none of the corroborating data that might have been expected have been found. Since the Egyptians rarely recorded events that were unflattering to themselves, one can try to explain away the lack of Egyptian records, but the lack of archaeological data from the Jewish settlement is troubling. Here the postulational character of historical reconstruction is obvious.

Some may object that if we can only postulate the existence of the past and its contents to account for present data, then vast stretches of the past will be left empty. There is something to this objection, but not much. It should be a truism that we can only know what we have evidence for; if there is no evidence for something, then we have no reason to believe in it. Of course this means that our theories about the past must be incomplete. Consider Stonehenge. There is virtually no chance that we will ever know the individual identities of the builders of Stonehenge, but we do know that it was built by people, and we can form some reasonable hypotheses about its purpose. Or consider the Northeast Woodland Indians before the coming of the Europeans. We know they were there because we have evidence of it—chiefly archaeological. We will never know their names or the details of their lives, but we can construct reasonable theories about how they lived from the data that we do have. In these cases, our theories are incomplete, but that does not make them false. One can know some things truly about a subject without knowing everything about it.

A further objection is that past persons are postulated to be human beings, and human beings, considered as a natural kind, are the sort of

entities that are observables. To say that past persons are not observables therefore seems to involve a contradiction. But what this objection
overlooks is the relative character of the terms *observable* and *observed*.
To say that x is observed is to say that x stands in the relation "___ is
observed by ___" to some y, which for present purposes we may take as
a variable ranging over some set of present-day human beings. Similarly,
to say that x is observable is to say that x stands in the relation "___
can be observed by ___" to some y. Observability therefore depends
upon the characteristics of the observer as well as those of the thing
observed. When a chemist says that a carbon molecule is observable,
he does not mean that it is observable to anyone, but to anyone who
has the necessary training and equipment. Thus for x to be observable
does not mean that any y can observe x, but that certain y's having
certain characteristics can observe x. The same obviously holds true with
respect to unobservability. Consider colors. Certainly colors are observable if anything is, but they are not observable for the blind. Moreover,
in this case they cannot be made observable to the blind. This is not a
case of acquiring certain training and equipment, as in the case of the
molecule; the disabling factor of the blind is such that it is impossible
for it to be remedied, and so for those unlucky folk color is not only
unobservable but unobservable in principle (i.e., such an observation is
for them physically impossible). Now consider the case of stars. Usually
stars as a kind are taken to be observables. But if inflationary theories
of the universe are correct, then there are stars we can never see, since
they are so far away from us that the light they emit can never reach
us. It is true that if we could travel to different regions of space than
the one we occupy, we could observe them, but for us to reach those
regions of space would require us to travel faster than light, which is
physically impossible. Such stars, assuming they exist, are therefore for
us not only unobservable but unobservable in principle, since for us to
observe them would involve the violation of the laws of nature. The
analogy to the case of historical persons is exact. Historical persons, such
as Moses, and historical events, such as the Exodus, no longer exist and
are not observable by us. The temporal distance between us and those
people operates like the spatial distance in the example of the stars. It
is perhaps true that we could have observed Moses had we lived in his
time and place (assuming of course that he really did exist), but we
cannot observe him now. And since time travel is an impossibility, we
cannot go back to his time to observe him, nor can he come forward
into our time where we can observe him. Moses is therefore not only
unobservable for us but unobservable in principle. Thus being a member of a kind the members of which would be observable if they were

present in our time and space does not imply that members of that kind not present in our time and space are observable, or even that they are observable in principle.

Moritz Schlick[7] held that a sentence was cognitively meaningful if it was verifiable, that is, if its verification was logically possible. Many things are logically possible that are not physically possible. Granted that observations of past persons and events are not physically possible, are they logically possible? There are well-known arguments that they are not. Suppose a scientist—call him "Quinn"—invents a time machine that allows him to travel back in time to the year after his grandfather was born. This supposition involves a contradiction, since if Quinn travels back before the date of his own birth, he would not exist and therefore could not travel to the year after his grandfather's birth. However, let us assume for the moment that Quinn's machine somehow allows him to travel in time without changing his own age. Then it would be physically possible for Quinn to murder his grandfather while he was still an infant. Therefore, Quinn cannot exist. So we have the contradiction that Quinn both exists and does not exist. Further, A. J. Ayer has shown that time travel is *logically* impossible. Suppose that Quinn, being a careful type, writes his will before he climbs into his time machine and zips back to September 1, 1750, where he stays for one week before returning to his own time—let us say 2005. Then Quinn's trip and his experiences in the eighteenth century occurred after he wrote his will. But his experiences in 1750 must have occurred before he wrote the will, since 1750 is before 2005. But no event can occur both before and after a given time unless the event is continuous, which in this case it obviously was not. Hence Quinn's trip involves a logical contradiction. Time travel is not only physically impossible but logically impossible. Thus Ayer has shown that direct observation of past persons and events is logically impossible and therefore impossible in principle.[8]

Ayer goes on to say, "From the fact that one cannot now observe an event which took place at an earlier date, it does not follow that the event itself is to be characterized as unobservable."[9] But this statement does not mean quite what it seems to mean, for Ayer says

> in dealing with statements about the past, we remarked that their analysis was not affected by the fact that they were expressed at times when it was no longer possible to observe the events to which they refer. The requirement that they should be verifiable was not held to entail that any particular person . . . should in fact be capable of verifying them. If one is to have any reason

for believing them one must, indeed, have access to some evidence in their favour, but such evidence need only be indirect. It is not required that one should perform the impossible feat of returning to the past.[10]

Ayer's point is that to make a statement such as "Vicksburg was captured on July 4, 1863" is verifiable, is to say that it *could have been* verified by direct observation at the time it occurred. The contrast Ayer is making is between something that no one could ever observe because it is self-contradictory, such as a spherical cube, and an event such as a battle that could be observed by a suitably positioned observer. But Ayer's argument implies that it is logically impossible for an observer now to observe a past person or an event, since that could only be done through time travel. The event in question was observable in its own time, but to claim that it is observable now involves a contradiction. To a present observer, it is therefore unobservable in principle.

One caveat should be entered here. Given the finite velocity of light, when we observe a distant star we are actually observing light that left that star a long time ago. In cases such as that, it seems to make sense to say that we are observing things in the past. But we are not; what we are observing is light emitted by that star long ago but only reaching us now, owing to the finite velocity of light. This case has no analogy to our observation of persons or events in the past of the earth. There is no medium with finite velocity reaching us from the Battle of Austerlitz.

But are the events and objects postulated to exist in historical theories real? Since the theory says they existed, they are real if the theory is true. But is the theory true? One cannot claim in any field of knowledge that one's theory is certainly true. What one can say is that if one's theory explains all of the known data about its subject, is consistent with all related theories, continues to explain novel data as they are found, and performs these functions better than any alternative theory, then it may provisionally be held as true—that is, as our best current estimate of the truth. As is true in every field, any given theory may turn out to be wrong, but our best-confirmed theories provide the best explanations that we have for the data time has left us. Furthermore, this sort of Constructivism does not involve a correspondence theory of truth. The real is what a true theory says is real; there is no metaphysical object lurking beyond that to which our theory must answer. Truth depends on the relation of theory to data, not correspondence. We thus avoid the problems of Representative Realism, yet we retain a realistic theory of the past.[11]

There is a further point to be made here. As applied to history, or science, Representative Realism gives us a dual standard of truth: the theory must copy reality, and it must be the best explanation of the data. It is possible that a theory meeting one standard might not meet the other. One can imagine a case in which a demon so selected the data we have that the theory that best accounts for them would not copy reality. But this sort of problem assumes that we somehow know what the reality is independently of the data we have. The difficulty is that we have no access to the reality except through the data. That being the case, the reality can only be what our best explanation of the data says it is. It follows that in a fairly trivial sense, our constructionist theory does provide a correspondence theory of truth, since our theory obviously corresponds to the world it describes. Unless there is some way of knowing the real that is independent of our data, the postulation of such an independent reality leaves us with an unknowable *ding-an-sich*. As an empiricist, I do not believe there is any way of knowing reality except through the theory that best explains our data, and I see nothing to be gained by the belief in an unknowable metaphysical entity.

But the question of biased data is not to be dismissed. In any body of data from a past society it is almost always the case that those who were wealthy will be overrepresented. Knowing this, the historian can stratify his set of data by wealth, weight the strata by the proportion of the population in the strata, and then proceed with his account. This requires a knowledge of the size of the past population and of the distribution of wealth within it, neither of which is easy to come by. But rough estimates of these should normally be sufficient, and such estimates can be devised from a variety of sources. For example, if the rich and the poor lived in different sections of the city, then estimates of the number of people in each section can be used. Or if, as in early Philadelphia, the rich lived on the main streets and the poor in the alleys, then again estimates can be made. Similarly, in farming areas the land quality varies from place to place. The rich will have the good land, and the poor will have what is left. And if one is very lucky, there will be documents such as the U.S. Census which is a gold mine of information of the sort needed.

Much of the skepticism promulgated by postmodernists such as Foucault apparently rests on the assumption that all Realism is Representative Realism. Having recognized that the metaphysical reality so assumed cannot be accessed by our investigations, they have retreated into some form of linguistic idealism according to which all that we can know is our own language. But this view is false. First, as lately shown, not all Realism is Representative Realism; the Constructivist Realism outlined earlier is not subject to these problems. Second, it denies the obvious fact that language refers to an external nonlinguistic world. This oversight may be due, at least in part, to the influence of Saussure, whose linguistic theory deals only with the relation of signs to concepts and ignores reference, but it leads to absurdities, such as taking texts to refer to themselves. Linguistic Idealism is no more credible than the other forms of Idealism, and considerably less so than Absolute Idealism.

The Constructivist Realism I outlined earlier is strongly contested by the AntiRealists. But the application to history of AntiRealist theories, such as van Fraassen's, raises some very interesting points. Van Fraassen holds that with respect to any scientific theory, we should believe as true those statements of the theory that refer to present observables only. He has no hesitation in using theories, such as those of quantum mechanics, that postulate the existence of unobservable entities in order to derive statements referring only to observables, but he holds that we have no basis for believing that any portions of these theories that involve unobservables are true, or that the entities they postulate are real. Thus to van Fraassen, scientific theories are black boxes that take as inputs only statements regarding present observables and have as outputs only statements regarding present observables; these we should hold to be true. But the contents of the black box—the theories themselves, with their claims for the existence of unobservable entities—we should consider merely instrumental, and no truth claims for them are legitimate.[12]

How does AntiRealism fare when applied to history? Consider, for example, the U.S. Constitution. It is generally accepted that this document was written in 1787 by a convention held in Philadelphia, and the names of the men who attended that convention are well known. How would the van Fraassen-type AntiRealist deal with the Constitution? On his theory, all talk of the Constitutional Convention, of Washington, Madison, Hamilton, Franklin, and so on, is merely instrumental; we must not believe that they are, or ever were, real, or that statements about them are true. We can talk about the document that is observable now, but we have no explanation of who wrote it or why. We can observe their signatures on the document, but since the men themselves are unobservable, we cannot explain how these inscriptions came to be there. Since an unreal cause cannot have real effects, we are left with no explanation at all of where the document came from, or why it is as it is. In fact, the AntiRealist faces a very interesting problem in dealing with history. Since the past people and events do not now exist, they are not observable, and therefore the AntiRealist cannot believe they are, or ever were, real, or that statements about them are, or ever were, true.

Now the AntiRealist will doubtless answer that whether the Founding Fathers are now observable or not, they are (were) the sorts of things that would be observable if they were present now, and therefore are observable in principle. But aside from this use of counterfactuals, which poses a problem for an AntiRealist, he is wrong in this conclusion. The Founding Fathers *are* unobservable *in principle*. They do not now exist. Since time travel is both physically and logically impossible, we cannot now go back to the eighteenth century to observe them, nor can they travel into our time where we can observe them now. It makes no more sense to talk of observing the Founding Fathers than it does to talk of observing quarks. It is impossible *in principle* that such observations as the AntiRealist demands can now be made of these men. For us, they are theoretical constructs whose *epistemological* status is not different from that of quarks. Thus the AntiRealist finds himself committed, in the case of history, to the unreality of the whole of the historical past.

The AntiRealist position of the van Fraassen type is, I believe, a position that is untenable. It would deny the reality of the deep past and leave us adrift in time, with no knowledge of how we got here, no sense of the cumulative experience of humankind that undergirds our beliefs, and no foundation for the standards and loyalties that inform our lives. It would rob historical accounts of any explanatory power, since the causes of real effects cannot be unreal, and leave us with a world that came to be we know not how, with practices the origins of which we could not explain, with objects such as Independence Hall that for all we know might have fallen from the sky, and documents such as the U.S. Constitution that might have arisen by spontaneous generation.

Van Fraassen's AntiRealism is an extreme form of empiricism that denies reality to anything not directly observable by us with our unaided senses. Michael Dummett's AntiRealism is a very different position. He views the Realist as being committed to a truth condition theory of meaning and to bivalence—the doctrine that every statement is true or false on the basis of some state of affairs. In an article published in 1978, Dummett held that with respect to statements about the past, the Realist is committed to the existence of states of affairs for the existence of which no effective decision procedure is possible. For if every statement is true or false, then regardless of whether or not we can determine its truth or falsity, we are compelled to assume the existence of a state of affairs that makes the statement true or false, even though we have no evidence for the existence of that state of affairs. Accordingly, he held that AntiRealism must be adopted.[13]

In his recent Dewey lectures, now republished and expanded in book form, Dummett says that he was not happy with his 1978 article and has been perplexed by the problem of the reality of the past ever since. He now tries to resolve this perplexity by rejecting extreme AntiRealism about the past. If such AntiRealism about the past were true, Dummett says that only statements supported by present evidence could be affirmed, and this he holds would mean that large portions of the past would vanish as evidence concerning them is lost or destroyed. "This conception," he says, "though not incoherent, is repugnant."[14] Indeed, Dummett holds that if the past and its contents are theoretical constructs based on presently existing evidence, then the past cannot be real; nothing would then exist but the present. Statements about the past could not refer to any real person or events, since none of these would be real. Such a position he regards as intolerable, and it is his intention to show, in these lectures, that what he calls a "justificationist" position can legitimate statements about the past without adopting Realism.

Dummett's theory of meaning is based on the intuitionist view of mathematics, which holds that a mathematical statement is meaningful only if there is an effective means of constructing a canonical proof for it. For empirical propositions, Dummett holds that meaningfulness requires that the statement either is or could be verified, where "verification" is widely construed as "having grounds sufficient to warrant asserting the statement." With respect to statements about the past, Dummett asserts his conviction that the truth of such statements is independent of whether or not there is present evidence for them. What is required for the truth of such a statement is that had someone been present at the relevant time and place in the past he could have observed the events referred to by the statement. That is, it is sufficient on the justification-ist view of meaning that the statement could have been verified if an observer had been there to make the observation.[15]

Dummett holds that on the justifictionist view of empirical state-ments, there is a "gap" between what the statement says is the case and what verifies the statement. Thus the statement "People in Afghanistan are starving" refers to the condition of people in Afghanistan, but it does not say how the statement is to be verified. The existence of this gap leads Dummett to introduce the distinction between what can be directly verified and what can be indirectly verified. Direct evidence for this statement would require eyewitness reports from Afghanistan on the situation there; indirect evidence could be obtained from data on death rates, food production, and so on. Both types of evidence can verify a statement, either together or singly. Thus some statements can be verified solely by indirect evidence.[16]

Applying this to history, Dummett holds that the truth of a state-ment referring to events for which we have no direct evidence can be affirmed by the use of a conditional: "If someone were to have been at hand at the relevant time, he could have observed an event of that kind."[17] Hitler's suicide was not an observed event. But the criterion for the truth of "Hitler committed suicide on April 30, 1945" is that had an observer been present in the right time and place in Hitler's bunker on April 30, 1945, he would have observed Hitler shooting himself.[18]

Dummett strongly emphasizes the fact that our knowledge, like our language, is not an individual possession but the common property of a community. Since he holds that all languages are intertranslatable, he takes this community to include all people. Much of what we know comes not from our own observations, but from reports of the observations of others. I may not go to Afghanistan to observe conditions on the ground, but others do, and their reports of their observations serve as direct evidence for me. But Dummett extends the boundaries of the community to encompass not only the living but the dead. Records of what people did observe in the past, memories of past events, and even memories passed down through a succession of generations are equally good evidence as the testimony of a living informant. The dead are as much members of our community as the living, and the observational reports of the dead are direct evidence for the truth of statements concerning the past events. But suppose no observer was present when a given past event occurred (e.g., Hitler's suicide). "Indirect evidence for the truth of a statement about a place where no observer was present must show that a suitably located observer could have made observations giving direct grounds for its truth: that is how indirect evidence must be related to direct evidence."[19] Given the sort of event that a suicide by shooting is, what is known about Hitler's bunker, and so on, we can hold that if an observer had been in the right place in the bunker at the right time, he could have observed Hitler's suicide.

Dummett notes that his justificationist position represents a step toward realism, but it does not go the whole way. Specifically, it does not legitimate bivalence; it cannot be assumed that every conditional whose antecedent is unfulfilled is either true or false. Such an assumption would be equivalent to assuming the world to be determinate independently of our experience. That, Dummett holds, is a realist position, and one that a justificationist cannot accept.[20]

There are several points on which Dummett's position seems to me to fail. First, he makes a great point of the degree to which to be observable means to be observable by some members of our community. This is, of course, true, but the claim requires qualification—it is not the case that all members of the community can be regarded as equally qualified observers. Hilary Putnam pointed out that our society, like every other, has people who are regarded as experts on certain subjects and whose testimony on those matters is awarded more weight than the testimony of others.[21] Reports of observers are testimony, and they must be evaluated by the usual rules for evaluating testimony—was the observer competent, did he or she have adequate opportunity, was he or she biased, and so on. In our society we simplify this problem by establishing institutionalized methods of certifying the competence of observers and criticizing the testimony they give. Chemists can speak with authority on chemical matters, but they are subject to review by other chemists. Reports on conditions in Afghanistan by President Bush's supporters will very likely not be accepted as direct evidence of anything but administration policy. The observations of all observers are not equal, and Dummett entirely ignores the myriad problems of evaluating evidence by assuming that they are.

Second, the extension of the community to include the dead is a mistake. Communications from the dead, particularly the long dead, are not addressed to those now living but to those who were the contemporaries of the dead. Those people were not members of our community, but of past communities, and much of our problem is to reconstruct just what those communities were, how their members communicated, and what those communications meant. Their writings involve terms and are based on conceptual schemes that are not ours, and the longer ago they died, the more likely are such sources of misunderstanding. No aspect of Kuhn's writing on the history of science is more admirable than his demonstration that past scientists were members of communities who believed in worldviews different from ours and whose observations were based on premises we now reject and in some cases report phenomena we are unable to reproduce. The same holds true for past communities in general; the New England Puritans saw the world in terms very different from ours. Anyone who reads the accounts of the Salem witch trials must be impressed by the fact that those people believed in and testified to the existence of things we do not believe ever existed. The literature of the past is filled with testimony of observations of witches, demons, angels, miracles, and all types of supernatural events that we find it impossible now to believe were real. To accept as true all of the observations reported by everyone in the past would leave us with a mass of contradictory claims. That is why in dealing with past observers, it is necessary to treat the artifacts that remain from them as data to be explained by devising hypotheses about them that account for these data. Thus, for example, if one looks at the statements regarding the beauties of slavery made by Southern writers such as Fitzhugh, the question is not just whether they are true or false but why they were made—what

purpose did the pro-slavery writer intend them to promote? The chief
significance of a statement by a historical figure may not lie in its truth
value but in what it tells us about the situation in which it was made
and the beliefs and desires of the writer.

Third, Dummett holds that if the past and its contents are constructs created to explain present evidence, then neither the past nor its
contents can be real.[22] Since this position is precisely the opposite of that
for which I argued earlier, it is important to see just where the issue is.
Dummett holds that one who regards the past as a construct from present
evidence is wrong. The mistake, as Dummett sees it, lies in confusing
the means of verification available to an individual with those available
to the community. The individual is indeed limited to presently existing
data, but since the community includes the dead as well as the living,
evidence that exists in the past is equally available as a basis for verification.
Since the past observer is a member of our community, in Dummett's
extended sense of "community," his observation should be accepted by
us as direct evidence, just as those are of a contemporary observer. But
how do we, individually or collectively, now know what someone in the
past observed? We can know this only by having available to us now a
document that we interpret as a record of those observations. But to
interpret the document is to hypothesize that an observer existed at a
given time and place, made those observations, and recorded them. This
hypothesis may be false; some stories about Lincoln were presumed to
be based on direct observation, but they have turned out to have been
invented by the so-called "public man."[23] To accept the document as
recording correct observations truly made at the time in question is to
adopt a hypothesis that accounts for the creation and characteristics of
the document. But there is nothing in this view to show that the past
and its denizens are not real. In fact, the view of our knowledge of the
past as a construct based on present evidence is inherently realistic, since
it takes past persons and events as explaining the existence and characteristics of present artifacts, and the cause of a real effect must itself be
real. None of Dummett's arguments will refute this.

The root problem here is the extent of the community of observers. Dummett wants the community to include all who have lived; at
least he assigns no temporal boundary to his community. But the existence of people in the deep past and of their observations are historical
hypotheses that have to be verified, and he presents no way of doing
that that would not involve a regress—that is, to confirm that observer
A existed and made observation X, we would need observer B to observe what A does, and similarly for B, and so on. Further, people in
the deep past operated with conceptual schemes often so different from

our own that to accept their observations as on a par with ours would result in a mass of contradictions that would make any coherent history impossible. It is therefore not possible to accept Dummett's definition of the community.

But what about Dummett's argument that if history is a theoretical construct postulated to explain present evidence, then as evidence vanishes over time so must portions of the past? Dummett is quite right, in the sense that, should evidence for some events in the past vanish, we would have no grounds for hypothesizing that those events ever occurred. Not only is he right, but it is easy to point out cases where this has occurred. Sumer is a prime example of a civilization lost to history but fortunately later recovered. Until the discovery of the Rosetta stone, much of Egyptian history was lost, since no one could read hieroglyphic writing; the same was true of the Maya, whose writing has only recently been decoded, and in the case of the Indus Valley civilization, we still cannot read their writing. There are indeed many cases where we know that past events must have occurred, but we have no way of knowing what they were. Human history before the invention of writing is precisely such a case. We know from archaeological investigations that people lived in certain regions, and we have some artifacts from which we can construct a few statements about their culture, but although their actions were observable at the time they occurred, and were observed by members of their own communities, we will never know what they were. These are simply facts about our knowledge of the past, and to raise them as objections to a particular view of historical knowledge is like cursing the wind.

Fourth, Dummett states his criterion for the truth of statements about unobserved events, as "if someone were to have been at hand at the relevant time, he could have observed an event of that kind." Thus consider the statement

(A) Hitler shot himself in his bunker on April 30, 1945.

According to Dummett's criterion, (A) would be true if the following contrary-to-fact conditional were true.

(B) If an observer had been present at the right place and time in Hitler's bunker on April 30, 1945, he could have observed Hitler shooting himself.

The problem of counterfactuals is not new and is still hotly debated. Yet I think no historian would hesitate to say that (B) is true. The reason is that we already know from other evidence that Hitler did shoot himself in his bunker on April 30, 1945, and shooting oneself is an observable type of event. Our willingness to affirm (B) thus rests upon our knowing that an event of the required sort did take place. How do we know that? Dummett says, "Indirect evidence for the truth of a statement about a place where no observer was present must show that a suitably located observer could have made observations giving direct grounds for its truth; that is how indirect evidence must be related to direct evidence."[24] Hence to affirm (B), we must already be able to affirm on the basis of other evidence that

(A) Hitler shot himself in his bunker on April 30, 1945.

(C) Shooting oneself is an observable type of event if done in the presence of an observer.

and

(D) The layout of Hitler's bunker was such that a suitably placed observer could have observed his suicide.[25]

But the truth of (A) cannot depend on the truth of (B) if the truth of (B) depends upon the truth of (A). Dummett's argument is circular. More generally, his claim that the truth of a proposition about the past requires that, had an observer been present at the appropriate time and place, he could have observed the event, either requires that we already know when and where the event took place and its character, or it leads to nonsense. Suppose I conjecture that aliens from outer space landed on earth on August 1, 9000, B.C. on the tip of Cape Cod. Surely had an observer been there at that time, he could have observed that event. But does that make the supposition true? I presume that Dummett meant his criterion to apply only to events that actually happened, and that means that we must already know that an observable event took place at a specific time and place.

In the expanded version of his lectures, Dummett has added a new argument. He considers four models of the relations of past, present, and future: (1) Only the present is real; (2) The future is real, but the past is not; (3) The past is real, but the future is not; (4) The past and the future are both real.[26] He then says:

On model (2) proper, it is acknowledged that the past has left traces, including our own memories. But . . . these traces, which are part of the present, are all that there is of the past: they constitute it.[27]

It is hard to see how an unreal past could leave such traces, but in any case those traces do *not* constitute the past; they constitute the evidence on the basis of which we postulate the existence and character of the past. Dummett then poses the following problem:

> Suppose that today [October 30, 2006], I scratch my right ear. By the truth-value link [the claim propositions do not change their truth values over time], if in a year's time you were to say "I scratched my right ear precisely a year ago," what you said would be true. But it may well be that in a year's time you have forgotten that trivial action, and that every trace of its occurrence would have dissipated. According to model (2), your statement, "I scratched my right ear precisely a year ago," would *not* be true.[28]

Call the statement "I scratched my right ear precisely a year ago" "A." What gives teeth to Dummett's example is that he knows that the ear-scratching event did occur a year ago. But if one did not already know this, then Dummett could not establish the truth of A from his counterfactual that had an observer been present a year ago, he could have observed me scratching my ear. As lately noted, Dummett's counterfactual regarding past observations presupposes that the events referred to occurred. If they did not, then one would be warranted in saying almost anything about the past that would have been observable had it occurred.

It does not follow that in 2006 A is false. What follows is that in 2006 there is no evidence for A, not that there is evidence for not-A. But since in 2006 there is no evidence supporting A, the statement cannot be asserted. If one wishes to preserve the thesis that a true statement is always true, then one would have to hold that in 2006 it is true, but unassertable, since there is by hypothesis no evidence for it. There are many statements about the past that appear to fit this description. Since many animals, including human beings, scratch their ears, we know that at some time in the past Plato scratched his right ear, but we cannot say exactly when he did so. All of the types of behavior we regard as being characteristic of human beings (eating, sleeping, evacuating, etc.) we must assume were done by historical actors, since we postulate them to have been real human beings, but barring some extraordinary evidence, we cannot say just when they so behaved. But

Dummett's case differs from these general statements in specifying the precise time when the ear scratching occurred. Since by the hypothesis Dummett framed, there is in 2006 and thereafter no evidence for A, A cannot be held to be true in 2006 or thereafter. If it were, then we should be faced with the problem of the status of true but unknowable statements. It does not follow that statements are true only at the time when they are shown to be true. The statement that the universe began with the Big Bang could not be asserted until Hubble discovered that it was expanding, but the theory itself we take to have been true for some 14 billion years, and so true long before it was known to be true. A statement once asserted as true may, however, become unassertable if all of the evidence for it vanishes, and this is the fate of countless statements about the past, but lack of assertability does not show that a statement is false, it simply shows that there is no reason to assume it. It seems to me that this is not very far from Dummett's own position, since he writes

> what exists is what can be known to exist. What is true is what can be known to be true. Reality is the totality of what can be experienced by sentient creatures and what can be known by intelligent ones.[29]

Assuming that "know" here includes probable knowledge, I would subscribe to this statement.

Dummett's position is peculiar. He is committed to a theory of meaning derived from intuitionist mathematics, and this has led him to espouse a type of AntiRealism. But at the same time, he believes strongly that statements about the past are, or can be, true and meaningful, and he rejects any form of AntiRealism that contradicts this belief. He construes the view that the past and its inhabitants are constructs resting upon present evidence as being a form of AntiRealism. On the contrary, I argued earlier that historical theories account for presently existing data that constitute the evidence for those theories. I also argued that while according to this view past persons and events have the *epistemological* status of constructs, they are *ontologically* real. They are indeed postulated, but they are postulated *as real*. It no more follows that one who holds all historical evidence to consist of present observations of artifacts must be an AntiRealist about the past than it does that one who holds that present observations supply the evidence of the existence of electrons must be an AntiRealist about subatomic particles.

Chapter 2

Evidence

This chapter deals with a number of problems concerning historical data. I look first at the question of what historical evidence is, and particularly what a document is. I then examine how historical documents are authenticated, using the example of the controversy over the Vinland Map. Next I discuss the problems of changes in spelling, grammar, and the meaning of terms. The importance of speech act theory for historical analysis also will be stressed. Then I will examine the problem of determining authorship and the perils of edited works. Finally, I describe the process of historical research.

⊸≫◈≪⊸

History explains the data that form the evidence for the historian's theories. Events enter historical theories as constructs within the theories. The theories themselves are attempts to explain the data and are good or bad depending upon their success or lack of it in doing so. So what, then, are the data that historical theories explain? In one sense, anything presently existing is a historical datum, since all objects of our experience have a past that could be investigated. For any object we can ask about its origin, its maker, its past history, and so on. These are all historical questions. And it does sometimes happen that an inquiry begins with the chance discovery of something that catches the historian's interest—an old letter, a picture, a teapot, or whatever. But most historians choose as their subjects some event or person believed to have existed in the past and then face the problem of finding the relevant data. That is, they start from the constructs, whose existence is taken for granted, and then have to work back to the data. However the inquiry begins, whatever they are to use as data must be something they can observe here and now. This point should be obvious, but it was so well put by Collingwood over half a century ago that his remarks bear repeating.

23

> Everything is evidence which the historian can use as evidence. But what can he so use? It must be something here and now perceptible to him: this written page, this spoken utterance, this building, this finger-print. And of all the things perceptible to him there is not one which he might not conceivably use as evidence on some question, if he came to it with the right question in mind. The enlargement of historical knowledge comes about mainly through finding how to use as evidence this or that kind of perceived fact which historians have hitherto thought useless to them.[1]

History is an empirical discipline, which means that it is based on ob-servations, and the only things that a historian can observe are those he can observe here and now.

What the historian actually confronts is an "object." That "object" may be material or immaterial; it may be an oral account or a story or a song, a teaching, or a practice such as shaking hands, but usually it is a physical object of some kind. The types of objects with which archae-ologists work—bones, tools, ruins of buildings, pollen residues, and so on—are all historical data on the basis of which they seek to reconstruct how the members of past populations lived. Archaeologists are of course historians, but those who label themselves "historians" are chiefly, and much too exclusively, concerned with the class of objects called "docu-ments." The necessary condition for an object to be a "document" is that it exhibits writing on its surface, but there are many objects, such as gravestones, monuments, instruments, and weapons, on which the amount of writing is slight and whose documentary status is therefore somewhat indeterminate. Obviously books, letters, treaties, and the like are documents in the full sense, and although archaeologists use such materials whenever they are available, they are usually associated with the work of historians. Here, as so often in academe, bureaucratic labels impose distinctions that make no sense.

Given a material object on which there is an inscription, how do we know that the inscription is writing? Although this may seem a daunting question, in fact it is not usually difficult to answer in practice. Writing has to be clearly distinguishable from markings due to natural causes or to animals, because those to whom the writing is addressed have to be able to make that distinction. We can in fact recognize something as writing without knowing what it means. Thus we know that the inscriptions on Harappan seals are writing, although we cannot read them; we know that Minoan Linear A is a system of writing, although we cannot interpret it; we knew that the Mayan glyphs were writing before we discovered what they meant. Of course this sets the problem of interpretation with which students of these matters must contend. Any living human language, no matter how odd from our point of view, can be learned by us and translated into our language.[2] But in the written languages of the past—the so-called "dead" languages that have no living speakers and are known only through surviving inscriptions—the problem is very different. Those systems of writing are for us uninterpreted formal systems that could have any number of models, and we have no basis upon which to decide among them. Our only hope here is a bilingual inscription, such as the Rosetta stone, which equates an inscription in the unknown language to one in a language already known. Such a bilingual inscription provides a key to unlocking the secret of the unknown language, though it requires years of work to extend this breakthrough into a full knowledge of the lost language. Even today, the construction of the first English-Sumerian dictionary is still in its early stages.

Suppose now that we have before us a sheet of paper with an inscription in English that bears a date, a salutation, and a signature. We will normally classify such an object as a letter written by the signatory to the person addressed on the date in question. What needs to be emphasized is that this is a classificatory hypothesis, and that it can be wrong. The letter may be a communication between other men of similar names; it may be a draft of a letter that was never sent, or a file copy of a letter sent but never received, or it may be a forgery. There are many well-known cases in which documents have been forged, sometimes for monetary reasons, but also for political or diplomatic or criminal reasons. Documents appeared during the 2004 presidential race purporting to contain information concerning George Bush's service in the National Guard that turned out to be fakes. In October 2002, a group of archaeologists announced the finding of an ossuary bearing the inscription "James the son of Joseph the brother of Jesus." An ossuary is a container for the bones of a deceased person. If this artifact had been genuine, then it would have been the first physical evidence of Jesus, and it would have had important implications for the Catholic doctrine of the perpetual virginity of Mary. It was not genuine. A committee appointed by the Israel Antiquities Authority found that the patina in the letters of the words "the brother of Jesus" was chemically different from that in the other words and was of modern creation. The ossuary itself and the first part of the inscription may be authentic, but the words relating "James" to "Jesus" are not. Obviously, if the entire inscription had been authentic, then the monetary value of the ossuary would have been very great.[3]

The most famous and puzzling forgery problem in the historical trade today is the case of the Vinland Map. This much publicized
controversy came to light in 1957. A rare book dealer, Laurence Witten, had acquired from an Italian book dealer a volume containing the
Vinland Map and the Tarter Relation. The map itself was on vellum
and showed "Vinilanda," clearly meaning "Vinlanda"—the Norse name
for North America. If genuine, this was the earliest map to display a
knowledge of the Norse voyages to the North American coast. The
Norse themselves did not make maps; at least there is no known case
of a Norse map. Knowledge of the Norse discovery of North America
was transmitted through sagas, not maps. The Tarter Relation is a single
quire of sixteen leaves; the outer and inner sheets are of parchment, the
rest of paper. The text is written on the first eleven leaves, two columns
to the page, and the remaining leaves are blank.[4] The text is an account
of the mission of Friar John de Plano Carpini to the Mongol emperor in
1245–1247. Carpini, a Franciscan friar, had been sent by Pope Innocent
IV to determine what dangers the Mongols posed to Europe as well as
to furnish information concerning the Mongol culture. Several reports
of this mission were issued in 1247, but the Tarter Relation bound with
the Vinland Map is unique; it is an account by a Franciscan friar C. de
Bridia based on information he had received from Carpini's traveling
companions. No other copy of this manuscript is known.[5] But the Vinland Map did not appear to have been originally bound with the Tarter
Relation; the wormholes in the two did not match. Then, two years
later, Witten found a copy of Vincent de Beauvais's Speculum historiale,
in which he discovered to his astonishment that the wormholes in the
map precisely matched those in the front of Vincent's Speculum, while
those in the Tarter Relation precisely matched those at the end of the
Speculum. The conclusion seemed obvious, that originally all three had
been bound together. Further, the handwriting for the Vinland Map,
the Tarter Relation, and the Speculum appeared to be the same.[6] The
paper on which the Tarter Relation and the Speculum were written had
the same watermarks. As Allan Stevenson wrote, "The Vincent and the
Tarter Relation seem to represent (virtually) one long *run* or supply of
paper. Thus one may argue that the manuscript was begun, probably,
not long after the paper was manufactured or at least supplied; and that
the paper dates from about 1440."[7] For these and other reasons, Yale
purchased the volume. But the controversy had only begun. Witten
and the Yale experts, including R. A. Skelton of the British Museum,
believed the map to date from about the middle of the fifteenth century
and probably to have been drawn at Basel in Switzerland. If so, then
knowledge of the Norse explorations had reached Southern Europe at

least half a century before Columbus sailed and could have been available to him. But was the map genuine?[8]

In an effort to settle the matter, Yale asked the Walter McCrone Company to examine the map. It was clear that the vellum on which the map was drawn was indeed old enough for the map to be genuine; the issue became the ink. McCrone found that the ink on the map contained anatase—an uncommon form of titanium dioxide, and that the crystals were rounded and smooth, typical of synthetic calcined anatase. Had the anatase been produced by grinding the mineral, as would have been done in the fifteenth century, the particles would have been jagged. McCrone concluded that the ink was post-1920, and therefore that the map was a forgery.[9] This did not end the controversy, but only exacerbated it. Further study of the map by Thomas Cahill and his colleagues at the University of California at Davis led to the verdict, "Our work argues strongly against the specific McCrone Associates proof that the map is fraudulent."[10] The dispute continued. Writing in *Analytical Chemistry* in 2002, Katherine Brown and Robin Clark found that the ink used in the Tarter Relation was iron gallotannate ink, whereas that used on the map was carbon ink. Using Raman microprobe spectroscopy, they found that the lines on the map were composed of two parts, "a yellowish line which strongly adheres via absorption to the parchment and an apparently overlaid black line." Anatase was found in the yellow lines. Though anatase could have been formed in the medieval preparation of iron gallotannate ink, the fact that the black ink is carbon based renders that possibility irrelevant. Brown and Clark note

> Had the VM [Vinland Map] been drawn in a medieval iron gallotannate ink, a yellowing at the borders of the ink such as that seen on the map might have been expected. Knowing that such yellowing is a common feature of medieval manuscripts, a clever forger may seek to simulate this degradation by the inclusion of a yellow line in his rendering of the map. However, this study has shown that (a) the black ink on the VM is carbon based making the natural occurrence of such a feature impossible and (b) that the VM shows no evidence of embrittlement of the parchment or associated parchment loss [which iron gallotannate ink would cause].[11]

They conclude, "The presence of a yellow line containing anatase, closely associated with a stable carbon ink, indicates that the VM is a modern forgery."[12] But others do not concur. Cahill rejects Brown and Clark's findings, as do some other experts. The controversy goes on.[13]

I have dwelt longer on the case of the Vinland Map than might have been expected to give some indication of the complexity of the issues involved and the difficulty in determining the authenticity of such documents. At this point, the most high-powered techniques of chemistry and physics are being employed in an effort to settle the question, and still the argument goes on. Today, a successful forger must be very sophisticated scientifically, but that does not mean that forgery is not still a problem. The dating of documents, the determining of when, where, by whom, and why they were produced, is what historians call the "external criticism" of the document. It is as vital today as it ever was, since what a document can be evidence for depends upon the answers to these questions. Historians who blithely accept a library's statement that a given document is such and such need to be aware that this is a classificatory hypothesis that can be false.[14]

The case of the Vinland Map shows how much can be done to determine the date and place of composition of a text by the study of the material on which it is written and the substances used to create the inscription. As should be obvious, the methods available for this are very powerful, but they all involve the correcting of history by history. Because we have detailed studies of the history of paper making, ink manufacture, book binding, and similar subjects, we can use these sophisticated methods to place a document in time and space. But there are other methods available that must be used.

A document is an artifact bearing an inscription. The physical characteristics of the inscription are also evidence. That handwriting varies from person to person is common knowledge, but it also varies over time. In the case of the Vinland Map controversy, the analysis showed that the legends on the map appear to have been written by the same scribe that wrote the Tarter Relation and the Speculum. There were differences: the map inscriptions were very small owing to the limited space available on the map; the Tarter Relation showed evidence of being written hastily, but the Speculum was carefully written. The writing style is upper Rhineland cursive book hand, which was widely used in Germany, Switzerland, France, Flanders, and Italy in the period 1415–1460.[15] Similarly, handwriting analysis often can be used not only to date a manuscript but to identify its author, if other samples of the author's handwriting are available for comparison.

Inscriptions have meanings, and if we can understand them, they furnish further clues. The meaning is not "out there" in the inscription; you can stare at an inscription in Minoan Linear A until you go blind, and you still will not know what it means. Putnam to the contrary notwithstanding, meanings are in the head. Meanings are conceptual;

they are not Platonic entities or physical objects. We *attribute* meanings to an inscription to form a text. That attribution can be wrong; all of us sometime have had the experience of finding that we attributed the wrong meaning to a word or sentence. The function of language is communication, and in order for it to perform that function, meanings must be shared among the members of the linguistic community. We usually discover that we have attributed the wrong meaning to an inscription when communication breaks down; someone cannot understand us, or we cannot understand someone. Alternatively, we find a passage in a text that seems unintelligible or peculiar, and we recognize that the writer meant something different by his words than we do. Meanings are part of our general theory of culture; to understand a culture one has to understand how people communicate and what they say to each other.

Every culture has a worldview—a conceptual system that the members employ to make sense of their experiences of the world around them, of each other, and of themselves. Such worldviews usually differ between cultures, often so radically that it is a major research project to decipher what statements by members of a different culture mean. Furthermore, worldviews are in constant flux, as new experiences of the society's members require revisions of past beliefs. It would not surprise a modern American scholar to find that his worldview is very different from that of the Aztec, but it is likely to be less obvious to him that his worldview differs from that of prior generations of his own society. Meanings change. Anyone who reads Shakespeare will find there words that are no longer in use, or that are now used with different meanings than they had in Shakespeare's time. But one need not go back to the sixteenth century to find evidence of such changes. Think of the words, "cool," "gay," and "square." A generation ago, all of these had very different meanings than they do now. To say of someone that "he is a gay man" meant in the 1940s that he was a lighthearted person; it had nothing to do with sexual orientation. Theodore Roosevelt called his program "the square deal," meaning that it was fair and honest. Word meanings can change very quickly, as can other items of the culture. When I was in college, every science student carried a slide rule; today, most undergraduates have never seen one. In my mother's day, every woman had a darning egg; girls today have no idea what they are. Cultures change, sometimes with startling rapidity, and the problems of interpretation multiply with every change.

As the phenomenon of meaning change implies, a given inscription can have more than one meaning. This is not only true with respect to change over time, but it can also be true of a text at one time. It is a common phenomenon that gangs and certain types of groups develop a set of "in" terms or sayings that have in addition to their common meanings a special meaning to the members but not to outsiders. The extreme case here is of course that of codes deliberately constructed to be unintelligible to any but the in-group. But in an even broader sense, an author may mean one thing by what he writes yet find that readers take him to have meant something else. As Stanley Fish, with his usual puckish humor, demonstrated, what one teacher wrote as a class assignment another could persuade his students was a poem.[16]

Many of the problems of interpretation come from thinking of languages as uninterpreted formal systems. Systems of *writing* whose meanings have been lost do have this character, but living languages do not. Reference is not a purely linguistic phenomenon, it is a psychological phenomenon. To refer is to direct attention to something. In the case of young children, reference usually begins with gazing and progresses to reaching and then to pointing. When words for objects are learned, they are substituted for gestures to refer to objects of interest. The child uses language to serve its communicative needs, and those needs involve directing the attention of others to things that interest the child. Only when language is considered in abstraction from its relation to the world does it appear as a formal uninterpreted system.[17]

Human life involves many constants. All human groups need food, drink, shelter, clothing, and heat, have sex, bear children, nurse, die, and so on. Every language has words for these matters because they are matters about which communication is essential and unavoidable. There has to be communication about how food is obtained, whether by hunting, fishing, harvesting, or whatever, and there has to be communication sufficient to effect a certain level of organization. The same holds true for the other constants. There are many respects in which languages can differ, but there are also certain matters about which human beings must communicate, and here there will be linguistic means for doing so.

It is a mistake to think that all concepts are expressed in words. Thus the Dani have only two color words—"mili" and "mola," for light and dark. But in color-matching tasks, they match colors just as we do, showing that they have the concepts, although their language has no words for them.[18] Thought is conceptual; it can usually be expressed in words, but it can be expressed by other means as well. Various symbolic systems exist in any culture, some of which are not linguistic, and discovering the concepts expressed by paintings, buildings, rituals, music, and other means is just as important as learning the linguistic system.

As John Austin taught us, words are used to perform actions.[19] The theory of speech acts is important because speaking and writing are actions done for a reason, and one needs to understand what act is being performed when a given utterance is made. The same words or sentences may be used for different purposes. Consider the sentence, "I'll be there." This could be a promise, a threat, or a statement of fact, depending upon how it is used. As Austin showed, an utterance is not only a locution having a specific meaning and reference, but it is an illocutionary act—an act performed in the making of the utterance, such as a promise or a threat. Discovering under what circumstances the utterance of a locution counts as a particular illocutionary act is essential to understanding how the language functions in a culture. Thus "You are out of order" performs a different act when uttered by the speaker during a House session or by one's physician. There is a wonderful story that during a debate about a small river, Senator Costigan of Colorado once remarked, "I could piss half way across that stream." The presiding officer roared, "Senator, you are out of order." "I know I am," replied Costigan. "If I weren't I could piss all the way across it."

Speech act theory is particularly important because very often the data historians use are not records of action but parts of the action itself. Thus a political campaign speech is not a record of the campaign, it is an instrument of the campaign, and it must be read accordingly. Candidates want to win votes, and what they say is determined less by truth than by what they think certain groups of voters want to hear. Similarly, diplomatic notes are not records of diplomacy, they are part of the diplomacy. It may well be to the advantage of one government to lie when dealing with another government, since the objective is not to leave a record for future historians but to influence how another government will act. Letters, sermons, speeches, tracts, treaties—all of these instruments are employed by their authors to bring about certain results. Even diaries and autobiographies are written with a particular audience in mind. No one who writes an autobiography for publication ever tells the whole truth and nothing but the truth. And there are even "historians" whose accounts are written less to tell the truth about the past than to further some political or social agenda of the author. True historians must constantly torture their sources to try to determine why they were written and what the author was trying to accomplish by writing them.

When a historian confronts a historical document that contains constative (i.e., fact-stating) statements, his first impulse is to ask if the statements are true or false. That, however, is the wrong question; he should ask "Why was that statement made?" And this is not equivalent to the question

> "What did the person who made it mean by it?" Although that is doubtless a question that the historian must ask, and must be able to answer. It is equivalent, rather, to the question, "What light is thrown on the subject in which I am interested by the fact that this person made this statement, meaning by it what he did mean?" This might be expressed by saying that the scientific historian does not treat statements as statements but as evidence; not as true or false accounts of the facts of which they profess to be accounts, but as other facts which, if he knows the right questions to ask about them, may throw light on those facts.[20]

Thus during World War II, President Roosevelt repeatedly told the American people that when the Allied landings in Europe came, Allied forces would land simultaneously at many different points. His statements appeared to be fact-stating statements. They were designed to have that appearance so Hitler would believe them and when the invasion came would hold back his forces until he knew all of the points at which the attack was being made. Roosevelt's statements were deliberately false; from the beginning the D-day plan was for a single landing only. But his statements fooled Hitler, who was slow to recognize that Normandy was the only landing site. Similarly, in 1850, Edward Hale published a letter on Irish immigration in which he wrote of the Irish, "In the epochs of written history, the pure [Celtic] race has done nothing positive for mankind, and been nothing but a monument of failure."[21] The historian may agree or not agree with Hale's statement, but aside from what it tells us about the concept of race at that time, the important question is why it was made. The answer is that Hale was trying to justify Irish immigration by convincing his fellow Bostonians that as a failed race the Irish would sink to the bottom of society, thereby freeing Anglo-Saxons from manual labor and enabling them to better their position by standing on the backs of the Irish. Probably Hale believed what he wrote, but the importance of the letter as evidence is that it indicates the conflict in New England over Irish immigration and the sort of solutions being proposed.

Meanings, spelling, and grammar may all change over time. Consider the following passage:

> For was it not a time when humane Worship and inventions were growne to such an intolerable height, that the consciences of God's saints and servants inlightened in the truth could no

longer bear them? was not the power of the tyrannicall Prelates
so great, that like a strong current carryed all down streame
before it.[22]

The spellings here are not incorrect. They were customary in the seventeenth century, as was the capitalization and punctuation. The sort
of standardization of spelling to which we are accustomed is a relatively
modern development and was still incomplete in the nineteenth century.
Andrew Jackson is said to have nothing but contempt for a man who
knew only one way to spell a word. Similarly, when one finds Jonathan
Edwards writing "the same object don't always appear alike agreeable
to the same person," it is not because Edwards was ill educated but
because this use of "don't" was proper English in the mid-eighteenth
century.[23] Consider, then, this passage:

> It is ordered, decreed and by this court declared; that the
> general or publick Treasure, or any part therof shall never be
> expended but by the appointment of a General Court, nor any
> Shire treasure but by the appointment of the Freemen thereof,
> nor any Town treasure but by the Freemen of that *Township*;
> except small sums upon urgent occasion, when the Court or
> the Freemen cannot direct therin, provided a just account be
> given therof.[24]

This text seems perfectly lucid, but it does not mean what a modern
reader would take it to mean. "Freeman" in Massachusetts in 1648 did
not mean a non-slave, it meant a Freeman of the Massachusetts Bay
Company, that is, it was a legal status enjoyed by only about one fifth
of the adult male population and was limited to Church members. Thus
what the law really does is place control over funds in the hands of the
Church members who ruled Massachusetts.

The determination of authorship often is one of the most difficult historical tasks. In many cases it cannot be done, at least on the
basis of presently known data. Biblical scholars agree that the Book of
Isaiah is the work of at least three different authors, but there is no
way to know who they may have been. In cases where the document
is handwritten, we have at least the handwriting to go on, but unless
there are other examples of that handwriting, where the identify of the
author is known, it has limited utility. Very often one is forced to try
to deduce from the text the characteristics of the author and then to
seek someone who has those characteristics. A particularly interesting
example of this is the problem of the "public man."

In 1879, the *North American Review* published "The Diary of a Public Man" in four installments. It purported to be a diary kept during the winter of 1860–1861. The editor of the *Review* stated that only selections from the diary were being published, covering twenty-one days between December 28, 1860, and March 15, 1861, during which time the diarist was in Washington, except for February 20, when he was in New York City. What made the diary important was that the diarist, who was not identified, recorded discussions with some of the leading political figures of the day—Lincoln, Douglas, Seward, and a number of others; he apparently knew everyone, and his views on the critical events of that secession winter provided striking insights into the mood and events of the time.[25] The "Diary" was accepted as authentic and was used as a historical source by a number of American historians, including Allen Johnson, Frederick Bancroft, James Ford Rhodes, Ida Tarbell, and W. E. Barton.[26] Only E. L. Pierce had cast doubt on its authenticity when Frank Anderson began his attempt to identify the diarist. Anderson at first assumed the diary was genuine. From the text, he drew up a list of eighteen characteristics that he thought the diarist must have had and sought to find someone who matched this profile.[27] Although difficult, this task was possible because the number of men who could have written the diary was limited. Having almost convinced himself that Amos Kendall was the diarist, Anderson discovered that Kendall had been in Philadelphia on a day when the diarist was in Washington.[28]

At this point, Anderson began to question the authenticity of the diary. He did not believe the diary was a total fraud. He wrote:

> One of the distinguishing features of the Diary, I had found, was that it reflected the newspapers of the day in a manner scarcely possible except for one who was reading them from day to day as they came from the press.[29]

But Anderson did not think it was genuine either. Because the diarist interacted with the leading figures of Washington, and because the newspapers of the time chronicled the activities and movements of these people day by day, Anderson could determine with some precision who could have seen whom and when. A close analysis of the diarist's accounts of his three meetings with Lincoln convinced Anderson that none of them could have taken place.[30] One particularly striking incident that the diarist recorded was that during Lincoln's inaugural address, Douglas held Lincoln's hat. The inauguration was viewed by hundreds of people, including reporters. Yet only one newspaper, the *Cincinatti Commercial*, carried this story, and only a few picked it up. Had such an incident occurred, Anderson thought it incredible that it had not been widely reported.[31]

Anderson concluded that the "Diary had as a nucleus a genuine diary, probably of a rather meager character which had been re-written and to which a good deal had been added from recollection and invention."[32] Proceeding on this hypothesis, he derived from the close study of the now-suspect text thirteen characteristics that he believed the diarist must have had:

1. He had been in Washington during the secession winter.

2. He knew personally many of the chief political men in Washington.

3. He had "the diary habit."

4. He was a man of the world with wide experience.

5. He knew the French language and literature.

6. He was a strong Unionist.

7. He knew a great deal about politics but was not a party man.

8. He was much interested in business.

9. He was either a New Yorker or someone who knew the New York leaders and conditions.

10. He disliked the Blairs, Stanton, and Senator Baker of Oregon.

11. He distrusted and feared the influence of extremists in both North and South.

12. He enjoyed ridiculing Caleb Cushing, Pierre Soule, and Charles Sumner.

13. He was on intimate terms with Seward and Douglas.[33]

Given this profile, Anderson searched for a person who fit it, and he found his man in Sam Ward, the brother of Julia Ward Howe, a man who seemed to fit the profile exactly.[34] Anderson's conclusion was that Ward had kept a diary in Washington in the secession winter, and that sometime later, probably shortly before 1879, when most of the leading figures mentioned in the diary were dead, he had embellished it with skillfully designed anecdotes, either alone or with the help of William Hurlbert and possibly Allen Rice, the editor of the *North American Review*.[35] That Rice knew who the diarist was seemed clear, both because he would not have been. likely to publish an anonymous diary without knowing where it came from, and because he closely guarded the secret of the diarist's identity to the day of his death.

Anderson's work of course did not go unchallenged. In 1953, Roy Lokken published "Has the Mystery of "A Public Man" Been Solved?,"[36] in which he argued that Anderson's arguments rested too much on circumstantial evidence and were inconclusive and even suggested that Anderson had shaped his profile deliberately to fit Ward. The two traded rebuttals in 1955 with I think Anderson having the better of it.[37] The evidence is not conclusive, but no one has made a better case for any alternative to Ward.

A different approach to the solution of authorship problems is illustrated by Frederick Mosteller's and David Wallace's solution to the question of the disputed *Federalist Papers*.[38] It is well known that this work was written by Hamilton, Jay, and Madison, and for most of the letters the authorship is not in doubt. But there were twelve letters for which it was unclear whether Hamilton or Madison was the author. Mosteller and Wallace tackled this problem in the following way. They studied a number of documents known to have been written by each man and determined the frequency with which certain words occurred in each man's writings. Then they counted the frequency with which those words occurred in the disputed letters of the *Federalist Papers* and constructed several probability models from which they could estimate the odds of a letter having been written by one man or the other. The results showed that the odds were overwhelmingly in favor of Madison as the author of all of them.

This case is unusual because there were only two possible authors, and Mosteller and Wallace knew who they were. Further, abundant writings by each man were available, including *Federalist* papers, the authorship of which was known, and from which each man's linguistic peculiarities could be determined. In most authorship cases, the problem is not so neat. But the techniques used by Mosteller and Wallace do offer ways of testing hypotheses about authorship by people for whom a reasonable amount of authenticated writings exists.

Once the historian has the document in printed form, he is apt to think that his troubles are over. They may not be. The text of the manuscript as it left the author's hand may not be identical to the text published. In the eighteenth century, books written in America often were published abroad, and their authors had no chance to correct proofs. Further, in works that go through multiple editions, authors may change the text from one edition to another. Probably the most famous case of this is the changes that Immanuel Kant made in the *Critique of*

Pure Reason between the first and second editions—changes that in some cases reflected major changes in his position. Many other cases of this sort are well known and serve as a warning to historians to be careful of which edition they use. But at least in these cases the changes were made by the author. Alas, in the eighteenth and nineteenth centuries, editors often took it upon themselves to alter or "improve" the author's text. A striking example of this is the alterations that editors made in Jonathan Edwards's *Treatise Concerning Religious Affections* from one edition to another. For example, in the first edition, Edwards wrote:

> In these words the Apostle represents the state of the minds of the Christians he wrote to, under the persecutions they were then the subjects of. These persecutions are what he has respect to, in the two preceding verses, when he speaks of the trial of their faith, and of their being in heaviness through manifold temptations.

This passage appears in the American Tract Society edition of 1833 as

> The Apostle here describes the state of mind of the Christians he addressed, while they were suffering those persecutions and "manifold temptations" referred to in the preceding verses, as the "trial of their faith."[39]

Such violence to a text would be intolerable today, but the practice was common in this earlier era. Any historian working on such texts must be very careful to make sure that the edition he uses is the one appropriate to his work. That does not necessarily mean that he must use the first edition. If the historian's subject cites the *Origin of Species* on a particular question, the historian should examine the edition his subject cited. The *Origin of Species* went through many editions during Darwin's lifetime, and he made substantial changes from one edition to another. Thus what Darwin said depends upon what edition one reads.

Having now reviewed some of the problems involved in determining what data are, we need further to look at the process of finding and utilizing data—that is, the research process. What the research process is is not obvious from historical texts themselves, which usually are narrative accounts that make no reference to the data upon which they are based. As Goldstein pointed out,[40] the actual data appear (if at all) in the footnotes and appendices, not in the main text. But a list of titles and page numbers does little to exhibit the process of historical research In fact, except on rare occasions, the actual *process* of historical research does not appear in the historical narratives at all. But without that process, there would be no history, narrative or other.

Suppose that, for whatever reason, a historian believes that an event occurred in the past. The first question he must ask is, what data relevant to this event *could* have been created? There may be *no* data. We would all very much like to know the first language ever spoken by a human being, but we never will know because no data concerning that event or events could have been created in a material or preservable form. But for most historical events, if we think they existed, we do so because some data concerning them have survived. On the one hand, in the case of a battle, there would have been witnesses who could have left written or oral accounts, or artifacts—weapons, armor, bones—that could be excavated, or possibly written orders or plans. Not every such account of a battle is believable—what Samson is said to have done in the Le Hi Valley is not. But the point is that whenever a battle occurred, there should be a witness' account or material or documentary evidence of it. On the other hand, it is almost certain that no account of the wedding night of Socrates and Xiantippi was ever created in any form. It might have been, but no one expects to find it. Thus the historians' first task is to predict what sorts of data *could* have been created concerning the event in question.

The second question is, if the data were created, have they survived? This is a very complex question. Suppose that there was a record of the last words of Nathaniel Bacon, the leader of the 1676 rebellion in Virginia. Then someone who witnessed his death wrote a record or told someone who wrote a record. What happened to it? Given Bacon's importance, someone might have thought it worth saving. But the chances of its survival depend very largely upon whether or not it came into the possession of an institution that had some procedure for preserving documents and some reason for doing so. Thus the Royal Commission sent to Virginia to deal with the rebellion might have preserved such a record. More generally, many institutions do have procedures for creating and/or preserving certain types of records. Church records, court records, legislative records, state records, tax records, and the like fall into this category. If the institution created the record and saved it, then there is a fair chance it has survived, but no guarantee—as witness the 1890 U.S. Manuscript Census that was almost completely destroyed by fire. If the institution simply collects and saves records, as historical societies do, then the chances of survival also are good. But many institutions and businesses create records and save them for a fixed period of time before destroying them to save the cost of storage. Once the record is in the possession of an institution or a business whose policy it is to preserve records, its chances of preservation are relatively good, though one must bear in mind the losses due to flood, fire, and war. When Sherman invaded South Carolina, the South Carolinians expected him to burn Charleston, so they moved their historical records to Columbia. Sherman burned Columbia instead.

But of course not all records come into the possession of institutions. Some are passed down in families or through private hands. Others are lost and then recovered in unlikely places—New England attics, antique desks, and so on. Some, like archaeological data, are still waiting for us in the ground. The chances of survival for such data are far less than for institutional data, but they do turn up—witness the Dead Sea Scrolls and the finds at Nag Hammadi. Most of these data, however, do not survive. Think of how many letters and e-mails you receive in a year, and ask yourself how many of these are still in existence at year's end. Every day tons of valuable historical data go up in smoke.

One must bear in mind that individuals and institutions do not usually create records or preserve documents for the benefit of future historians. Records are created for a purpose—congressional reapportionment, protection against prosecution, estimation of profits or sales trends, and so on. What a record contains is what is useful for the purposes of its creators, and utility may decline over time. A business that preserves records of profits in order to protect itself against tax penalties will not feel it necessary to preserve those records once the time defined by the statute of limitations has expired, and it will probably destroy the records at that point. Medical records are generally destroyed after the patient dies. In short, the creation and preservation of data are actions done for certain reasons, and those reasons affect what is recorded and what is preserved.

Given that data regarding the event in question were ever created, and given that they have survived, the next question is, where are they? The historian has to find them, and that means he has to predict where they could be. This sounds like an impossible task, but fortunately for the historian there is a veritable forest of guides and directories that identify and catalogue collections of documents. These cover the holdings of most libraries and institutional repositories, state or private. And now there are online search engines such as Google and Yahoo that permit users to search for and access an ever-increasing body of data. Much of the training of graduate students in history consists in learning how to use those aids to find what they need. But this of course assumes that the data are archived somewhere and indexed and included in some guide. If the person or event is famous, then the chances are fair that this is the case, though it does not follow that all of the relevant data are in the cited archive. Thus it is easy enough to find where the papers of John Dewey are, but that all of the surviving Dewey papers are there is another matter. Dewey carried on an immense correspondence; there are almost certainly Dewey letters still in private hands. But the research process is probably best illustrated by those cases in which one is researching an individual whose papers have never been archived. I will therefore discuss an actual case of this sort that I was involved in, though the names of the persons and places and certain facts have been changed for obvious reasons.

The subject is Dr. James O. Hart. He is known to have been a physician of some note in Cheyenne, Wyoming, and a medical directory says he was born in 1891 in Kansas City, Missouri, and received his M.D. from the University of Nebraska. No papers written by him are known to exist. The problem arose in the writing of a history of Wyoming doctors when a letter surfaced from one Arthur Cummings saying that Hart had changed his name. Who, then, was he, and why the change, if change there was?

The first step was obviously to contact Cummings and find out why he thought Hart had changed his name. But this proved to be a dead end. Cummings knew only that his grandfather had said that Hart had changed his name, but he knew nothing more. The next obvious move was to find Hart's descendents. Those turned out to consist of a granddaughter who was still alive and who provided a genealogy of the family drawn up by her grandfather, going back to an early Massachusetts clergyman named Urian Oakes and an early Connecticut minister named Luther Hart. She also told us that Hart was a member of the Sons of the American Revolution (SAR), and showed us a directory of the SAR to prove it. The genealogy might have been conclusive, but it was not. Hart had every birth, death, and marriage date for every ancestor on both the Hart and Oakes lines from the founding of New England to his own time. This was indeed possible, but it was a little too good, particularly since there appeared to be no family Bibles in which such records had been kept. The granddaughter was able to tell us that Hart had been a devout Presbyterian, but she knew nothing about any name change and dismissed the idea as absurd.

Hart had received his M.D. from the University of Nebraska, which meant that there should be a student record of him there. There was; it showed that James Oakes Hart was awarded the M.D. in 1920, that he had done both his undergraduate and medical studies at Nebraska, and that he had matriculated in 1915 under the same name. But it also showed that he had transferred credits from Creighton University and from "St. Mary's." The birth date was given as 1891. Creighton

University is a Jesuit school; why would a devout Presbyterian go to a Jesuit school? Predictably, Creighton had a student record for Hart. His transcript showed that he had matriculated in 1912 as James Oakes Hart and had left without graduating in 1914. It gave his birth date as 1890, not 1891, and his father's name and address as James O. Hart, Murray, Nebraska. It also showed that he had previously attended "St. Mary's Academy" in Kansas. St. Mary's turned out to be a Jesuit school that combined a high school with a college and was located in St. Mary's, Kansas. The school was defunct, though the buildings are still used by the Catholic Church, but the records were in the Jesuit Provincial Archives in St. Louis. And there we found a surprise. Hart had been a student there from 1910 to 1912, but under the name of James Benedict O'Hart. There was no doubt that this was James Hart; his father's name and address were the same, except that this time the father's name was given as James O'Hart; the birth date was 1890, and there was a notation on his record that a copy of it had been sent to Creighton in 1912. It did therefore appear that there had been a name change, and this conviction was strengthened by finding that one of his classmates was Oscar Cummings, who was the grandfather of Arthur Cummings. But if O'Hart had changed his name legally, then there should have been a court record of that fact, and we could find none in any county in which we knew he had lived. If, then, there was a change, it was apparently never made legally; he just did it on his own. If this were true, then Hart/O'Hart had then created a false genealogy for himself and used it to join the SAR.

The data we had so far strongly suggested that Hart/O'Hart began life as a Catholic, probably an Irish Catholic, from Murray, Nebraska. The U.S. Manuscript Census for 1900 showed James O'Hart, age ten, living on the farm of James O'Hart Sr., outside of Murray. It also showed a woman named Trask, listed as a housekeeper, and her son, listed as a hired hand, but no Mrs. O'Hart. To track Hart/O'Hart year by year, we turned to the school records, which were on a closet shelf in the office of the superintendent of schools for Cass County, Nebraska. Having located the school district in which his father's farm lay, we searched the records for that district and found James O'Hart listed from 1900 to 1910, but nothing before 1900. Why not? Since no mother was living on the O'Hart farm in 1900, according to the census, it was a fair assumption that she was dead; divorce was very unlikely at that time, especially if the O'Harts were Catholic, as the evidence indicated they were. The young child might therefore have been taken in by relatives—grandparents or siblings living in the area, particularly if the mother had died while the child was an infant. Searching the

school records for 1897 district by district brought us eventually to
James O'Hart, age seven, in a school several miles from his father's
farm, but with the parent listed as P. O'Hart, which meant he was living
with P. O'Hart. Turning again to the 1900 census, we found Patrick
O'Hart, wife Catherine, with four children living on a farm in the correct school district. The school records showed that James O'Hart had
entered school at age five and had attended that school until 1897; he
was not listed for 1898 or 1899. The 1880 U.S. Manuscript Census
showed James and Patrick O'Hart listed as sons of Edward O'Hart
living on a farm just north of Manley, Nebraska, so Patrick and James
were brothers. The plat atlas showed the location of the three farms, all
quite close together. But we needed to be sure James O'Hart was the
father of Hart/O'Hart rather than Patrick. Nebraska did not institute
birth certificates until 1904, but if the O'Harts were Catholic, then there
should have been a baptismal record. From the *Catholic Register* for 1890
we found that in 1890 the nearest Catholic Church to Murray was in
Plattsmouth—the county seat, and there at the Church of the Holy Spirit
we found a baptismal certificate certifying that James Benedict O'Hart
had been baptized in June 1890 with parents James O'Hart and Mary
Ann Quinn O'Hart and witnesses Patrick O'Hart and Catherine Quinn.
So we were now sure that James Oakes Hart was really James Benedict
O'Hart, son of James O'Hart, and it was a fair guess that Catherine
Quinn was his mother's sister and probably became Patrick O'Hart's
wife. We were able to confirm that from a newspaper notice of their
marriage in December 1890. That would make it logical that the child
had lived with Patrick and Catherine, if his mother had died when he
was very young. To determine that, we located the Catholic cemetery
closest to Murray, and there we found the gravestone of James O'Hart,
who died May 12, 1925, and Mary Ann O'Hart, who died February 3,
1891. Reasonably enough, James had placed the infant with his brother
and sister-in-law, who also was his wife's sister.

　　We still did not know where the child was in 1898 or 1899. Where
could he have been? Although there were grandparents in the area, we
found no evidence that he was living with them. If he was not with
the family, then the alternatives were limited, but one possibility was an
orphanage. The *Catholic Register* showed only one Catholic orphanage in
the region at that time, located just outside of Omaha. There we found
the records; he was placed there in 1898 by his father and withdrawn
early in 1900, again by his father. The records gave no indication why
he was there. So far the institutional records could take us, but we
needed more. We succeeded in tracing Patrick and Catherine O'Hart
to Washington State where, we found a granddaughter still alive. She

remembered hearing her grandmother, who she confirmed was Mary Ann O'Hart's sister, talk about James O'Hart's action of putting the child in the orphanage as a punishment for misbehavior—a punishment she had strongly opposed. And her brother, Catherine's grandson, had a letter that Hart/O'Hart had written to "Aunt Katie" in 1926 describing his mistreatment in the orphanage, his hatred of the nuns who ran it, and his rage at his father for having committed him. We had, therefore, a fairly complete record of Hart/O'Hart from his birth until he got his M.D., and we knew that he had changed his name. Why? One reason was obvious. He was an Irish Catholic in a time and place where being Irish and being Catholic meant you had two strikes against you. But we suspected there was more, that he blamed his father for his incarceration in the orphanage and wanted to break away from him. Further, it was quite clear that he wanted status; he wanted to "be somebody" and to be respected. That is clear from the fake genealogy.

Urian Oakes and Luther Hart were real people, and their genealogies were known. What Hart/O'Hart did was invent ancestors to serve as links to those genealogies and so to pass himself off as the descendent of notable New England divines. How could he have gotten away with this? It was not as difficult then as it would be now, but it was not that easy either. Since his St. Mary's records were all in the name of O'Hart, his options for change were limited. O'Hart is an Irish name; Hart is not. By dropping the apostrophe and substituting a period, he could plausibly claim that the "O'Hart" on the St. Mary's transcript was a clerical error for "O. Hart." That left him needing a middle name beginning with "O." How he learned about Urian Oakes we do not know, but that discovery may have suggested to him the idea of the fake genealogy. Wherever he got that idea, he carried it out well enough to fool the SAR. So a third-generation Irish Catholic farm boy from Nebraska became the heir of two distinguished seventeenth-century Puritan families with ancestors on both sides who had served in the Revolution.

I have gone through this case in detail at the risk of some tedium to illustrate the nature of the process involved in the research. At every point, the historian asks himself, if the situation was as I think it was, what should I be able to find, and where should I be able to find it? It should be obvious that the process consisted of a series of predictions and inferences as to what and where the data would be that were then followed up and confirmed or infirmed. In a case such as Hart's, having determined that the family did not have a satisfactory answer, one looked for the points at which Hart's career intersected with institutions that made and preserved records and followed that strategy as far as it would go. The final pieces were filled in from recollections of living persons and documents held by one wing of the family, but even without those one could have made a pretty good guess at the reason for his name change, though the added information helps explain why he was so obsessed with respectability. He was a budding juvenile delinquent who made good.

The Hart case differs from the usual case because there was no secondary literature on it; no books or articles had been written about James Hart. There were no Hart papers, unless one includes the fake genealogy, no library collections indexed in a guide. Here everything had to be done from scratch. The case also illustrates how difficult it is to recover information even on a moderately distinguished man born just over a century ago. The usual historical case is much easier, because historians build on other historian's work and receive assistance from "saints" in the form of librarians and archivists who collect, organize, and index information so that historians can access it easily. If it were not for them, the sheer magnitude of the data produced, for example, by the U.S. government would make it impossible for scholars to use. But for most research projects, once one has read through the hundred or so books and articles on the subject, it is still necessary to get to the manuscript sources, or—depending on the field—the original artifacts. Seeing a document as it was written is not the same as seeing it in print, and not only because the editor may have altered it, but because not everything written is ever reproduced in its entirety. When I was researching Charles Peirce in the manuscript collection at Harvard I recall turning over an envelope and finding that Peirce had written on the back, "If a woman be well dressed, her soul will be serene." I knew then that he was a great philosopher.

There is a further point that should be made here. It is often said that unlike scientists, historians cannot predict. The claim has been used to show that history cannot be a science. Whether or not history is a science seems to me not to be a question worth arguing, but the question of prediction is important. What has usually been meant by the claim that historians cannot predict is that they cannot predict the events of the past. What could it mean to say that one can predict the American Revolution or the Civil War or the Great Awakening? There is, however, a sense in which such talk of prediction does make sense. If one has an explanation of the occurrence of the event in question such that had one had that knowledge of those explanatory facts prior to the event, one could have predicted it (and no one has such knowledge of the aforementioned three events), then it is not illogical to say that the event was predictable. This is why simulation studies are so valuable; they allow such claims regarding retrospective predictability to be tested.

But what historians really predict is what data they can find and where they can find them. Scientists may predict many things, but fundamentally what they predict is what they will observe under certain conditions. The same is true of historians; they predict what observations they can make and often what those observations will tell them. But historical predictions are subject to problems to which scientific predictions are not. One can predict that events that took place in a legislature were recorded, but sometimes they were not, as Patrick Henry's famous speech in the House of Burgesses that bordered on treason was simply not recorded by the clerk.[41] Or, one can know that data were collected and ought to have been preserved but were not—as the burning of the 1890 United States Census shows. Think of all of the towns in Europe that had their records destroyed in World War II, despite their efforts to preserve them. Luckily for them, many of these could be restored since the Mormons had been there and photographed them. But a negative outcome of a search for historical data does not usually mean the same thing that a negative outcome of a physics experiment would mean, because there are so many factors that can account for it. Nevertheless, we proceed by prediction, inference, and test, because there is really no other way to proceed.

The description of the research process given earlier ignores certain practical but vital considerations. As should be obvious from the description of the Hart/O'Hart case, a considerable amount of travel, time, and money was involved. Notoriously, historians work alone, or at most with one or two partners, and there is little research money available for them from their universities, or anywhere else. These constraints may be mundane, but they have critical consequences for historical research. Historians find themselves faced with a trade-off between the information they might acquire by further research and the costs—in money and time—that would be required to obtain it. These constraints are very real; the money constraint is obvious, but the time constraint is often more important. Young historians must publish, or they perish; older ones have more leeway, but the pressure to publish is unrelenting. Research costs money. Suppose that the investigator in the Hart/O'Hart case was from a university in New York. Then he would have had to travel to Omaha, Lincoln, and Plattsmouth in Nebraska, to St. Mary's in Kansas, to St. Louis, and to Washington State. St. Louis may not be as expensive as New York City, but it is not cheap either. To put the matter in slightly different terms, a scholar who has exhausted what he believes to be the main body of materials about his subject, and yet knows that there are likely to be other data elsewhere, has to weigh the expected gain in data from such travel against the costs in time and money and decide whether or not the theory he has constructed is likely to be substantially changed by the data that still might be found. For most historians, there comes a point at which they say, "I have enough," and they get on with publication, even though they are well aware that there is a nonzero probability that someone else, using the data that they could have but did not find, will use it to demolish their theories. In the heaven of pure theory, such dilemmas would not exist, but in this vale of tears, they do.

Chapter 3

Explanation

What constitutes a historical explanation? This question has been so central to the debates over the philosophy of history over the last sixty years that it would be irresponsible to ignore it. I have therefore included this chapter, which deals much more with philosophical issues than with historical ones. The conclusion that what best explains human action is what is often called "folk psychology"—that action is caused by desires and beliefs—will surprise no historian, since it is how historians have always explained human actions. But the argument that supports that conclusion is not simple and will chiefly interest philosophers. Readers who are not interested in the philosophy of history may find this chapter difficult and wish to skip to chapter 4.

⌘

The word "explanation" has various meanings. Michael Scriven, for example, speaks of explaining the "rules of Hanoverian succession," meaning a detailed exposition of what those rules were.[1] This is of course a legitimate use of the term *explanation*, but it is not the meaning that will be discussed here. What we shall be concerned with is *causal* explanation—explanations of how and why events and actions took place. Were it not for the cumbersomeness of the term, I would use "causal explanation" throughout, but I will assume the reader understands that when the term *explanation* is used in this text, it abbreviates "causal explanation."

Although this issue of explanation is as old as the writing of history, the modern debate began in 1942 with Carl Hempel's "The Function of General Laws in History" in which he presented a theory of explanation for history that he and Paul Oppenheim subsequently developed into a general theory of scientific explanation.[2] According to Hempel, an explanation of an event, E, consists of three parts: one or more general laws asserting that always upon the occurrence of events

47

of types $C_1. \ldots C_n$, an E-type event follows, a statement that in the case in question events of types $C_1, \ldots C_n$ did occur, and the logical deduction that upon this occasion E occurred. Thus the schema is

Always C_1 and . . . and $C_n \rightarrow E$
On this occasion, C_1 and . . . and C_n occurred
Therefore, on this occasion, E occurred.

Since this claim about how they explained events was news to historians, Hempel modified his claim slightly by admitting that a rough sketch of such an explanation might do for history, but the modification was trifling. In subsequent papers, Hempel developed a schema for probabilistic explanations that was no more helpful to historians than his original model.[3]

The difficulties with Hempel's model, known as the "covering law" model, since the general laws are supposed to "cover" the particulars in question, are many. It is doubtful that this model fits all actual explanations, even in physics, but it certainly does not fit what happens in history. Without reviewing the enormous literature that this debate has generated, two points can be made. First, if historical explanations require covering laws, then where are the laws? Rather obviously, they are in embarrassingly short supply. There are few, if any, such historical laws, and if the social sciences are pressed into service to fill the gap, the lack of such laws in social science leaves us not much better off. Second, the explanations historians actually give are usually given in singular causal sentences (e.g., "Truman granted diplomatic recognition to Israel because he wanted to carry New York in 1948"). If such a statement connecting events C and E is "covered" by a general law, we have an explanation satisfactory to a Hempelian. But what if it is not? And since in fact we rarely have the general laws, this is the important question.

Suppose that under conditions K, C does cause E. Then most would agree that the occurrence of E is explained if K and C obtain. But without the general laws, how do we know that in conditions K, C causes E? Donald Davidson has held that we can still assert the singular causal statement as true even without the general law, provided that we have good reason to believe that such a law exists, even though we do not know what it is.[4] But in essence what this comes down to is a judgment call. Why not simply judge that in K, C causes E and be done with it?

Singular causal statements occur in every field of empirical inquiry, so the issue here is broader than just history. If we accept the claim that all laws that account for the occurrence of events are causal laws, then we appear to be caught in a circle. We seem to be unable to establish that a given sequence of C and E is causal without a law, and we cannot tell what uniformities of the world are lawful without knowing what causes what. How do we escape from this circle? It will help us to look back to David Hume, from whose writings the modern theory of cause derives. As is well known, in the *Treatise* Hume claimed that when cases of causal interaction are closely observed (e.g., the collision of billiard balls), all that can actually be seen is the temporal priority of the cause, the contiguity in time and space of the cause and effect, and the constant conjunction between the cause and effect.[5] Hume seems to have been somewhat doubtful about the importance of contiguity. In the *Enquiry*, he gave a somewhat different definition of cause:

> We may define a cause to be *an object, followed by another, and where all the objects similar to the first are followed by objects similar to the second.* Or in other words *where, if the first object had not been, the second never had existed.*[6]

Here contiguity is dropped from the list of empirical indicators, and the counterfactual is added. Explicitly, Hume held that the empirical indicators were not enough to define causality; he insisted that causation involved a necessary connection between cause and effect. According to Hume, the constant conjunction in our experience of a C-type event with an E-type event leads us to associate the idea of the cause with that of the effect, since association by contiguity is one of the "laws" of mental actions. This association becomes habitual, or "customary," and so we have an impression of reflection of this customary connection; it is from that impression of reflection that the idea of the necessity of the causal connection arises,[7] and it is this that underlies the counterfactual formulation.

It is obvious that Hume was not a "Humean," as that term is used today. The so-called "Humean" view is that constant conjunction (i.e., regularity) is the criterion of laws, and singular sequences of events are causal only if they instance such laws. The connections among the events constituting the regularity are taken to be purely contingent, and all necessary connections are denied. This is clearly *not* Hume's position. For Hume, regularity was an empirical *evidence* of causality, but causality could not be defined by regularity.

The problems with Hume's theory have been a subject of considerable recent discussion. Modern writers reject out of hand Hume's mechanistic psychology, and so his account of causal necessity. But none of the purely empirical marks of causation are adequate either. Temporal

priority is a doubtful criterion. In Newtonian physics, masses act simultaneously upon each other. It has even been suggested that backward
causation is possible, though as far as I know, no convincing case of
it has been described. In any event, the claim of temporal priority is
clearly too strong. As for contiguity, this seems to be a matter of which
scientific theory one believes. In Newtonian physics, there is action at
a distance; in Einsteinian physics, there is no action at a distance; in
quantum mechanics, no one really knows. The issue therefore seems to
be an empirical one, and not one to be settled by definition. Whether
contiguity in time is a necessary mark of causation also seems to be an
open question. As Patrick Suppes has noted, in Freudian theory, events
in childhood have effects years later.[8] Nor does constant conjunction
fare much better. Many regularities in experience are not directly causal,
and so are not lawlike. Day follows night, spring follows winter, but
no one thinks that night causes day or winter causes spring. These are
common cause problems, but there are also purely accidental regularities—such as Nelson Goodman's example of all of the coins in his pocket
being silver.[9] Hume rejected the notion that regularity was sufficient for
causality, being all too well aware of the occasionalist interpretations of
Malbranch and others,[10] and he insisted that causality involves necessary
connection. But how is one to know if a regularity is due to a causal
connection if the definition of causality depends on regularity?

In a widely influential book of the 1970s, J. L. Mackie tried to
answer this problem by proposing the following definition of cause:

> X occurred and Y occurred and in the circumstances, Y would
> not have occurred if X had not.[11]

Mackie takes the singular causal statement as primary and introduces
the element of necessity by the use of the contrary-to-fact conditional.[12]
As lately noted, Hume himself suggested this line of approach in the
Enquiry, but Mackie makes it central. A regularity is not accidental if,
given the right conditions, the effect would not have occurred if the
cause had not occurred. But how do we know if the counterfactual is
true? Mackie thinks of counterfactuals as suppositional.

> A non-material conditional statement introduces a supposition
> (the antecedent) and asserts something (the consequent) within
> the scope of that supposition. The conditional "If P, Q" can
> be paraphrased by "Suppose that P; on that supposition, Q";
> or again by "In the possible situation that P, Q also." This ac-
> count holds for all non-material conditionals; a counterfactual

adds to this the suggestion that the antecedent does not hold in the actual world.[13]

This in effect is a possible world analysis, although Mackie does not believe in real possible worlds. And since the counterfactual is not true in the actual world, he holds that it cannot be true or false.

It is not a long step from Mackie to Robert Stalnaker and David Lewis and the full-blown theory of possible worlds semantics for counterfactuals. As Saul Kripke showed, possible worlds can provide models for modal logics.[14] Thus "Necessarily p" is true if "p" is true in all possible worlds, and "Possibly p" is true if "p" is true in some possible world. It is obvious that here "Necessity" and "Possibility" act like quantifiers over possible worlds. But the range of a quantifier can be restricted, in which case the range includes only the possible worlds that satisfy the restrictions. For example, if we are concerned with what is physically possible under the laws of nature that hold in "i" (our actual world), then the possible worlds accessible from "i" are limited to those that have the same physical laws that we have. In this case, for "p" to be necessary, it must hold in all the worlds accessible from "i"—that is, all those with the same laws of nature that obtain in our world. But it should be noted that "i" is not always among the possible worlds accessible from other possible worlds. Thus, for example, if we want to know what is possible in a morally perfect world, it is fairly obvious that our world "i" is not among those accessible from the perfect world.[15]

But what are possible worlds? Stalnaker takes them to be properties that could have been instantiated in the actual world but were not; Lewis takes them to be metaphysically real alternative worlds. It is David Lewis who gives the most thorough and detailed elaboration of the theory of possible worlds, and so I will focus on his work. It seems clear that there are real possibilities; Al Gore might have been elected in 2000; it is possible that a vaccine against AIDS will be developed in the next decade, and so on. Lewis holds that such statements refer to a way the world might have been or might be—hence to worlds like ours except that Gore was elected or the vaccine is developed. Such worlds Lewis calls "possible worlds." A statement such as "The next president of the United States will be female" is shown to be possible if there is an accessible possible world in which it is true. But a statement such as "Jones built a spherical cube" is impossible because the term "spherical cube" is contradictory and Jones's project must fail in every possible world. But one must be very careful of the terminology here. A statement "p" is true in an accessible possible world if it satisfies its truth conditions in that world, but for a statement to be true in an accessible *possible* world does not make it true in our *actual* world; rather, if "p" is true in an accessible possible world, then "p" is *possible* in our actual world. This point is often put somewhat differently, as the statement that "Possibly p" is true in the actual world if "p" is true in an accessible possible world. Thus it is correct to say that if "p" is true in an accessible possible world, it is possible in our actual world, or that "Possibly p" is true in our actual world if "p" is true in an accessible possible world. What one cannot say is that "p" is true in our actual world if it is true in an accessible possible world.

An infinite number of possible worlds exist. Lewis orders these in terms of similarity to some world chosen as a reference point—in our case, to our actual world. The point is that for a statement to be held possible in our actual world, it should be true in the accessible possible world, or worlds most similar to the actual world—that is, where its being true compels the least amount of deviation from our actual world. For example, "The next president of the United States could be female" would be true in a world in which the U.S. Constitution was amended to require the president to be female, but obviously the possibility of any such amendment is vanishingly small. One would therefore prefer a possible world in which the current electoral procedures would lead to the election of a female, since that would require less deviation from the actual world.[16]

There is, however, a real problem in extending this possible worlds apparatus to deal with counterfactuals. A counterfactual conditional such as "If Gore had been elected in 2000, then the United States would not have invaded Iraq" can be shown to be true in some nearby possible worlds and is therefore possible in our actual world. But what we want to know is whether the counterfactual is true in our actual world. Lewis sets out the truth conditions for counterfactuals as follows. He holds that possible worlds are grouped into nested "spheres" surrounding a given world, with each sphere containing real possible worlds, and with the spheres ordered by the similarity of their worlds to the given world. The actual world is therefore the center of a concentric set of "spheres" or sets of possible worlds so ordered that the sphere closest to the actual world contains those possible worlds most similar to our actual world. A sphere is said to be "antecedent-permitting" if it contains at least one possible world in which the antecedent of the counterfactual is true,[17] and a possible world is an "antecedent-world" if the antecedent is true in that world. Then Lewis gives the truth conditions for counterfactuals of the form "If A had been, then B would have been" as

(1) there is no antecedent-permitting sphere around i [the given world], or

(2) the consequent holds at every antecedent-world in the smallest antecedent-permitting sphere around i.[18]

What this comes to is that a counterfactual is true if it is vacuously true, or if it is true in the possible world or worlds in which both its antecedent and its consequent are true and which is most similar to the actual world. But true of what? What does a counterfactual being true in a possible world have to do with its being true in our world? The antecedent of a counterfactual is by definition false in the actual world—that is why it is a counterfactual. Why should we care if it is possible to imagine circumstances in which it would be true if those circumstances are not those of this world? If this means that the actual world *could have been* that possible world, then how do we prove *that* counterfactual claim? To do so, we would have to employ the counterfactual "q": If the actual world W were identical with the possible world X which is an antecedent-world for "p," and the consequent of "p" is true in X, then the counterfactual "p" would be true in the actual world. But this leads immediately to a contradiction, since the antecedent of "p" is false in the actual world but must be true in the possible world X if X is an antecedent-world. Hence, W and X cannot be identical. Indeed, since the antecedent of a counterfactual is false in our actual world, our world can never be an antecedent world as required by Lewis's definition of truth for counterfactuals. The theory of possible worlds does not give us a way of determining which counterfactuals are true in our actual world.

The problem of counterfactuals is not new, and much has been written about it, and about the problem of conditionals generally. "Conditional" is a syntactic category. Beyond the fact that a conditional is false if its antecedent is true and its consequent false, it has no semantic implications. Any two indicative sentences can be yoked together in a syntactically proper conditional. Thus "If the sky is blue, then the sea is deep," "If gold is heavier than lead, then Sophie is pregnant," and "If sugar is sweet, then Everest is four feet high" are all perfectly proper conditionals, though it is hard to see why anyone would assert them. As far as the syntax is concerned, it makes no difference whether the antecedent is true or false; thus "If Bush is arrogant, then 2 + 2 = 4" and "If Columbus discovered Greenland, then Napoleon won at Waterloo" are substitution instances of the same conditional schema as the preceding conditionals, namely, "If _____ then _____." However, a counterfactual conditional of the form "Had A been the case, then B would have been the case" does have the semantic implication that the antecedent is false. One cannot say "Had Nixon been elected president in 1968, then he would have sought to subvert the U.S. Constitution"; the syntax implies that he was not elected in 1968 when in fact he was. Such a statement is semantically ill formed; it is like saying "Since Jones was dead, he ran the marathon." Furthermore, contrary-to-fact *causal* conditionals have further semantic implications. Consider, "If Jackson had been at Gettysburg, then the South would have won the battle,"[19] "If Kennedy had been president in 1965, then U.S. combat troops would not have been sent to Vietnam," "If Truman had run in 1952, then he would have defeated Eisenhower." What these sentences assert is that there is a causal relation between what the antecedent asserts and what the consequent asserts. Such statements are true or false; certainly Robert E. Lee believed the first to be true; many believe the second to be true; no one thinks the third is true. But what are they true or false *of*? They are true or false depending upon whether or not the referent of the antecedent bears a causal relation to the referent of the consequent in the actual world. So obviously we run in a circle; such a counterfactual is true if there really is such a causal relation and false if not. Instead of supplying the required necessary connection of cause and effect, a causal counterfactual depends upon that relation. The counterfactual analysis of causation does not advance us one inch.

The apparent hopelessness of this approach has led a number of philosophers in recent years to emphasize the priority of causes rather than laws. One of the leaders among those has been Nancy Cartwright, who has been a vigorous critic of the established philosophy of science. In her 1983 book, *How the Laws of Physics Lie,*[20] she flatly declared, "Really powerful explanatory laws of the sort found in theoretical physics do not state the truth."[21] Her more recent (1989) book, *Nature's Capacities and Their Measurement,*[22] presents what amounts to an inversion of the Humean program.[23] Instead of seeking to reduce singular causal facts to regularities, Cartwright takes singular causal facts to be primary[24] and regards regularities as *evidence* of causal relations. What singular causal facts establish is the existence of "capacities," which she describes as follows:

> Properties may carry a variety of different kinds of tenden-
> cy—tendencies to behave in certain ways, to bear certain fixed
> relations to other properties, to evolve in a particular manner,
> or to produce certain kinds of effects. For all of these I use the

general word "tendency"; "capacity" is reserved for a special subset of these—those tendencies which are tendencies to cause or to bring something about.[25]

Capacities are those causal powers that attach to properties; they are ontologically real,[26] and they are the fundamental factors in the explanation of what happens in nature.[27] Capacities are taken to be stable. What we observe is singular causal facts. Observation and experiment can establish that in certain test populations these singular causal facts are repeated.[28] But we go beyond this when we generalize more broadly that certain capacities are causally connected to certain properties.[29] Thus we have a three-tiered structure.

> At the bottom we have individual singular causings. At the top we have general causal claims, which I render as statements associating capacities with properties—"Cash-in-pocket can inhibit recidivism" or "Inversions have the capacity to amplify." In between stands the phenomenal content of the capacity claim—a vast matrix of detailed, complicated, causal laws.[30]

David Armstrong has presented a theory that, although different from Cartwright's, also gives priority to singular causal sequences (i.e., token-token relations). For Armstrong, the fundamental constituents of the world are states of affairs—x's being an F, for example,[31] and states of affairs are the terms of causal relations. The causal relation is a non-relational attribute of the sequence of states of affairs and is conceptually primitive. "It is not to be further analyzed conceptually."[32] As Hume correctly saw, from our experience we acquire the notion of regularities as a feature of the world, and "we *bring together* our experience of singular causation and our experience of regularity. We come to think that singular causation brings forth its effects in such a way that, roughly, the same type of cause brings forth the same type of effect."[33] But regularities alone do not give us laws. Even when we reach the statement, "It is always the case that something's being an F and having R to a further thing of the sort G causes the further thing to become H," we still have the problem of explaining the regularities.[34] Armstrong's answer is that causality holds not only between tokens but between types. "The fundamental causal relation is a nomic one, holding between state-of-affairs types, between universals."[35] This higher-order relation of types is itself a universal linking universals, and cases of singular causation instantiate the higher-order laws. Thus for Armstrong, as for Cartwright, singular causal sequences are primary, but they instantiate causal laws.

The difference between a lawful regularity and an accidental one is that the former instantiates a causal law, whereas the latter does not. But if causality accounts for law, then how can we identify causes?

There are really two questions here: Is "cause" a univocal term? Is causality perceived? The Humean position is that cause is univocal—all causality is regularity causality. But in recent years there has been an increasing amount of controversy over this issue. Richard Miller holds that there are three varieties of causality.

> The elementary varieties include pushing (for example, the wind's blowing leaves), giving sensations or feelings (for example, a sting's hurting), and motivating action (for example, fear's motivating flight). Someone who does not recognize any of the elementary varieties, or someone who is not led by growing experience of them to group these varieties under the same label, does not have the concept of cause.[36]

H. L. A. Hart and A. N. Honore hold that "there is not a single concept of causation but a group or family of concepts. These are united not by a set of common features but by points of resemblance, some of them tenuous."[37] They distinguish three concepts: producing a desired effect "by the manipulation of an object in our environment,"[38] under which they include making a difference in the normal course of events, interpersonal transactions, in which one person causes another to act by giving him reasons for doing so,[39] and opportunities for doing something.[40] They particularly emphasize that while the first concept does require some type of generalization, the second does not: "The statement that one person did something because, for example, another threatened him, carries no implication or covert assertion that if the circumstances were repeated the same action would follow."[41] The third category takes two forms: the provision of an opportunity, and the omission of or failure to provide something. Opportunities may be either conditions or causes, but omissions are another matter. "Clinton's failure to reinforce Cornwallis led to the surrender at Yorktown" does appear to be a genuine case of causality. Thus whether one regards these various meanings of "cause" as representing different concepts or as varieties of one concept, there are clearly substantial differences among them, and any analysis of causality will have to take these differences into account.

Is causation perceived? Hume denied that it is, but his views of perception are hardly those of modern psychology. There are now substantial grounds for saying that causality is perceived in at least some cases. To make this clear, one should first look at what Hume considered the paradigm case of causal interaction.

Here is a billiard ball lying on the table, and another ball moving toward it with rapidity; they strike; the ball which was formerly at rest now acquires a motion. This is as perfect an instance of the relation of cause and effect as any which we know either by sensation or reflection. Let us therefore examine it. It is evident that the two balls touched one another before the motion was communicated, and that there was no interval betwixt the shock and the motion. *Contiguity* in time and place is therefore a requisite circumstance to the operation of all causes. It is evident, likewise, that the motion which was the cause is prior to the motion which was the effect. *Priority* in time is, therefore, another requisite circumstance in every cause. But this is not all. Let us try any other balls of the same kind in a like situation, and we shall always find that the impulse of the one produces motion in the other. Here, therefore, is a *third* circumstance, viz., that of *constant conjunction* betwixt the cause and the effect. Every object like the cause produces always some object like the effect. Beyond these three circumstances of contiguity, priority, and constant conjunction I can discover nothing in this cause.[42]

In a series of ingenious experiments, A. Michotte examined the question of whether or not causality is perceived. One of these experiments involved an apparatus designed to produce phenomenal experiences that closely replicated Hume's example.[43] The apparatus consisted of a screen in which a horizontal rectangular viewing slit was made, and two disks, one smaller than the other, on each of which a black arc was drawn a half centimeter wide. The two disks were mounted with the smaller in front of the larger so that they could rotate about a common center behind the screen.[44] The arc on the smaller disk ran along the disk's edge for some distance and then turned sharply inward toward the center. When the disks were rotated, the portions of the arcs appearing in the viewing slit were seen as rectangles. By rotating the disks, the arc segment from the larger disk could be made to appear to approach the apparently stationary arc segment from the smaller disk until they touched, at which point the motion of the first segment ceased, and the second segment moved away. The apparent motions of the arc segments replicate exactly the motions of the billiard balls in Hume's example. This phenomenon Michotte named "direct launching." Subjects viewing it uniformly *perceived* the first segment as causing the motion of the second.[45]

The modern reader will hardly be surprised by this; the reply will be that the subjects' responses were due to interpretation. But they seem not to have been. Known cases of causation, such as the alignment of iron filings by a magnet, do not produce a *perception* of causality.[46]

Further, in the case of direct launching, the perception of causality was overwhelming, even when the subjects knew how the apparatus worked, and so knew that there was no actual causality involved. As Michotte remarks, "All the causal impressions mentioned in this book have occurred in the presence of observers who knew perfectly well that 'in reality' no causal influence was operating."[47] In other words, the perception of causality was cognitively impenetrable; knowledge had no effect on it. This strongly indicates that the perception of direct launching as causal is the result of a specific module—that is, that we are programmed to perceive causality under such conditions. The existence of other such hardwired perceptual modules is well established, and their characteristic feature is that they are cognitively impenetrable. Such a module would be innate, so its presence should be detectable even in very young children. This is just what Alan Leslie and his coworkers have shown to be the case.[48] It seems clear then that, Hume to the contrary notwithstanding, we do directly perceive causality in certain cases.

Locke, Hume, Mill, and empiricists generally have denied the existence of innate ideas. But they took this position in opposition to the innateness of classical rationalism. Since Noam Chomsky's work in linguistics and the cognitive revolution in psychology, empirical evidence has steadily accumulated that human beings, like other animals, are hardwired to perceive the world in certain ways. This recent innateness has little in common with classical rationalism, though some of its adherents have thought it has[49]; it is based on experimental findings and is as solidly empirical as any work in modern psychology. And the findings are hardly surprising. On evolutionary grounds alone, the ability to recognize certain relations in the world as causal would obviously advantage any species so endowed, assuming of course that there is a real world in which causal relations obtain.

What about the other varieties of causality? David Armstrong and Evan Fales have both argued that we have a direct perception of pressure on our own bodies as causal. As Armstrong summarizes his and Fales's argument:

> (1) The pressure is felt as having a location, a point or area on our own body. (2) It is felt as having a magnitude. (3) It is felt as having a direction in space. (4) Where there is more than one force applied to more or less the same part of the body, these forces can sometimes be distinguished from each other, for example, by direction. (5) Felt forces can be felt to add together in a way that depends on their respective magnitudes and directions.[50]

As Armstrong and Fales note, these properties correlate nicely with the properties of force vectors in physics. It is surely undeniable that we do perceive pressure on the body, and it does seem to be perceived as causal.

As for motivating action being causal, the wonder is that anyone has ever denied it. Even Calvinists, who deny the freedom of the will, believed that one's actions were caused by one's motives. The problem for them was, what determined one's motives? According to our New England forerunners, sinners seek sin not because they are forced to do so against their wills but because they love sin, and the reason they love sin is that they have inherited this proclivity from the original sin of Adam and Eve. Sin, they believed, is the natural state of human beings; only the grace of God can enable people to love virtue. That is why the Puritans were forever scrutinizing their own motives or, as Edwards put it, their "affections." So if even predestinarian Calvinists believed motives caused actions, those who denied determinism have had no problem in concluding that their motives caused their actions. Today, for most people in this country, it is taken for granted that their actions are caused by their motives and beliefs. Hence, the most common way of accounting for someone's actions is to cite his motives and beliefs.[51]

What about opportunities and omissions? Opportunities seem to involve a departure from the normal course of events that allows an event to occur that in the normal course would not have occurred. Thus the householder who forgets to lock his door when he leaves his house gives the burglar an opportunity for robbery that would not have existed if the door had been locked. In this case, one could argue that the unlocked door was a condition for the burglary rather than a cause. But in the fourth game of the 1941 World Series, with two out in the ninth inning and Tommy Henrich at bat with two strikes on him, Mickey Owens dropped the third strike and so allowed Henrich to reach first base, providing the Yankees with an opportunity that changed the outcome of the ball game. Here it does seem clear that the opportunity had a causal role. Omissions are somewhat different. To take the stock example of the train wreck caused by the failure to throw the switch, what is assumed is a causal chain of which the throwing of the switch is one link and which would normally lead to there being no train wreck. The chain is broken by the failure to throw the switch, which produces a different causal chain leading to the wreck. The omission itself is an event which presumably has a cause, but is *it* a cause? Apparently it is; as a result of the omission, one causal chain is initiated in place of another. This case does not seem to fall under any of the other categories discussed earlier.

If, then, in cases such as direct launching, pressure on the body, and motivation, we do perceive causal relations directly, then there are some singular causal statements that are known to be true on the basis of perceptual experience. If I touch a red-hot stove, then I burn my hand; if I hit my thumb with a hammer, then it hurts, and so on. Furthermore, it is a fact of experience that such sequences occur repeatedly, and it is often possible to determine empirically what similarities in conditions must obtain for them to do so. From such observed cases of causality, we can, by induction, generate generalizations in obvious ways. But although we can thus account for *some* regularities as causal, such as "always touching a red-hot stove burns your hand," the laws so generated are relatively low level. If we are to gain significant explanatory power from causes, then something more is needed.

It is generally agreed that if in conditions K, C causes E, then if K and C occur followed by E, the occurrence of K and C explains the occurrence of E. It would be nice if one could say here just what causation is. Unfortunately, I have no idea what causation is, and as far as I can tell, no one else does either. Efforts to analyze causation as some sort of energy transfer have failed to satisfy anyone but their proposers,[52] and I doubt that with our present tools it is possible to say just what causation is. But the fact that we cannot solve the metaphysical problem does not mean that we cannot recognize instances of causation when we meet them. There are, as Michotte demonstrated, many cases that we directly perceive as causal. Further, there are observable phenomena that serve as *evidences* of causality. As both Hume and Cartwright have pointed out, regularities are evidence of causality. They are by no means infallible evidences. There are many regularities, such as day following night or spring following winter, that are the results of common causes. I doubt that anyone ever thought that night caused day, but those who believed that at dusk the sun passed beneath the earth to emerge the next morning after its subterranean journey recognized that a causal process was involved, even if they misdescribed it. There are also purely chance regularities, such as all of the chairs in this room being made of wood. Yet regularities remain one of the chief evidences of causation. As Charles Peirce wrote:

> Uniformities are precisely the sort of facts that need to be accounted for. That a pitched coin should sometimes turn up heads and sometimes tails calls for no particular explanation; but if it shows heads every time, we wish to know how this result has been brought about. Law is *par excellence* the thing that wants a reason.[53]

Regularities are among the most salient features of the world, and the most important. Without them, all foresight, planning, and action would be impossible and, as C. I. Lewis once remarked, we should all be dead within the week.[54] Yet we have no explanation for regularities except other regularities or causes. The former obviously leads to a regress; only the latter gives us a "reason." And if causes are responsible for regularities, then regularities are evidence of causes.

A second type of evidence for causation comes from experiments and observations. The classic paradigm for these is Mill's methods. Consider a fairly typical controlled experiment to test the claim that variation in X causes variation in Y. The investigator constructs a situation in which (ideally) all of the factors other than X that are considered possible influences on Y are controlled. Then the investigator varies X. If the variation in X is followed by a corresponding variation in Y, and if there is no variation in Y when X is constant, then one concludes that the variation in X caused the variation in Y. This is a straightforward application of the method of difference: the behavior of Y when X varies is compared to its behavior when X is constant. Of course the experiment must be repeated to show that the first result was not accidental, but if repetitions of the experiment show the same result, then we conclude that we have an instance of a causal relation. This need not yield a general law. As James Woodward has shown, what is necessary is that the relation between X and Y be invariant over some continuous range of the variables and/or conditions. But if that is obtained, we have clear evidence of causation.[55]

A third type of evidence is provided by true counterfactuals. This claim will seem odd to some, but it should not. The aforementioned experiment was carried out by an investigator; that is, the investigator acted to produce the experiment when he chose to do so. A counterfactual would hold that under the conditions described, if X were to be varied, then Y would exhibit a corresponding variation. In other words, the counterfactual claims that the same result would occur if the experiment were performed at times when it is not. To deny this is to say that there is a time at which the performance of the experiment would yield a different result. But the answer to that is, name the time! If the investigator can produce the result *whenever he or she chooses*, then unless the action of the experimenter causes the result, we have reason to accept the claim that there is no time at which the performance of the experiment would not yield that result. Denial of this argument is like those debates as to whether or not I could have raised my arm at a time when I did not. Barring external constraint or physiological impairment, if I can raise my arm whenever I choose to do so, then it is silly to deny the counterfactual, "I could have raised my arm five minutes ago," when in fact I did not.

This example should remind us of the importance of action. As Lewis frequently pointed out, tests of the sort described earlier involve actions on the part of the investigator, and this is true not only with respect to experiments but observations as well. The fact that the investigator can perform the experiment or observation at will means that the connection of X and Y must be stable. There are of course phenomena to which this argument does not apply: a solar eclipse can be observed only on specific occasions. But even this rare event is repeated in a sufficiently long time frame. In those cases where the experiment or observation is under our control, that fact means that there are possible experiments and observations that could have been made but were not. To be convinced that the behaviors of X causes the behaviors of Y is therefore to be convinced that the counterfactuals relating to experiments and observations not made are true. Conversely, if we can assert the truth of such counterfactuals, then we have further evidence that X causes Y.

Some regularities are invariable, thus fitting the paradigm defined by Hume and Mill, but many are not. Where regularity is partial only, we usually talk in terms of probability. But probability arises in two ways. On the one hand, probability is a function of our ignorance. Thus in the kinetic theory of gases, we explain the relation between pressure and temperature in terms of probability. But our physical model of gases is that gases are composed of molecules that move according to deterministic laws. It is the impossibility of our simultaneously calculating the velocities, masses, directions, and positions of all of the molecules in the gases that forces us to use probabilities. On the other hand, in quantum mechanics, the objective state of affairs is believed to be describable only by probability laws. Here the indeterminacy is taken to be in the objective world. As far as I know, this sort of indeterminacy has been shown to exist only in the quantum world; in the world of molar objects, probability laws reflect our uncertainty and ignorance regarding the causal features involved. But this does not mean that such laws are not explanatory; as Suppes showed, the case for probabilistic explanation is irrefutable.[56] But I agree with Armstrong, that "what a probabilistic law gives us is not probabilistic causality but a certain probability that causation will occur."[57]

The actual situations in which we find causal activity in the world are considerably more complex than indicated earlier. As Mackie noted, very often a given type of event E has multiple causes; a fire may be started by a struck match, lightning, a cigarette butt, or in a number of other ways. Further, causes usually act only under certain conditions; fires do not burn unless oxygen is present. These complications are well known, and many writers have dealt with them, particularly John Stuart Mill,[58] but something needs to be said about them here.

The difference between a cause and a condition is, to put it mildly, vague. Some have said that a cause precedes the effect, whereas a condition persists after the effect—for example, the oxygen in the atmosphere does not disappear when the match is struck. Obviously this description is inadequate. Gravity continues to act while a body falls and thereafter, yet it is surely a cause of the body's motion. Being alive is a condition of dying rather than a cause, yet life terminates at the moment of death, whatever the actual cause of death may be. What is a condition in some cases—for example, the presence of oxygen for combustion—may be a cause in other cases—for example, the sudden combustion of sodium metal due to exposure to oxygen. It is therefore virtually impossible to draw a hard and fast line between causes and conditions, and what is taken to be one or the other will depend upon the particular objective of the inquiry. One could lump together all causes and conditions of a particular effect and call the whole lump the cause, but this would certainly violate common usage; no one would mention being alive as a cause of a man's death. But in particular cases, the distinction is usually clear enough. If the condition is understood to be that in the absence of which the cause does not operate, then we may collect these conditions into what Mackie called a "causal field" and express the causal relation of C to E as "In the causal field F, if C then E."

It is often the case that a given effect may be the result of multiple causes. As every reader of detective fiction knows, death may be caused in a variety of ways. Thus a causal regularity will often have a disjunctive form—if A or D or H then E. Moreover, the causes are often conjunctions of factors; neither drug X nor drug Y acting alone may be sufficient to kill a man, but X and Y acting together may be lethal. Thus our regularity may have the form, "If ALK v BDG v CHJ → E." If now, following Mackie again, we understand by a cause C being a necessary condition for an effect E that whenever E occurs C occurs and by C being a sufficient condition for E that whenever C occurs, E occurs, then the complete formula (ABC or DGH or JKL) represents a condition that is both necessary and sufficient for E.[59]

Of course there are a lot of further problems here. No regularity of our experience is more invariable than night following day, yet no one supposes that day causes night. This is a case of common cause; the existence of the regularity does indicate the presence of causality, though it requires further investigation to identify what the true cause

is. The real countercase is accidental regularities, such as the coins in
Goodman's pocket being made of silver. These are regularities that are
purely chance occurrences, and chance admits of no causal explanation. Here regularities do not indicate causation. But since in chance
regularities, there is no reason the regularity should persist beyond any
given term if the events of the series are independent, the probability
of such chance regularities being extended diminishes as the sequence
grows. Thus one could easily attribute five successive heads in a series
of coin tosses to chance, but one would hardly accept that explanation
for 100 successive heads. Goodman's pocket may contain nothing but
silver today, but if this is an accident, one would be very surprised if he
carried nothing but silver every day for a year. It is thus often possible
to distinguish chance regularities from causal ones.

The problems of identifying the causes of regularities are many and
are well known (e.g., preemption, trumping, etc.). These problems are
aggravating, but they do not make our lives impossible.

At an even higher level, we find more abstract laws linking deter-
minables[60] and theories that postulate the existence of constructs that
play causal roles (e.g., electrons). The road from the perception of direct
launching to the splitting of the uranium nucleus by neutron bombard-
ment is long and difficult, but the fact remains that we have no other
explanation of why some of the regularities of nature are lawlike except
that they involve causal relations.

Finally, the view here advanced seems to me to provide the only
satisfactory solution to the problem of causal counterfactuals. To say that
under conditions K, had C occurred then E would have occurred is to
say that in K, C causes E. Such a statement is true or false; if there is
a real causal relation between C and E, then the causal counterfactual is
true; if not, not. What the causal counterfactual is true *of* is the causal
relation between C and E in the actual world. The antecedent, C, is
not true in the actual world, since the statement is counterfactual; the
consequent, E, may be true or false in the actual world. But what the
statement asserts is that there is a real causal relation between C and
E in the actual world, and it is true or false accordingly. It must be
emphasized that we are talking here about *causal* counterfactuals only,
and not all counterfactuals are causal, even true ones. "If the sum of
the first ten positive integers were not 55, the sum of their cubes would
not be 3025" is a true counterfactual but not a causal counterfactual.
Lewis has even held that there are counterfactuals with true antecedents.
But the fact that any two indicative statements, one of which is false,
can be put into a counterfactual syntactic form does not show that
such statements need be taken seriously. A proposition such as "Had

it been the case that the sun came up this morning, I would have cut the grass" is not true or false; it is ill formed, since it employs a form that requires the antecedent to be false to make a statement in which the antecedent is true. This is not a problem, it is a mistake. As far as causal counterfactuals are concerned, we need look no farther than the actual world to know whether they are true or false.

The fact that some causal relations can be perceived has a special relevance to questions of human behavior. We perceive ourselves as motivated to act by our desires or aversions, with our actions guided by our beliefs. When we act, we generally do so to attain some objective or goal that we desire, and we employ the means we do because we believe they will allow us to reach our goal. This claim says little more than that human action is purposive—a claim that I think no one can deny. But it is useful to include here not only the instrumental beliefs referred to but also our beliefs concerning how our reference individuals and groups will respond to our actions, and our beliefs concerning the degree of control we have over the situation. Going to the grocery store is a simple enough purposive action, but in doing so we take it for granted that the car will start, that we can complete the drive both ways without an accident, and so on. Climbing Mt. Everest is a rather different matter. One might desire to do so, and believe one knows the means necessary to do so, yet doubt one's ability to perform the feat. Similarly, we all know that we are often encouraged or discouraged to attempt something by the views of our reference individuals and groups.

Explanations of action of the sort just described are often derided as examples of "folk psychology" that some sophisticates would have us believe have no validity. But why is it that the "folk" so uniformly believe in the adequacy of this sort of account? The obvious answer is because they perceive these factors as causally responsible for their actions. If I ask a man why he bought a particular make and model of car, it is quite a sufficient explanation for him to say that he wanted the safest car he could find, and that he believes this particular one is the safest, that his wife likes this model, and that he can afford it. What more could he say? The explanation is complete. It is therefore important to point out that the variables cited earlier are those used in Isek Ajzen's theory of planned behavior,[61] a theory that has acquired an impressive amount of experimental support. That the "folk" recognize these variables as crucial for explaining action is simply one result of the fact that they perceive these variables as playing key causal roles in accounting for their actions. And the fact that they are key variables in Ajzen's highly successful psychological studies adds evidence of the fact that they are causal factors in our actions. The strict application of Ajzen's theory to historical subjects is nearly impossible, because it requires a knowledge of the subject's subjective probabilities, and in the usual case such information cannot be obtained from historical data.

An actor's perceptions of the causes of his behavior are obviously private. For observers who wish to explain his behavior, there is therefore the problem of determining what the actor's wants and beliefs are. This sort of diagnostic problem arises all the time in human affairs and is one with which the social sciences have been much concerned. For example, one way to find out why actor A does what he does is to ask him; this is certainly the usual approach in such cases. But A may lie; for innumerable reasons, he may not want his true motives known. Or A may not be available to be asked; he may, for example, be dead, so that all we can know of him is what the historical records give us. But there are other indirect methods of finding out what A believes and wants. Very often observations or records of his behavior are sufficient to reveal what his goals are and how he believes they can be attained. And it is often possible to identify who his reference individuals or groups are. Further, A does not usually attempt an action unless he believes he has enough control over the situation to make success possible. He may of course be wrong, but it is unusual for someone to attempt something he thinks he cannot do.

Perceptions can be in error. I may perceive the animal across the street as my dog, and yet find out that it is not. The same is true regarding causes. Freud taught us that we are not always aware of why we do what we do or believe what we believe. When the behavior of someone we are observing appears to us irrational, one way of accounting for this is by postulating psychodynamic processes of which the subject is unaware. This is always a risky procedure because, on the one hand, it is too easy, while, on the other hand, it is too hard. It is too easy because one can always dream up some motive or other that might account for someone's behavior and construct a psychohistory of the individual that will make it seem plausible. This is particularly easy in the absence of data that might constrain one's creativity. It is too hard because finding good evidence that someone is motivated by drives of which he is unaware is very hard, and finding evidence for the occurrence of events that might have produced a repression of desires or beliefs is often impossible. Such explanations must be used with considerable circumspection.

In dealing with human behavior some types of causal processes have not received the attention they deserve. The first of these is rule following. If one considers one's daily behavior, then it will be clear that most of it is done according to rules. Thus in driving to work, one's behavior is governed by a set of rules for operating a motor vehicle. At work, one is, for the most part, following prescribed rules and routines. In talking with colleagues, rules of proper behavior must be observed. At meals, there are rules governing the use of dishes, flatware, glasses, and so on. Even in dealing with one's family, rules must be observed. Perhaps most obviously in speaking to others, or one self, one is following linguistic rules without which communication is impossible. Rules are such a pervasive feature of our lives that we are rarely aware of them. They are a significant part of our culture.

One must distinguish clearly between satisfying a rule and following a rule. One's behavior can satisfy a rule purely by accident. Thus given a rule to "choose only red things" in a candy store, one might happen to pick only red things because one likes cherry flavoring; here one's behavior satisfies the rule, but one could not be said to be following it. Following a rule requires seeing to it that one's behavior fits the rule. That does not require that one be conscious of the rule, although one often is. Thus we all follow linguistic rules in our speech. Most people would be hard pressed to state the rules they are following, but they are aware of their failures to follow them and will try to correct themselves if they misspeak. A young child may say, "I eated it; I mean I ate it." The correction shows that the child is following the rule, although it is unlikely that he could state it.

Rules are normative. They tell us what ought to be done in certain circumstances. Hence, they can be violated, either deliberately or inadvertently. Following a rule involves *adopting* the rule—that is, it requires a psychological commitment to following the rule. Why should one do that? Obviously, because one is taught to, but the reasons go far beyond that. Life is chaotic enough; to make social interaction manageable, one must be able to predict how others will act, and others must be able to predict our actions. Usually rules attach to some group of actors who, in particular circumstances, will be expected to follow the rules. That means others expect that in the proper circumstances the actors will follow the rule, and they usually disapprove of actors who fail to do so. That disapproval acts as a negative sanction on the actors. Such sanctions may be internal (e.g., guilt or shame), but often they are external and sometimes formalized so that some group or person has the duty of sanctioning actors as they do or do not perform the expected behavior under the prescribed circumstances. Thus the driving code is enforced, not only by swearing motorists and the risk of accident, but by police officers whose job it is to enforce the code. Similarly, at work most people are subject to supervisors who can punish or reward behavior as it does or does not conform to the rules. People may even be committed to following rules that they dislike and obey only because they dislike the negative sanctions for disobedience even more (e.g., prison inmates). This structure of actors, expectors, and sanctioners is pervasive in our culture and most others. The existence of such rules explains much of our behavior. Americans are taught to eat with their forks in their right hands; when they use knives, they shift their forks to their left hands and pick up their knives with their right hands. American agents in Europe in World War II sometimes gave themselves away by forgetting that Europeans eat with their forks in their left hands. Each culture has its rules for the use of flatware, but they happen to be different—a fact of which the Gestapo took full advantage.

Table manners are rules learned early and are informally enforced. Laws represent the formalization of such rules backed by coercive sanctions. Thus the *Laws and Liberties* of 1648 in Massachusetts contains a law prescribing that every witch shall be put to death. As this statute makes clear, rules are defined over the sets of persons believed to exist in a given culture, whether we now believe such persons existed or not. The government of Massachusetts in the seventeenth century did believe that there were real witches and acted accordingly, most notably in the case of Salem Village in 1692. Rules are culture specific; one drives on the right in the Untied States, on the left in England. And they involve those persons believed to exist in the worldview of the society that subscribes to them.

Explanations by rules are not covering law explanations. Rules are not laws; they are normative statements of what ought to be done. Hence, a rule explanation must involve not only the statement of the rule but the added statement that the subject involved is committed to following the rule. If these are given, then it will follow that the subject will probably perform the action required by the rule in question, if he is able to perform it and believes that he is able to perform it. Rules thus can function to predict and explain the behaviors of actors where there is evidence that the actors are committed to following the rule. It is the commitment to following the rule that provides the causal force.[62]

Rules are a major part of the culture of a society, and like other components they can change over time. They also vary between different subsets of society. Rules of dress vary by the sex of the wearer and by the wearer's age.[63] In our society and in many others, they also vary by class, where they become characteristics of refinement.

> Epitomizing the new refinement was the changing use of the fork.
> Through the first half of the nineteenth century most table forks

were made of iron or steel with two sharp prongs. One held such
a fork in the left hand and, after cutting a piece of food, raised
the morsel upward with the fork still in the left, and then used
the flat, rounded blade of the knife in one's right hand to put the
food in one's mouth. But as the two-tined fork yielded to forks
with three, then four tines (and often of silver), the cumbersome
and characteristically American procedure developed, whereby
one transferred the fork from left to right after cutting a piece
of food, and only then raised it to one's mouth.[64]

As this passage illustrates, there is a close relationship between changing
rules for the table and the changes in material culture—a relationship
that holds for other sectors of the culture as well. There are innumerable
examples of rules governing the behavior of groups and the interactions
among groups. Thus

A gentleman [meeting a lady] should remove his hat from his
head with the hand farthest from the person saluted. This turns
the hat from instead of toward them. If you see that the person
saluted is going to stop to shake hands, use the left in order to
leave the right free.[65]

The history of rules and rule changes forms an important part of cultural
history, and one that has recently received increased attention.

The second causal process that requires emphasis is plans. We
normally act with a considerable amount of foresight. We do not rush
about madly seeking to satisfy each impulse as it occurs; rather, we plan
what we will do and when and how we will do it. This is obvious in
an individual's daily life; before going to the market, one thinks about
what one will need and makes a list of what to buy. This is even more
obvious where multiple people are involved. Group actions require co-
ordination, which in turn requires planning who will do what, when,
and how. Planning is a fundamental part of human action.

Plans may or may not be normative. Individual plans may have
either character; group plans usually are normative, because for the
plan to work, each member must act as the plan requires, and failure
to do so disrupts the actions of others. When a particular play is called
in a football game, each player has a specific role to play, and failure
to do so will bring swift sanctions from fellow players and the coach.
For example, the receiver who does not follow his assigned route on
a particular play will hear about it loud and clear. Thus, as in the case
of rules, satisfying a plan must be distinguished from following it. To

follow a plan requires a commitment to do so, and it is the commitment that provides the causal force. But where there is a plan and the
actors are committed to following it, the probability is high that they
will do so.

It is common to refer to *the* problem of historical explanation.
There is no one such problem. Historians are concerned with many different things. They may have to explain physical events (climate change,
variations in sea levels), natural events (agricultural blights, fish or animal
migrations), interactions between natural and social events (epidemics,
environmental destruction or pollution), social events (wars, revolutions),
and so forth. They are called upon to explain individual behavior, group
behavior, interactions between individuals and groups, the behaviors of
organizations, states, or armies, cultural changes—such as the rise and
fall of religions, political systems, or economic systems—and so on.
In other words, historians have to account for what happened in the
past that affected human beings, and the range of such factors is vast.
Some of these may be amenable to covering law explanations, some to
statistical explanations, and some to an explanation by singular causal
statements. There is no one type of explanation that covers all of the
phenomena with which historians must deal. The problems of historical
explanations are therefore just as great as the problems of explaining
what people do in the present world.

How then do historians choose their subjects? There is no rule here;
historians select the subjects that happen to interest them. A variety of
factors will affect this choice. In their graduate training they often find
subjects that their teachers encourage them to pursue, or their interests
may stem from their childhoods, from stories told to them by adults,
or from their own reading. But there are also discernable effects of the
society in which they grow up. For example, prior to the 1960s, the
abolitionists did not inspire much interest. Many considered them to
have been crackbrained idealists, and how they won was puzzling. Then
in the 1960s, historians saw social movements whose dynamics were
similar to that of the abolitionist movement. These movements grew
stronger the more they were denounced and repressed; they courted
arrests and saw them as badges of honor; they were devoted to idealistic
goals and acquired passionate support. Suddenly it was possible to see
in action how such movements worked, and so to understand better
how abolitionism had become so powerful. This revelation generated a
good deal of research and scholarship.

Or, consider the sudden flowering of social history—of books
on the poor or "common" people, described as writing history "from
the bottom up." This too was due, to a considerable extent, to the

1960s's influence. Historians are not isolated from their societies, and the changing ideological beliefs of the society often affect the problems they choose to work on.

One might think that when historians deal with problems of the sorts that in the modern world are dealt with by the social sciences, the sensible thing to do would be to apply to the past events the social scientific theories that are applied to corresponding events today. This makes perfect sense, *if* there is a satisfactory social science theory covering the case, and *if* the theory is applicable. But it needs to be pointed out that, first, the success of the social sciences in explaining present phenomena is not very impressive, and second, that applying a theory from the social sciences, which means a theory developed on the basis of modern American or European data, to a society from a different era may create more problems than it solves.

To take the first point, probably the most sophisticated social science just now is economics. But, notoriously, economic forecasts are often far off the mark. Further, there are quite different economic theories currently in use that yield quite different accounts of present phenomena. There are still supply side economists among us, despite the dismal records of supply side measures. As will be noted in some detail, attempts to explain the Great Depression by Monitarists and by Keynesians come to very different conclusions. Obviously one should make use of the social sciences when possible, but one should not delude oneself into thinking that one is dealing with physics.

The second point is even more critical. Past societies are not copies of present societies; they differ in technology, institutions, customs, norms, and beliefs, and in innumerable other ways. They are different cultures, and people in those cultures may not behave the way we do in our culture. The attempt to shoehorn past social phenomena into the categories of our contemporary theories is almost certain to lead to trouble. One egregious example of this is Robert Fogel's and Stanley Engermann's *Time on the Cross*,[66] an attempt to apply current economic theory to the antebellum South. The fact that current economic theories assume a free labor force rather than slavery did not deter Fogel and Engermann. For example, they compared slave maintenance costs to the wage income of free labor, the slave diet to the diet of free workers, slave housing to the housing of free workers, and similarly for clothing and medical care. But the maintenance cost of a slave was what was required for subsistence, whereas the wages of free labor were (according to economic theory) what was required to induce workers to work. No matter how slave maintenance cost is calculated, and there are serious problems with the way Fogel and Engermann calculated it, these are not comparable quantities. Similarly, Fogel and Engermann estimated slave housing by the number of square feet in a slave cabin, but the number they used was for an exceptionally large slave cabin. They compared this to the sleeping space in the very worst New York slums in 1893. It should be obvious that housing quality involves a good deal more than the square footage, and equating total square footage, on the one hand, to sleeping space, on the other, is certain to yield biased results. Similar remarks apply to their estimates of diet, clothing, and so on. These problems all arise from the attempt to make the material well-being of slaves comparable to that of free labor so that they could apply the categories of standard economic theory to slavery. In fact, those categories do not apply to slavery, and the result is a very misleading picture. They completely ignored as well the phenomenon of slave resistance, since they had no convenient modern category under which to place it. One should hardly be surprised that their work produced weird results, including, for example, the claim that slave labor was more efficient than free labor. The present is not the past, and one must be very careful in applying current theories to the past.[67]

What differentiates historical explanations from present-day explanations is not that history requires some special forms of explanation, but that historical data differ from other present data. A social science investigator working on a current problem has the capacity to generate new data at will. The constraints on his doing so are usually money and time, though sometimes political and legal limitations are involved. The historian usually has a far more limited body of data to work with and cannot increase his base of data at will. Sometimes the database can be expanded by finding new materials previously overlooked or by lucky finds, as happened, for example, in the discovery of the Dead Sea Scrolls. But usually historical data are increased by finding a way to extract new information from objects long known to exist. A good example of this is the impact of the computer on our ability to manipulate large bodies of data. The "New Political History," pioneered by Lee Benson, is a case in point. The utilization of all the county election returns for the country in a study of a past election would be impossible if it were not for the computer. But even so, historical data usually are fragmentary, and the processes by which they are preserved are not ones that generate random samples out of past populations. As a result, problems that nowadays would be researched by the use of interviews, questionnaires, observations schedules, and the like usually cannot be attacked by these methods in history. One cannot interview the dead. Many contemporary theories cannot be applied historically for the simple reason that the data necessary for their application no longer exist or were never collected in the first place. Historians use whatever data they can find and adapt their explanatory strategies to fit the data they have. What is common to historical explanations is the attempt to determine what caused what, and any type of explanation that can solve that problem is legitimate in history.

.

Chapter 4

Theory

I have described historical "interpretations" as theories. In this chapter, I hope to substantiate that claim by examining a number of examples of such theories. I distinguish four levels of historical theories: those dealing with particular subjects, which may include such things as particular periods, those dealing with hypothetical states of affairs for which direct evidence is lacking, expressly formulated historical theories, and so-called "grand theories." Examples of each type are discussed here.

⬟

By a "theory," I shall, following W. V. Quine, mean a set of logically consistent sentences about some subject. This is a minimal definition; it does not require the sentences of the theory to be true. Thus we speak without hesitation of the Newtonian theory of mechanics, the Aristotlean theory of the four elements, and the Ptolemaic theory of astronomy, although none is currently regarded as true. Those who advance such theories, however, do believe that they are true. Nearly enough, the set of logically consistent statements about a subject that one believes to be true may be taken to be one's theory concerning that subject.[1] In terms of this latitudinarian definition of "theory," it should be obvious that what a historian calls an "interpretation" is actually a "theory."

Are historical theories consistent? Often they are not. Historians do not think much about consistency, and often they lack the tools necessary to determine whether their theories are consistent. But they do not knowingly advance theories that are inconsistent; they want their theories to hang together, and they assume that if they do, then they are consistent. As far as this belief rests on a conscious justification, it is that if, as historians believe, their theories are true, then they must be consistent, since true statements cannot contradict each other. A theory, all of whose statements are true, must be consistent, and historians do strive for the truth.

75

Historians' theories are intended to tell us what happened in the past and why. Accordingly, they deal with events, persons, and facts. But a more careful analysis of such theories shows that what they actually explain are the data; historical facts, events, and persons, being unobservable because they no longer exist, are part of the theory and are asserted to have existed because by doing so historians can account for their data. Thus the whole structure of facts and theory rests on an observational base of presently observable data; these data provide our only access to the past, and in the final analysis these data are accounted for by the theory.

There is, of course, an interaction between theory and data. It usually is the case that the data accounted for are those that best support historians' theories. Data that are not supportive of the theory then have to be "explained away" as "irrelevant" or "insignificant" or are simply ignored. Historians accept this procedure as inevitable. It is generally accepted in the trade that the use historians make of data is "selective," meaning that they emphasize what they consider the most "important" data or, otherwise put, the data that will best fit their theories. It is not surprising, under these circumstances, that historians' accounts of the same subjects often disagree.

Historical theorizing takes place on several levels. At the first level, a narrative history is produced that constitutes the historian's account of a particular subject. Although the account appears purely descriptive, underlying it are theoretical assumptions, explicit or implicit, that govern the organization of the narrative, the selection of data, and the distribution of emphasis in the account. A second level of theorizing becomes apparent when the historian believes some state of affairs to have existed but does not have the evidence to prove or disprove it. Here the hypothesized state of affairs is introduced with such support as it has, but reliance is placed on how that hypothesis fits in with other components of the account—that is, on the coherence of the account when the hypothesis is included, as compared to when it is not included. A third level is reached when the historian explicitly formulates a theoretical hypothesis to account for a wide range of data and offers confirming evidence for them. Finally, we have the level of "grand theory," dealing with the rise and fall of civilizations, or the past, present, and future development of a social institution or a nation, or a religion, and so on. In what follows, I examine examples of each of these levels chosen from a variety of fields.

An example of the first level is provided by Arthur M. Schlesinger's *The Age of Jackson*,[2] a narrative history of the Jacksonian period, brilliantly written by one of the most gifted writers among present-day historians.

Schlesinger frames the conflicts of the era in terms of the Hamiltonian tradition, on the one hand, which called for government support of wealth and manufacturing, and which he sees as continued in Henry Clay's "American System," which called for protective tariffs to build up domestic manufacturing, internal improvements to facilitate inter-state trade, and a national bank to hold government funds and regulate the currency. The Jeffersonian tradition, on the other hand, called for minimal government interference in the economy, limited manufactur-ing, and a nation of freehold farmers. Jackson's election in 1828 was seen as a triumph for the Jeffersonian point of view, but Jackson was a Jeffersonian with a difference.

Jackson did oppose the use of federal money for internal improve-ments within the borders of a state, as he made clear by the Maysville veto. He also opposed the Bank of the United States and vetoed the bill rechartering the Bank. He viewed the Bank as a monopoly, which in Smithian terms, it was—a private bank granted special privileges by the government. But Jackson's views went farther; he was a hard-money man who opposed the issuance of banknotes by private banks. Since at that time the federal government issued only specie, the actual circulat-ing currency of the country consisted of banknotes that were essentially IOUs issued by the banks. The value of these notes fluctuated depending on what people thought the likelihood of their redemption was, and the volume of the note issue varied with banks' expectations of good or bad times, so that the money supply was unstable in quantity and value and varied with popular confidence. The monetary system was thus peculiarly liable to violent fluctuations. While Jackson accepted the use of bank paper such as bills of exchange in commercial transactions, he wanted to eliminate the circulation of small denomination banknotes. This led to a series of actions against the banking system, including the veto of the recharter of the Bank of the United States, the removal of federal deposits from the Bank, the specie circular, and, under Van Buren, who succeeded Jackson in office, an attempt to establish an independent trea-sury by the federal government that would handle currency matters—a proposal enacted under Van Buren but repealed later by the Whigs.

Jackson's monetary views created a problem for Schlesinger. While Eastern working men may have supported hard money, Westerners did not. They did support Jackson's attack on the Bank of the United States, because one of that institution's functions was to force other banks to limit their note issues, and Westerners wanted not fewer banknotes but more. Thus the continued support for Jackson in the West, despite his hard-money policy, has to be explained, and Schlesinger does so by claiming that Jackson's personal popularity in the West was enough to offset the lack of appeal of his monetary policy. On the tariff, Jackson failed to move until the Nullification Controversy forced the issue. While affirming the indissoluble character of the Union, he and his supporters arranged a compromise on the tariff that undercut the Nullification movement and resolved the issue.

Schlesinger strengthens the support for his thesis by a review of developments in three states—Massachusetts, New York, and Pennsylvania. He stresses the development of Workingmen's Parties, unions, and even strikes, as well as the rise in New York of the Locofocos, representing the working-class radicals in their battle against the more conservative wing of the Democratic Party, centered in Tammany Hall. The analysis of these three states is used to show the class character of the political strife, with the Jacksonians representing the "producing class" (i.e., the workers and farmers). It is significant that in his discussions of New York, Schlesinger makes only four casual references to AntiMasonry.

Schlesinger follows the fate of the Jacksonians through the Whig victory of 1840 and Polk's victory in 1844. As the forties passed into the fifties, the slavery issue increasingly became the dominant political issue in the nation. Schlesinger argues that the Jacksonians became the leaders of the antislavery movement. The Democratic Party split over the issue with Van Buren leading the Free Soil ticket in 1848, and by 1850 the political realignment that would create the Republican Party and leave the Democratic Party as the party of conservatism was well under way. The last Jacksonian in Schlesinger's view was Andrew Johnson, and with the capture of the Republican Party by business leaders, Jacksonianism was dead.

Schlesinger ends his volume with a discussion of Jacksonianism's failure to develop a lasting ideology. The Jacksonians, he believes, were caught between a traditional and sentimental allegiance to Jeffersonianism and the need for the intervention of a strong government to curb the increasing power of the business community or, as Herbert Croly was to put it, the need for Hamiltonian means to achieve Jeffersonian ends.[3] This left the antigovernment position up for grabs, and those who grabbed it were the business leaders. Despite the rhetoric, each party when in power, asserted strong government intervention in the economy and when out of power opposed it. The Jacksonian economic issues did not become dominant again in American politics until the end of the nineteenth century, and Schlesinger, writing in 1946, had the good fortune to be able to believe that with the New Deal they had achieved at least a temporary victory. How temporary the victory was is now tragically apparent.

What underlies Schlesinger's narrative account is the belief that the "real" conflict of the Jacksonian era was a class conflict between the working class, including urban workers, artisans, and small farmers, on the one side, and the business class, including the emerging manufacturing and commercial classes and wealth in general, on the other. Jackson is presented as the hero of the "producing class"—that is, the working class, and his opponents such as Nicholas Biddle, Henry Clay, and Daniel Webster as representing various segments of the moneyed class. This class conflict model is supported not only by data concerning the political conflict at the national level but also by Schlesinger's examination of Massachuetts, New York, and Pennsylvania, which were the most industrialized states in the union at that time. This model of "Jacksonian Democracy" is quite explicit in Schlesinger's pages and informs his whole narrative. Clearly, it is a theoretical model used to explain the data and the events of the period.

To bring out the degree to which theories at this level can differ, it is worth comparing Schlesinger's analysis to that presented fifteen years later by Lee Benson.[4] Benson's book focuses on only one state—New York—but New York was the largest state, one of the two most industrialized states in the country, the home of some of the leading Jacksonians, such as Van Buren and Silas Wright, and one of the states Schlesinger used as an example to illustrate his thesis. If the class conflict model does not work for New York, then Benson held that it probably would not work anywhere. Moreover, Benson addressed directly the question of whether or not the "Concept of Jacksonian Democracy" was a viable one. He defined this concept as follows:

> 1) Andrew Jackson and his successors led (really or symbolically) a particular political party; 2) the party drew its leaders from certain socioeconomic classes or groups; 3) the party received strong mass support from certain socioeconomic classes or groups; 4) the party formulated and fought for an egalitarian ideology that envisioned not only political but social and economic democracy; 5) the party implemented a program derived from or consonant with its egalitarian ideology; 6) the opposing party drew its leaders and mass support from different socioeconomic classes and social groups, and opposed egalitarian ideas and policies.[5]

This is clearly the concept of Jacksonian Democracy used by Schlesinger, and it also constitutes a theory in the sense described earlier.

Benson sees little continuity between the "parties" of Jefferson and Hamilton and those that emerged in the 1830s. Of course the names of the Founding Fathers were invoked by latter-day politicians, but these invocations were largely ceremonial. By the 1830s, mercantilism was dead, and the issues of the 1790s had given way to very different ones in the 1830s and 1840s. Further, Benson argues that there were no parties in any modern sense in New York prior to 1830, and that what emerged after that was a new development, not the resurrection of the earlier divisions.

The event that initiated the development of New York political parties was, as Benson sees it, the Anti-Masonic movement, which began in 1826 with the disappearance and alleged murder of William Morgan, a renegade Mason who had written a book revealing the secrets of Masonry. Morgan's disappearance was blamed on the Masons and gave rise to a conspiracy theory according to which the secret brotherhood had become an evil force that had captured positions of power and privilege in the nation and was in the process of creating a ruling elite. Anti-Masonry expanded its agenda to include the demand for the abolition of secret societies, for equality for all white men, an end to special privileges, majority rule, an end to monopolies, abolition of imprisonment for debt, and similar radical proposals. The movement practically destroyed Masonry in New York, but it grew into a broader egalitarian movement whose particular target was the Albany Regency, whose leader was Van Buren. The Regency was involved in many activities opposed by the Anti-Masons, particularly the granting of bank charters and the Safety Fund that the Regency had established to help guarantee the solvency of the state's banks and that was portrayed by the Anti-Masons as a monopoly designed to serve the privileged few. In the resulting political battles, the Anti-Masons joined with the Workingmen's Party against the Regency—that is, against the Jackson men. The Regency responded by opposing the Anti-Mason's reforms, such as abolition of debt imprisonment and defended its banking policy.

At the same time, the policy of the Jackson men was based on the concept of the negative liberal state—that is, a state that confined its activities to the protection of persons and property. The Jackson men were firm believers in states' rights and vigorously opposed Clay's American System, with its call for tariffs, internal improvements, and a *national* bank. Jackson's Maysville veto was one expression of this policy; his veto of the recharter of the Bank of the United States was another. But that veto also offered the New York Jackson men a chance to divert the antibank issue from New York to the national level, and recognizing that the equalitarian drive of the Anti-Masons was costing them votes, they adopted the Anti-Masonic rhetoric to attack the Bank of the United States as a monopoly. This was perfectly consistent with their states' rights negative government view and allowed them to turn the enemy's flank.

As Benson argues in detail, there is no evidence for class voting in New York, and in no sense can the New York Jackson Party—that is, the Democratic Party—be called the party of the workers and farmers. Using the election of 1844 as the basis for his analysis, Benson analyzes the backgrounds and social status of the Democratic and Whig leaders and finds that they were relatively well off and cannot be differentiated on economic grounds. But when Benson examines the actual voting behavior of the electorate, other differences appear. Most striking is the role of ethnocultural and religious differences. Group by group, he shows that the immigrant Catholic Irish, Germans, and Catholic French all strongly supported the Democratic Party. The Protestant Irish, Welsh, Scottish, and English immigrants voted Whig. African Americans and Huguenots voted solidly Whig; so did "Puritans," that is, men of New England origin and evangelical faith. Of the native born (excluding African Americans and Huguenots), the majority voted Democratic. Furthermore, Anti-Masonry flourished in western New York in what is known as the "burnt-over" district—burnt over by evangelical religious revivals. This evangelical Protestantism, with its call for moral and religious reform, disposed its adherents to demand government action on behalf of its programs and emphasized a positive liberal state—one that actively intervened in society to promote the "general welfare"—in contrast to the negative liberal state championed by the Democrats.

Benson also analyzes the basis and voting patterns of the Liberty Party and the American Republican Party. The Liberty Party was at that time the more important of the two. Its strength lay in rural areas, especially in central and western New York, and among people with strong evangelical religious beliefs determined to reform the world. They were generally better educated than the average and usually were former Whigs. Indeed, Democratic victories in the 1840s owed much to this siphoning off of Whig voters by the Liberty Party. Thus contrary to Schlesinger's argument, that Jackson men led the fight against slavery, Benson's analysis shows just the opposite.

The point here is that the picture of the Jacksonians that Benson presents is in most respects contradictory to the one presented by Schlesinger. Benson sees the Jacksonians as wedded to a concept of the negative liberal state. This made them a natural home for those who emphasized states' rights, and so of course for the Southern slaveholders. But it also made them a natural home for immigrant groups that found assimilation into American society difficult—particularly the Catholics. Conversely, the Whigs emphasized a positive liberal state. In economic matters, this meant Clay's American System, designed to promote the rapid economic development of the nation. It also meant active moral reform, ranging from Bible and Tract Societies to Home and Foreign Missionary work. Such reform often involved government action—the issue of the Sunday mail, for example, active church-state cooperation, and most important, abolition. It was not the Jackson men who led the antislavery crusade but the radical Whigs, determined to remake the world according to their religious and moral principles.

Benson concludes that the Concept of Jacksonian Democracy is not only useless but that it has misled historians in their interpretation of the pre-Civil War period. He finds no evidence of class voting; instead, he proposes an ethnocultural-religious model of voting behavior. More broadly, he sees the whole era as one in which egalitarianism became the ideology of all parties—a development that he attributes to the transportation revolution. He also stresses that since all parties were in substantial agreement on the basic questions of political and economic doctrine, elections tended to be decided by local issues. The Concept of Jacksonian Democracy has obscured the actual situation by attributing to the men of the Jacksonian era conflicts that were not theirs.

Comparing these two interpretations of the Jacksonian era, one might well wonder if Schlesinger and Benson are talking about the same people. But they are, and to a considerable extent they used the same sources. The major difference is that in the fifteen years that separate these books, mechanical and electronic methods of analyzing large quantities of data had been developed. This enabled Benson to use actual voting statistics as data in a way that had not been possible for Schlesinger. Yet their interpretations differ not only in their general theses but in the "facts" they cite. Schlesinger ignores the Anti-Masonic movement that Benson regards as crucial to an understanding of New York politics; Benson ignores the hard-money doctrine that Schlesinger regards as so vital to understanding the Jacksonian views. Where they deal with the same events, they construe them in opposite ways. Thus for Schlesinger, Jackson is a prototype of Franklin Roosevelt; for Benson, he is just the opposite. Yet Schlesinger and Benson are two of the most respected American political historians. Surely it must be evident that their "interpretations" are theories that determined how they interpreted their data.

The second level of historical theorizing is well illustrated by Elaine Pagels's book *Beyond Belief*[6] and her hypothesis concerning the Gospel according to this John. That this Gospel poses a problem is well known.

The four Gospels usually are divided into the synoptic Gospels—Matthew, Mark, and Luke—and the Johannine Gospel. It is generally agreed that Mark is the earliest, written probably around 70 A.D. No one knows where it was written, though some scholars think it was written in Syria. Its authorship is unknown. Matthew and Luke probably were composed in the 80s. Who wrote the Gospel according to Matthew we do not know; it is very unlikely to have been the apostle Matthew. This Gospel is by far the most Hebraic, laying great stress on the way Jesus fulfilled the Old Testament prophesies in order to prove that he was the Messiah. Luke is believed to have been written by Luke the physician who was the traveling companion of Paul and also the author of the Book of Acts. Matthew and Luke both used Mark as a source; their chronology is his, and many of the passages of Mark are reproduced in their texts, sometimes verbatim. Both also used a further source that scholars call "Q"; no copy of Q is known to exist now, but there are enough passages common to Matthew and Luke, but not in Mark, to indicate another source, and the way this material is incorporated into their accounts indicates that neither of the Evangelists used the other as a source. In addition, each undoubtedly used other sources, presently unknown. There are, then, a great many similarities among the synoptic Gospels; they tell the same story, although with some significant differences.

The Gospel according to John is a wholly different matter. The date of composition is estimated to be around the end of the first century. But the story John tells is different than that told by the synoptic Gospels. The chronology is different: in John, one of Jesus' first acts is the driving of the money changers from the Temple; in the synoptic Gospels, this is one of Jesus' last acts. Jesus' age is different: in the synoptic Gospels he is a young man approximately thirty years old; John says he is "not yet fifty," which would clearly put him in his late forties. While John includes many of the events included by the synoptic writers, he includes some they do not and excludes some they do. But the differences go far beyond these. In the synoptic Gospels, as Pagels has noted, Jesus is presented as a man, though one specially chosen and endowed by God.[7] In John, Jesus is presented as God incarnate—God himself in human form. These are very different texts.

That the synoptic Gospels and the Johannine Gospel contradict each other is not a new discovery. At the time the New Testament canon was formed, there were arguments as to whether or not the Johannine Gospel should be included.[8] Why it was included has puzzled scholars. Burnett Streeter held that when the New Testament canon was formed, there were many so-called "Gospels." The problem was, which were authentic? His argument was that those included were vouched for by the leading churches as having apostolic warrant.[9] But things have changed since Streeter's day. In 1945, at a place in Egypt called Nag Hammadi, an Egyptian, Muhammad Ali, unearthed a six-foot jar containing a large number of hitherto unknown, or known only by reputation, early Christian texts. That there had been such texts was known from the attacks upon "heresies" by Irenaeus and other early church fathers, but now it was possible to actually read them, and in particular to read the Gospel according to Thomas. Although fragments of this Gospel had been found earlier, this was the first time the whole text became available. What these so-called "Gnostic" texts showed was that during the first several centuries after the death of Jesus there had been far greater diversity of opinion about who Jesus was and what he had taught than anyone had previously recognized. Probably even now we have only found a few of the variants that flourished in this era. The differences were very substantial and reveal the existence of different traditions concerning Christianity taught by many different writers and preachers.

The Gospel according to Thomas, as reproduced in Pagels's book,[10] consists of 114 of Jesus' sayings. It is not a connected narrative of Jesus' life and work as are the synoptic Gospels, but it is similar to what Q is believed to have been—a collection, in no particular order, of Jesus' teachings. There has been an intensive debate over when it was written,[11] over its relation to the synoptic Gospels,[12] and more recently over its relation to the Gospel according to John,[13] and all of these are still debated. Although some have held that the communities that gave rise to the Gospels according to John and Thomas had no contact with each other, Ismo Dunderberg writes, "More recently a few scholars have recognized in the Johannine writings signs of a debate with the views which are now attested by the Gospel of Thomas."[14] Gregory Riley has taken a stronger position.

> The elements present and positions countered, in the peri-
> scope [sayings in John] cohere well with those in the Gospel
> of Thomas, and lead to the conclusion that the Gospel of
> Thomas was already at some stage of completion, either writ-
> ten or oral, and that its contents were known to the author of
> John, probably through verbal contact with members of this
> rival community.[15]

Riley sees "evidence of reciprocal debate" between the Johannine and Thomasine communities and holds that the Johannine Gospel "was written in part as a reaction against, and a correction of, the earlier Thomas tradition."[16]

There are many issues between the Johannine and Thomasine Gospels; Riley has focused on the debate over resurrection, but as Pagels has shown, what most distinguishes the Gospel according to Thomas is its claim that Jesus held all men to have access to God within themselves. According to this Gospel, Jesus said:

> The Kingdom is inside you, and outside you. When you come to know yourselves, then you will be known, and you will see that it is you who are the children of the living Father. But if you will not know yourselves, you dwell in poverty, and it is you who *are* that poverty.[17]

Again, Thomas says:

> Jesus said, "If you bring forth what is within you, what you bring forth will save you. If you do not bring forth what is within you, what you do not bring forth will destroy you.[18]

But Thomas goes even farther, attributing to Jesus the saying "whoever drinks from my mouth will become as I am, and I myself will become that person, and the mysteries shall be revealed to him."[19] According to Thomas, then, all people have within them access to divine truth; the Kingdom is here now, but people do not see it. To find it, all they have to do is look within, and then they can become like Jesus himself.

These teachings are clearly heretical from the standpoint of John and his followers. The contradictions between the two Gospels led Pagels to the following conclusion:

> Thomas and John clearly draw upon similar language and images, and both, apparently, begin with similar "secret teachings." But John takes this teaching to mean something so different from Thomas that I wondered whether John could have written his gospel to refute what Thomas teaches. For months I investigated this possibility, and explored the work of other scholars who also have compared these sources, and I was finally convinced that this is what happened.[20]

In the Johannine text alone one finds the denigration of Thomas as "doubting Thomas," and as not a true disciple. Further, the message of John is that it is through belief in Jesus as divine, and *only* through such belief, that one can be saved. There is, for John, no search within; Jesus is the light and the way and the only light and way. If Pagels is

right, then John and Thomas represent two irreconcilable interpretations of Christianity.

Irenaeus was one of the key figures, and perhaps *the* key figure,
in this controversy. He had been a student of Polycarp's in Smyrna and
had heard Polycarp talk of "John," whom he took to be the apostle,[21]
so from the start he was prepared to grant authority to the Johannine
text. But more than that, what Irenaeus wanted was a unified "catholic" (i.e., universal) church. The sort of doctrine found in Thomas
leads to schisms and variant interpretations. Its antinomian tendencies
have been evident throughout Christian history and were abundantly
clear in the fragmentation of the Christian community in Irenaeus's
day, as his five-volume *Refutation and Overthrow of Falsely So-Called
Knowledge* makes abundantly clear.[22] What Iranaeus found particularly
offensive was the doctrine of second baptism—that ordinary baptism was
merely the first step in the life of faith, but that a second baptism was
required to attain the status of children of God. This doctrine divided
the Church into ordinary members and an elite who claimed a superior understanding of God.[23] To destroy the doctrines that promoted
such divisions and chaos among Christians became Irenaeus's goal; he
insisted not only on the inclusion of the Johannine Gospel but on its
primacy.[24] And when, following the conversion of Constantine in 312,
the emperor called the council at Nicaea in 325 to codify Christian
doctrine in a form that would provide a framework for a universal
church, Christian leaders such as Athanasius were able to seize the
opportunity and establish the sort of creed Irenaeus had dreamed of,
following the doctrines of John.[25]

No one knows who wrote either the Gospel according to Thomas
or the Gospel according to John; almost certainly they were not written
by the apostles, whose names they bear. But if Pagels is right, that the
Gospel according to John was written to refute the Gospel according to
Thomas, then that fact explains why it was such a perfect instrument for
Irenaeus. And with Irenaeus, we do know the beliefs that guided him
and the desires and intentions that motivated him. We can give a causal
explanation of why Irenaeus insisted on the inclusion and primacy of
the Johannine Gospel. Believing that this Gospel had apostolic warrant,
and that it showed the way toward the unification of all Christians in
one Catholic church, he had every reason to insist that not only was
John's Gospel a true one but that the synoptic Gospels should be read
through the lens of John.

That Irenaeus prevailed was the result of events that occurred long
after his time and that he could not have foreseen. He was but one of
many who opposed the Gnostic teachings and abhorred the divisions

within the Church, but his was a particularly influential voice, and later Church leaders such as Athanasius carried out Irenaeus's agenda.[26] In his list of the twenty-seven books of the New Testament—the earliest-known such list—Athanasius included the Gospel according to John as one of the four Gospels. Thus Pagels's theory gives us a coherent explanation of why this Gospel was so important that it had to be included in the canon—an explanation in terms of the beliefs and desires of Christian leaders and the opportunity offered by the transformation of Christianity from a persecuted sect into an imperial church.[27]

The Gospels also offer us a beautiful example of the role of facts in historical accounts. Consider the baptism of Jesus by John the Baptist. Mark simply records this event.

> It happened at this time that Jesus came from Nazareth in Galilee and was baptized in the Jordan by John.[28]

But this creates a problem, since the fact that John baptized Jesus seems to imply that John was superior to Jesus. In Luke also, the baptism is simply reported: "During a general baptism of the people, when Jesus too had been baptized."[29] But this is preceded by an elaborate history according to which the mothers of John and Jesus were kinswomen, both of whom were informed of their coming maternity by the Angel Gabriel, and the superiority of Jesus to John is fully established.

Matthew deals with the matter as follows:

> Then Jesus arrived at the Jordan from Galilee, and came to John to be baptized by him. John tried to dissuade him. "Do you come to me?" he said; "I need rather to be baptized by you." Jesus replied, "Let it be so for the present; we do well to conform in this way with all that God requires." John then allowed him to come. After baptism Jesus came up out of the water at once.[30]

Here the roles are reversed; Jesus is the superior and orders John to perform the baptism. And in John's Gospel, the baptism of Jesus by John the Baptist disappears entirely. John proclaims Jesus but does not baptize him. In other words, the "fact" of the baptism vanishes.

Looking at these four texts, how is one to decide whether or not John ever baptized Jesus? Most scholars accept the baptism as a fact, but a fact that the Evangelists found embarrassing. Thus both Matthew and Luke include it but construct their Gospels so as to reverse the implied superiority of John, while the Johannine Gospel, which is the only Gospel that holds Jesus to be divine, excludes the baptism entirely. Since the bias of all of these writers is against the inclusion of the baptism, the fact that three of them do so, two of them grudgingly, speaks in favor of the truth of the account in Mark. In other words, where an account involves something that goes against the bias of the author, there is more reason to believe it, since the bias of the author would lead one to expect its exclusion if it were not so well known to have occurred that it could not be excluded. That, however, does not stop John from deleting it entirely, since he is writing later than the others and his Gospel gives to Jesus so exalted a position that any hint of subordination is intolerable

"Facts" occur in historical theories as posits to account for data. The data here are the accounts given by the four Gospels. Since one of the four does not mention the baptism, these accounts are not consistent. To resolve that inconsistency, we require an explanation of why the "fact" is included in three of them and not the fourth. The earlier sketch outlines such an explanation. If we take Mark's account to be true, then the baptism poses a problem for the other Evangelists. Matthew and Luke think it occurred as Mark says, but they restructure their texts to eliminate the implied subordination of Jesus to John. But the author of John, whose text exalts Jesus, preferred to exclude the baptism entirely. One thus concludes that Mark's account of the baptism is true, and this explains why the others differ from it in terms of the interests and biases of their authors.

While all historical accounts are theoretical, Pagels's account of the relation between the Gospels according to John and Thomas is more explicitly so. It helps explain why the two Gospels are so radically opposed, and why John's Gospel, which differs so notably from the synoptic Gospels, should nevertheless have been considered of such importance that it was included in the canon of the New Testament. It also helps explain why that canon developed in the way it did, gives us a clearer insight into the nature of the so-called Gnostic controversy, and sheds light on the actions of the Council at Nicaea. This is of course an empirically testable theory, and one that will surely be reexamined in light of further finds, but it accounts for the presently known data remarkably well.

What I have called the third level of theorizing is the explicit formulation by the historian of a theory at a level of generality that is designed to make it applicable to a wide range of phenomena. One of the most famous examples of this in American history is the Frontier Thesis of Frederick Jackson Turner, to which we will come in due course, but a more recent example is Lee Benson's theory of voting behavior, put forward in his 1961 book on Jacksonian Democracy. Benson states his thesis as follows.

> The wider the area of agreement on political fundamentals, the more heterogeneous the society (or community), the larger the proportion of its members who have high levels of personal aspiration, and the less centralized the constitutional system, then the greater the number and variety of factors that operate as determinants of voting behavior.[31]

Benson holds that there was, in Jackson's time, general agreement on political fundamentals. The political theory hammered out between 1763 and 1787 had become canonical in the United States and was accepted by everyone. Certainly the society was heterogeneous, and it was rapidly becoming more so as a result of large-scale immigration from Europe. The constitutional system was decentralized, and the wealth of economic opportunity that existed encouraged high aspirations. Given this situation, ethnocultural and religious hostilities became the major determinants of voting behavior. Since the Catholic Irish flooded into the Democratic Party, the Protestant Irish went to the Whig Party. In other words, for the Protestant Irish, the Catholic Irish constituted a negative reference group, and vice versa. Similarly, the English immigrants went to the Whigs because they could not stand the Catholic Irish. Catholics generally went to the Democratic Party while Protestants went to the Whigs. These ethnic and religious hostilities that the immigrants brought with them from Europe and the British Isles thus reappear in the United States as determinants of voting behavior. This ethnocultural model of voting behavior advanced by Benson has been the dominant theory in political history since 1961, as is evident in the work of Richard Jensen,[32] Paul Kleppner,[33] and many others. Further, picking up on V. O. Key's famous article that introduced the concept of critical elections—an election "in which there occurs a sharp and durable electoral realignment between parties."[34] Benson distinguished voting cycles in New York where each cycle was initiated by a fluctuation phase in which the critical election occurred and a stable phase during which the realignments established in the fluctuation phase persisted until the next fluctuation phase. In New York, the first fluctuation phase began in the period 1826–1827; from 1832 to 1853, the voting percentages were relatively stable. A second fluctuation phase began in 1853 and lasted until 1860; the second stable phase ran from 1860 to 1893.[35] These findings, and the theory that led to them, were developed by Benson on the basis of historical data from New York, but they turned out to be consonant with the theory of political behavior advanced by Angus Campbell, Philip Converse, Warren Miller, and Donald Stokes in *The American Voter*[36] and show that, contrary to what has often been claimed, historians can and do generate theories that explain not only their specific data but theories that have broader applications to other cases.

At this third level of theory also are found the applications to the past of theories drawn from contemporary social science. These theories are often explicitly stated, but whether they are explicit or implicit, such applications pose genuine problems. The theories of contemporary social science are generally based upon American or European data from the recent past. Anthropology is an exception here because of its use of non-Western data, but most anthropological studies are based on contemporary populations. Past cultures often contain beliefs in entities of a sort not currently thought to be or to have been possible existents. They also often involve types of behavior that, were they to occur in our present culture, would be judged irrational or even pathological. To attempt to apply our social science theories to historical cases involves considerable risk of misunderstanding, and of failing to recognize that what appears to us irrational may well have been perfectly rational in the cultural context of the time. Similarly, we are often faced with documents that contain testimony to the occurrence of events that were explicable in terms of the past culture but that we have difficulty in accepting as genuine occurrences at all. Thus, for example, consider the following:

> In the afternoon the pots hanging over the fire did dash so vehemently one against the other [that] we set down one that they might not dash to pieces. I saw the andiron leap into the pot and dance and leap out, and again leap in and dance and leap out again, and there abide. . . . Also I saw the pot turn itself over and throw down all the water. Again, we saw a tray with wool leap up and down and throw the wool out and so many times.[37]

This is eyewitness testimony from a man not known to have suffered from hallucinations. The explanation given by the author was witchcraft, and within the culture of New England in the seventeenth century, such an explanation was considered plausible. As all students of seventeenth-century New England know, the Puritans believed in the existence of witches; since witches are mentioned in the Bible, they could hardly do otherwise. Modern historians do not believe in witches, and so they must try to find alternative explanations for what happened in New England.

By far the most famous case of witchcraft in seventeenth-century New England was the outbreak at Salem Village in 1692. The story has been retold so many times and is so well known that only the briefest reminder is needed here. It began with the illness of Betty Parris, the nine-year-old daughter of Salem Village minister Samuel Parris, and her cousin Abigail Williams, presumably stimulated by the superstitions of Parris's slave, Tituba. The girls' trances, wild behavior, and seizures led to a diagnosis of witchcraft. The disorder quickly spread among a group of girls, and when questioned as to the identity of the witches attacking them, they began to name names. The result was an epidemic of accusations in which over 150 people were jailed and nineteen were hung, since witchcraft was a capital crime in New England. The epidemic ended when the governor prorogued the court and imposed new rules of evidence that made uncorroborated "spectral evidence" no longer sufficient for conviction. "Spectral evidence" meant that the "specter"—likeness—of the witch appeared to the bewitched, usually attacking them, but since no one but the bewitched could see the specter, someone so accused could mount no defense. For just this reason, New England law required that spectral evidence be corroborated by a second witness, but in the Salem Village case, the requirement of corroboration was dropped, and spectral evidence alone was taken as sufficient. As far as this was justified, it was by the belief that the devil could not appear as the specter of an innocent person. Neither the governor nor the leading ministers doubted the reality of witches or specters. But Increase Mather and other leading ministers pointed out that according to the Bible the Witch of Endor appeared to Saul in the form of the prophet Samuel, thus showing that the devil could indeed appear in the form of an innocent person. The governor suspended the court, and when the trials began again it was under new rules of evidence. Only three people were convicted of witchcraft under the new rules, and these the governor reprieved.

What is the modern historian to make of this remarkable episode? None of the modern writers has accepted the Puritan belief in the reality of witches, so an alternative explanation has been sought. In 1974, Paul Boyer and Stephen Nissenbaum published a study that focused on the nature of the conflicts within Salem Village and their psychological effects on the accusers.[38] Salem Village, in their view, was an anomalous settlement—it was not a legal town but an area of settlement on the outskirts of the town of Salem. The village was divided between those who wished to become a separate town and those who wished to remain part of Salem. This division reflected the conflict between the rapidly growing mercantile capitalism of Salem and the more traditional

Puritanism of the agricultural community farthest from Salem. It also reflected the increasing prosperity of the mercantile-oriented group and the declining economic position of the farming group that was running out of land. The separatists had succeeded in establishing a village church, but the villagers closest to Salem usually continued to belong to the Salem church. The village divisions had become crystallized into factions, the separatists headed by the Putnam family, the nonseparatists by the Porter family. As Boyer and Nissenbaum show, the bewitched who made accusations came from the separatist areas of the village, those they accused from the nonseparatist sections closest to Salem. The village was thus the scene of bitter factional feuding, but it also lacked the usual institutions for dealing with such conflicts—it had no town government of its own, and even the church represented just one of the village's factions.

How did these animosities translate into witchcraft?

> Ultimately, then, Salem witchcraft, by reducing real human beings to a single set of threatening impulses and temptations which they seemed to embody, was a kind of allegory-in-reverse. Self-purgation through allegorical projection: this was hardly a style of thinking alien to the late-seventeenth-century Puritan mind.[39]

Given the great emphasis the Puritans placed on communal peace and harmony, anger could not be openly expressed, and so it was repressed and projected onto others believed responsible for the troubles that caused it.

In 1982, John Demos published a study of witchcraft in New England as a whole in the seventeenth century.[40] This study had little to say about the peculiarities of the Salem Village case but sought to account for the phenomenon of witchcraft more generally. This perspective allowed Demos to relate witchcraft occurrences to a variety of types of events: natural disasters such as epidemics, fires, crop failures, and the like,[41] "signs" such as comets, eclipses and earthquakes,[42] and internal controversies—controversies within the town—occurring several years prior to the outbreak.[43] In fact, Demos finds that witchcraft outbreaks rarely occurred during internal controversies but followed them.[44] In this respect, Salem Village is atypical, since controversy continued through the outbreak. Demos also finds that external controversies (i.e., controversies with other religious groups, such as Quakers and Baptists) European nations such as Spain, France, and Holland), and Indian wars inhibited witchcraft.[45] The latter finding is not surprising, since external conflict usually produces group integration. Of these various causes, the most important seems to have been internal conflict. As Demos remarks, "Conflict was inherently problematic, not to say calamitous, when set in the scale of New England values."[46] While conflicts took many specific forms, Demos remarks:

> Witchcraft laid bare—and, in a sense, controlled—a critical point of tension in New England society: cooperative values versus individualistic ones.[47]

But as Demos points out, in New England, conflict was never just conflict. For the Puritans, all aspects of life, particularly of community life, were set on a cosmic stage as battles between the forces of the devil and those of God. New England was not just an English colony; the Puritans saw themselves as God's chosen people on an errand into the wilderness to carry out a divinely appointed mission.[48]

How did these social factors lead to witchcraft? Demos draws extensively on Freudian theory to provide an answer.

> (1) "Projection" was everywhere central to witchcraft accusations. And projection, with its "oral" foundation, rates as one of the earliest of all the psychological "defenses." (2) Witchcraft belief displayed important elements of "magical thinking," especially with respect to implicit stereotypes of women. (3) The symptoms and fantasies associated with witchcraft suggest a certain vulnerability in the "self system." Here, too, the genetic line leads far back toward infancy. (4) The same evidence, considered from the standpoint of "ego qualities," underscores the issue of "autonomy" (and its negative correlate, "doubt"). And this issue is said to belong especially to the "second stage" of psychosocial adaptation, encompassing roughly the second and third years of life. (5) The extreme symptoms of one particular victim-group, the "afflicted girls," denote unresolved conflicts in relation to "maternal objects." And the cast of those conflicts seems largely "pre-Oedipal."[49]

There is, then, a good deal of agreement between Boyer and Nissenbaum and Demos, though Demos develops the psychoanalytic analysis much more fully than Boyer and Nissenbaum.

In 1987, Carol Karlsen published a study of the relation of sex and witchcraft in New England.[50] That witches were generally female is agreed upon by everyone. Of the 342 people accused of witchcraft in

New England between 1620 and 1725 whose sex can be determined, Karlsen notes that 267 were women.[51] Furthermore, of women accused, the majority were married women,[52] chiefly between ages forty and fifty-nine,[53] and many of the younger women accused were daughters or granddaughters of older accused women.[54] Women widowed and without brothers or sons were particularly liable because, Karlsen argues, these women stood to inherit property, thereby disrupting the usual custom of male property ownership. "Dissatisfaction with one's lot was one of the most pervasive themes of witches' lives,"[55] Karlsen argues, and those women who gave expression to their dissatisfactions, particularly in the form of anger, were particularly liable. Indeed, as Karlsen sees it, women who rebelled against the gender code of New England were most often seen as witches. This rebellion could take the form of sexual misconduct,[56] of occupations such as midwife, healer, or religious leader,[57] or tavern keeper,[58] but particularly of lying and pride.[59] Of the characteristics of these women, Karlsen lists "discontent, anger, envy, malice, and pride," the last being, in Puritan eyes, the very essence of sin.[60] But as Karlsen sees it, particularly conflicts over economic resources, especially land, underlay the resentments and anger that led to witchcraft. Sons resented mothers whose inheritance of property diminished their own, but given the Puritan emphasis on honoring one's parents, such resentments could not be openly expressed. Thus:

> These resentments [against their mothers] came out, but they were not directed at the men who were their principal sources. Rather, they were expressed as witchcraft accusations, primarily aimed at other women, who like accusers' own mothers vied with men for land and other scarce material resources.[61]

Here one has at work repression, displacement, and projection. Women who accused other women were acting similarly,[62] but given the hierarchical nature of Puritan society, including Puritan families, not only did wives stand in subordinate relation to their husbands, but daughters stood in subordinate relation to both parents, especially their mothers. As Karlsen puts it, "To be numbered among God's elect, women had to acknowledge this service as their calling and *believe* they were created for this purpose."[63] It was not their own mothers they accused but surrogates for them.

In 1993, Bernard Rosenthal published a study of the Salem Village witch episode that takes a somewhat different point of view.[64] All of the scholars discussed earlier assumed that the accusations of witchcraft in Salem Village were made in good faith and sought psychological explanations for them in terms of repression, displacement, and projection. But in 1764, Thomas Hutchinson held that at least the charges made by the circle of Salem Village girls were lies. Rosenthal comments:

> In refined and more sophisticated forms in modern times, elaborate explanations emerged through theories of psychology, biochemistry, and social interaction. All have had in common a powerful impulse to reject what appears as simplistic the view that at the core of the accusations resided simple fraud. For people who read at supermarket counters about two-headed babies from UFOs, the concept of real witchcraft at Salem comes easily. For scholarly advocates of competing modern theories, Hutchinson's view that fraud lay at the center has simply emerged as a quaint simplification to be challenged through sophisticated insight. Still, no explanation, under scrutiny, has held up as well as that understood by Hutchinson, as well as by a lot of people in 1692.[65]

When they testified at the trials of those they had accused, the girls backed up their accusations that witches were attacking them by sticking pins into their bodies by producing real pins for the court to see.[66] That was not a problem for the court in 1692, since a witch's specter was believed able to manipulate physical objects. But psychological projections do not produce real pins. There is no other apparent explanation for the pins but fraud.

Further, it is well established that many of the confessions the court wrung from the accused—sometimes by torture[67]—were lies. Confession did not

> in general represent hysteria, although people were surely agitated and frightened; rather, it represents a desperate logic, rational and correct, that the safest way out of the web of accusation was through confession, accusation, or claims of affliction. We do not need to look for exotic theories to explain the behavior of the "girls of Salem" once the rules became clear. Thus, a script emerged in which accused, accusers, and the judiciary had a vested interest; The accusers and the judiciary needed the ritual of confession to legitimize their activities, and the confessors needed the continuation of the ritual to avoid the gallows.[68]

Those who confessed and named others as witches lived; those who maintained their innocence to the end were hung. And that many

confessed falsely to save their lives is evident from the number of subsequent recantations.[69]

The "girls of Salem" were not all girls. Some men joined the ranks
of the accusers, including John Indian—the husband of Parris's houseslave
Tituba, and a number of others.[70] Nor were the court's hands entirely
clean. Rosenthal argues convincingly that George Corwin, nephew of
Jonathan Corwin, who was one of the judges in the trials, took the opportunity to seize the property of accused witches for his own profit.[71]
But Rosenthal does not deny that some of the accusations may well have
been sincere. His point, rather, is that many of them clearly were not,
and that his fellow historians have been so concerned not to disparage
the beliefs of another culture that they have overlooked the possibility
that the girls did it "for sport."[72]

A belief in witches does not require psychological processes such
as repression or projection. The Puritans lived in a world dominated by
invisible spiritual beings whose actions determined the fate of humans.
Given their scientific and religious worldview, those beliefs were perfectly
rational. That witches existed was for them a certainty, since they are
referred to in the Bible. Moreover, their traditional knowledge provided
clear descriptions of how witches act. All of this was included in the
knowledge they inherited from their tradition. There is no doubt that
seventeenth-century New England Puritans did believe in witches. Had
they not, the accusations of the girls would have been without effect.
It was just because everyone knew how witches acted that the charges
were believable. And there is no doubt that most of those involved in
what happened at Salem Village did truly believe that witchcraft was
afoot. Since modern historians do not believe in witches, they have had
to seek alternative explanations for what happened, and so psychological
theories have been invoked to provide them. But this does not exclude
that the girls also lied, and psychological theories do not account for
real pins. But if the girls did lie, then the lies they told still show the
systematic features pointed out by Boyer and Nissenbaum, Karlsen,
Demos, and others. The accusations were made against certain people,
but not others; the accused had specific characteristics of age, sex, and
status; they lived in one area of the town rather than another, and they
had particular economic interests. If the girls were lying, then their
choices of targets were not random but conformed to divisions clearly
established within the village. Psychological processes such as projections
seem to have played an important role in this affair, even if the girls
used props to support their claims.

The argument over Salem witchcraft is a cautionary tale about the
dangers of applying current theories of social science to the explanation

of historical events. Such applications are often useful, but one must be very careful to make sure that the theories really do apply. No one knows what the motives of the "girls of Salem" really were; even when they subsequently recanted, what they said later does not tell us what they thought in 1692. Rosenthal is surely right in pointing out that there is convincing evidence of some fraud, but even if that is true as an explanation of some part of the behavior of the girls, it provides, at best, a partial explanation of this incident.

I have dwelt on the Salem Village case in more detail than was perhaps necessary because it illustrates so well the problems involved in applying contemporary social science theory to the past. But as Benson's work shows, such applications can be done. Benson discovered the voting cycles in his data; he also found in Key's famous article an explanatory theory that could account for them, and that would fit his data. Similarly, he used the concept of negative reference groups that came from the American Soldier studies[73] and was further developed by Robert K. Merton.[74] But in all cases, the applicability of these concepts to his nineteenth-century data was thoroughly tested. And the voting cycle theory was then found to be consonant with the theory of maintaining and realigning elections of Campbell, Converse, Miller, and Stokes. This is one of the few cases in which a historian has developed a general theory of broad application on the basis of historical data. The witchcraft cases represent a different situation. Psychological theories are usually stated in universalistic form, even if their supporting evidence is drawn from the current students in Psych. 1. Certainly this is true of Freudian theory. And certainly the Salem Village affair, when viewed from the standpoint of our contemporary theories, seems to involve abnormal behavior with which Freudian theory is well equipped to deal. But belief in witches, and the behavior of witches, was not abnormal in New England culture. The concepts of repression, displacement, and projection offer one very attractive way of accounting for the behavior of the "girls of Salem." But other possibilities need to be taken into account. One does not have to accept the Puritan belief that the girls really were bewitched. As Rosenthal has shown, "simple fraud" may have been at the root of the whole tragedy.

The final level of historical theorizing is what I have referred to as "grand theories," theories that offer explanations of the rise and fall of civilizations, or of historical "progress," or that present some particular scheme of historical development. It is characteristic of such theories that they not only claim to explain historical events but also attempt to predict the future. Such theories, whether they are those of Hegel or Marx or Toynbee or Spengler, have not fared well and are rightly rejected by most historians. Not only have their descriptions of the past proven inaccurate, but their attempts to predict the future have uniformly failed. Yet interestingly enough, one such theory has been widely accepted within the trade and still receives rather uncritical celebration—Thomas Kuhn's theory of scientific development. Because it is the only such theory currently held in good repute, and because it is a "grand theory," it requires some comment.

Thomas Kuhn was a historian of science who made a number of important contributions to that field. He has also had an enormous influence beyond the history of science, and in general history as well as other fields one now finds that Kuhnian terms, such as "paradigm" and "normal science," frequently recur. The reason for this extraordinary influence in the humanities and social sciences generally is that the theory of scientific development Kuhn presents does three things: (1) It asserts that scientific theories can never be true descriptions of reality (2) By diminishing the claims of science, it emboldens humanists to believe that their theories are of equal merit to those of science. (3) It provides a simple developmental model that can be applied to other subjects.[75] But it has often not been recognized that Kuhn's theory is more than a theory of the history of science; it is a theory of science per se, of the nature of science, and so of science past, present and to come. It is, in fact, a grand theory in the same sense as those of Marx or Toynbee.

What Kuhn claims is that a field of inquiry becomes a science only with the adoption of a "paradigm," where "paradigm" is defined as a concrete scientific achievement that includes "law, theory, application, and instrumentation together" that will serve as an exemplar, is "sufficiently unprecedented to attract an enduring group of adherents away from competing modes of scientific activity," and is "sufficiently open-ended to leave all sorts of problems for the redefined group of practitioners to solve."[76] Paradigms such as Newtonian mechanics and Einsteinian relativity, once adopted, become the framework within which subsequent research is carried out; such research, focused on the problems defined by the paradigm, constitutes what Kuhn calls "normal science." But, Kuhn holds, normal science *always* leads to "anomalies"—that is, to problems that cannot be solved within the framework of the paradigm. When these anomalies become numerous enough and important enough, they change from being simply unsolved problems to being countercases, and scientists recognize that the old paradigm is no longer adequate. This creates a "crisis" for science, the result of which is a scientific revolution that results in the invention of a new paradigm that can solve the problems the old one could not, and so the establishment of a new period of normal science. This process of paradigm adoption, normal science, anomalies, crisis, and revolution is taken to be definitive of scientific development.[77] It is, as Paul Hoyningen-Huene points out, "a universal phase model of scientific development"[78] and is asserted as true of science itself past, present, and future. It is no less a "grand theory" because of its focus on science than are the theories of Marx and Hegel.

It would not be appropriate here to undertake a detailed critique of Kuhn's theory. It must suffice to point out briefly certain features of it. The most important is that if Kuhn is right, then no scientific theory can ever be true. If a theory were true, then it would not lead to anomalies, and without anomalies—that is, failures of the paradigm theory to solve certain problems—there would be no crises, no revolutions, and no new paradigms. That would mean the end of science as Kuhn conceives it, and since he sees his theory as universal, that cannot happen. Those who have taken Kuhn as their authority in holding that scientific research does not lead to truth have read him correctly. It need hardly be said that Kuhn's theory has found little support among scientists.

Not surprisingly, in view of his grand theory, Kuhn denies that there is "progress" in science. He defines progress not in terms of an approach to truth, since he denies that possibility to science, but in terms of "ontological convergence."

> I do not doubt . . . that Newton's mechanics improves on Aristotle's and that Einstein's improves on Newton's as instruments for puzzle-solving. But I can see in their succession no coherent direction of ontological development. On the contrary, in some important respects, though by no means in all, Einstein's general theory of relativity is closer to Aristotle's than either of them is to Newton's.[79]

But ontology is clearly the wrong place to look for progress, as Kuhn's own history of astronomy shows.[80] If, however, one looks at the ability of scientific theories to predict and control natural phenomena, then the evidence of progress is unmistakable. Our medicine is better than Galen's, our physics is better than Aristotle's, and our chemistry is better than Boyle's, where by "better" is meant having greater explanatory power and scope. To deny scientific progress may be a startling assertion, but it is clearly wrong.

Kuhn has also argued that different paradigms are incommensurable—that is, there is no common measure by which they can be compared.[81] In defending this view, he has held that the change from one paradigm to another involves a "conversion" or "gestalt switch" so that adherents of different paradigms live in different worlds.[82] This claim has created enormous confusion among Kuhn's readers that could have been avoided if Kuhn had distinguished understanding a theory from believing a theory. It is perfectly possible for an adherent of one paradigm to understand a different paradigm. In the physics curriculum of my university, Newtonian mechanics is still taught, although neither the students nor the faculty consider it true. It would be absurd to argue that after Einstein developed general relativity theory, he no longer understood Newtonian theory. Kuhn himself has recorded his discovery of what Aristotle's physics meant,[83] but he did not become an Aristotlean. Adopting a theory as true though may involve a "conversion" experience of some sort. That does not mean that one no longer understands what one previously believed. Kuhn is correct in holding that some terms of a theory cannot be separately learned but must be learned together—"force" and "mass" in Newtonian theory, for example.[84] But that does not show that the theories cannot be compared with respect to explanatory power and success in predictions.

A further ground for claiming incommensurability is, according to Kuhn, that when paradigms change, what is considered a problem or a solution also may change, so that revolutions bring not only gains in explanations but losses as well.[85] Thus Kuhn notes that the corpuscular theory of matter had by Newton's time largely banished occult properties from science. Yet Newton's theory made gravity an innate, occult property of matter. As Newton's theory became firmly established, efforts to explain gravity mechanically were abandoned, and "innate attractions and repulsions joined size, shape, position, and motion as physically irreducible properties of matter."[86] The corpuscularian insistence that bodies can act on each other only by contact had to be abandoned in the face of Newtonian gravity's ability to act at a distance. But what this argument comes to is that what appeared from the point of view of the prior theory to be a problem or problem solution or explanation of the data may turn out to be none of those from the point of view of the succeeding paradigm. If one assumes, as Kuhn would not, that the succeeding theory is superior to its predecessor, then such losses will involve no lack of progress, since riding the science of false theories would be a step forward rather than backward. Only from the standpoint of the prior theory would it follow that the move from one paradigm to another involves a real loss, but that is to assume that the sequence of theories does not represent an advance. The argument does not therefore show that the sequence does not represent an advance, since it assumes that as a premise.

Finally, Kuhn has propounded a theory of scientific "development" modeled on Darwinian evolution.[87] The central claim of this argument is that the sequence of scientific theories represents development from a starting point, not development toward an end point, and the great utility of the Darwinian analogy for Kuhn is that Darwin is well recognized to have been right in rejecting teleology in nature. But the rejection of teleology in nature cannot be held to imply a rejection of teleology in human action, since human action is blatantly teleological. Furthermore, Darwinian evolution involves two fundamental principles—fortuitous variation and natural selection. If the analogy holds, then one would expect to find sequences of theories that show random variation from the original theory, so that the result would be a plethora of variant theories. Manifestly, this is not what the history of science shows. If there were such a plethora, then Kuhn would need some equivalent of natural selection to eliminate the unsuccessful variants. His answer has been the scientific community, and in 1970 he emphasized that after the revolution the community reestablishes a consensus around a new paradigm theory.[88] But what is there about the scientific community that brings about this new consensus on the new paradigm? Kuhn was never able to answer that question.[89] The closest he ever came was to cite unity as a value embraced by all scientific communities,[90] but this simply translates the fact of consensus into a value that is then used to explain the consensus. Furthermore, unity is a value in many other types of communities (such as religious communities) that has been notably unsuccessful in preventing them from undergoing repeated divisions. It does not therefore provide an answer to Kuhn's problem. In his later work, perhaps just because he could not answer this problem, he began to emphasize that scientific revolutions result in "speciation,"[91] that is, new specialties appear as variants, so that something of the proliferation required by fortuitous variation is claimed to occur. But this argument also fails to solve the problem. First, it does not address the central question of why, in the wake of the Newtonian revolution, physicists came to a consensus on Newtonian physics, and after the Einsteinian revolution, they came to a consensus on relativity theory. In other words, the original problem of how and why consensus is reestablished is still there. Second, the new specialties that appear are not competitors of the new paradigm or of each other but usually involve using that new theory and others to attack a special set of problems. Molecular biology is not a competitor of either molecular or biological theory but a further development of both of them. The original problem of consensus remains and recurs for each specialty, and it is crucial to Kuhn's theory; it is also unanswered. What Kuhn will not admit is that the selective agent is nature, because to do so would involve him in problems in holding that science does not lead to truth.

Acclaim for Kuhn's theory has come very largely from nonscientists and is a testimony to the inferiority complex of humanists who have envied the progressive character of science and have bemoaned the lack of this characteristic in their own fields. In literature, for example, it is at least arguable that the greatest epic poem ever written was the *Iliad*, composed some 3,000 years ago. It would be very hard to argue that the drama has improved since Shakespeare or the novel since Tolstoy. But although no one can deny the genius of Isaac Newton or the magnitude of his achievement, our physics today is superior to his, as his was superior to Aristotle's. Science does progress, Kuhn to the contrary notwithstanding.

The track record of grand theories is not impressive. While many involve shrewd insights and useful concepts, their efforts to project processes they claim to have identified in the past into predictions of the future have been notably unsuccessful. It is generally agreed upon that Marx was a brilliant social thinker whose theories made an important contribution to our understanding of social processes, yet his attempt to predict the future course of social development was a disastrous failure. Similarly, Kuhn has made important contributions to the history of science, but his general theory of scientific development is untenable. This is not the place to enter the argument as to whether or not the future of human society and institutions is predictable; suffice it to say that no theory of social science or history presently known gives any evidence of being able to do so successfully. Historical theories deal with the past, not the future, and their task is to tell us what has happened, not what will happen.

There is a further point to be made. It has been widely held in recent years that neither scientific theories nor any other theories can be true. The authority cited for this claim is usually Kuhn. As noted earlier, Kuhn's claims for this view are without warrant. He built that assumption into his model of scientific development and then argued from the model to that conclusion—an obviously circular argument. It may or may not be possible for scientists, or historians, to discover the truth, but Kuhn's argument that they cannot is fallacious.

Chapter 5

Narrative

The literary form most commonly used by historians is the narrative. In this chapter I discuss the nature of the narrative and some of the claims made by narratologists concerning the virtues of the narrative. The chapter concludes with an examination of the work of one of the chief champions of narratology—Hayden White.

⊰◇⊱

In recent years, largely as a reaction against the "covering law" model, there has been a flood of writing about history as an interpretative and a narrative discipline. It should be emphasized that this description does not apply to all types of historical works. Some are analytic and expository, seeking to convey an understanding of beliefs or behavior patterns at a particular time and place. Perry Miller's *The New England Mind: The Seventeenth Century*[1] is a classic example of such a work, although Miller's work is also explanatory. Some are critiques of theories advanced by other historians; Peter Temin's *Did Monetary Forces Cause the Great Depression?*[2] is a good example. Some are applications of contemporary theoretical models to the explanation of past events; Fogel and Engermann's *Time on the Cross*[3] and Peter Temin's *Lessons from the Great Depression*[4] are illustrations, and there are other varieties as well. The narrative form is chiefly used to deal with events in temporal sequence. It seems to be assumed that an "interpretative" treatment of a historical subject must be in narrative form, though why this is so is unclear.

The word "narrative" refers to a particular literary form. It is remarkable that while there is much talk about narratives, it is very hard to find a definition of just what a narrative is. Most writers seem to agree that Aristotle was right in saying that a narrative must have a beginning, a middle, and an end, but beyond that there is rather astonishing vagueness. W. H. Dray, who as usual is clearer than most, specifies

103

the following criteria for a historical narrative. (1) It must "display the true temporal succession of its elements, as in chronicle, although the elements need not be cited in their order of occurrence." (2) "It must ascribe them to a central subject." (3) It must relate at least some of its elements to others in such a way that they explain the others, in any of a number of senses of "explain." (4) It must relate some of these elements to succeeding elements "with a view of displaying their significance." (5) It must show by displaying connectedness "that the various elements were parts, phases, or stages of a developing whole of some kind." It follows that the narrative will have a beginning, a middle, and an end, so that "the story told will have the formal characteristic referred to as "closure."[5] To this other writers would add a variety of further stipulations. Noel Carroll adds comprehensiveness.[6] Francois Furet adds that "all history of events is teleological history; only the "ending" of the history makes it possible to choose and understand the events that compose it."[7] Lawrence Stone says, "Narrative is taken to mean the organization of material in a chronological sequential order and the focusing of the content into a single coherent story, albeit with subplots."[8] Edgar Kiser adds, "Narratives are not just sequences of events, but are tied together by a central theme or plot."[9] Margaret Somers says, "It is possible to identify four features of a reframed narrative particularly relevant for the social sciences: (1) relationality of parts; (2) causal emplotment; (3) selective appropriation; and (4) temporality, sequence, and place."[10] William Cronin writes:

> We configure the events of the past into causal sequences—stories—that order and simplify those events to give them new meanings. We do so because narrative is the chief literary form that tries to find meaning in an overwhelmingly crowded and disordered chronological reality. When we choose a plot to order our environmental histories, we give them a unity that neither nature nor the past possesses so clearly.[11]

And, again, "narratives—unlike most natural processes—have beginnings, middles, and ends. Stories are intrinsically teleological forms, in which an event is explained by the prior events or causes that lead up to it."[12] Donald Spence holds that narratives must have "self-consistency, coherence, and comprehensiveness," and he describes the narrative as an "understandable Gestalt."[13] Seymour Chatman distinguishes the "what" of narratives, which he calls its "story," from the "way," which he calls its "discourse"—a division he equates to the Russian formalist's division into *fabula* and *sjuzet*.[14] Jean-Francois Lyotard claims, "Narration is the quintessential form of customary knowledge."[15] Indeed, with the exception of some aspects of science, Lyotard seems to regard narrative as the form of all knowledge.[16]

Michael Scriven tells us, "Literary critics have often written of the criterion of 'inevitability': it is said that a good play must develop in such a way that we are surprised at each development, i.e., cannot predict it, but then see the development as necessary, i.e., can explain it."[17] That is, each development surprises us as it comes, but by the end each is seen to have been necessary to produce the outcome.

These characterizations of narrative seem to me obscure and ambiguous. A far superior analysis is given by William Labov in his analysis of narratives of personal experience, drawn from several age categories of African American speakers. His basic definition is this:

> We define narrative as one method of recapitulating past experience by matching a verbal sequence of clauses to the sequence of events which (it is inferred) actually occurred. . . . The clauses are characteristically ordered in temporal sequence: if the narrative clauses are reversed, the inferred temporal sequence in the original semantic interpretation is altered.[18]

The basic structure is elaborated in what Labov calls the "fully formed narrative" by adding to it further elements that characterize the narratives in his sample.

1. abstract

2. orientation

3. complicating action

4. evaluation

5. result or resolution

6. coda[19]

"The abstract not only states what the narrative is about, but why it was told."[20] The orientation sets the scene: it identifies "the time, place, persons, and their activity or situation."[21] The complicating action is the sequence of narrative clauses. The evaluation is "the means used by the narrator to indicate the point of the narrative, its raison d'etre: why it was told, and what the narrator is getting at."[22] The result tells how the action ended, and the coda "returns the listener to the present time."[23]

This scheme was developed from first-person oral autobiographical narratives, told in response to the investigator's questions. Its application to historical narratives requires some modification. If a historical narrative contains an abstract, then it is usually given in the preface or the introduction. An orientation is always necessary to introduce the narrative and to locate it in time and space. The complicating action (i.e., the narrative itself) may be taken as matching a sequence of linguistic units (which are usually larger than the clause) to a sequence of historical events, so that changing the order of the linguistic units would change the order of the events referred to. The evaluation functions to tell the reader why this narrative is worth reading. As Labov says, the purpose of the evaluation is to forestall the rejoinder, "So what?"[24] Labov cites a number of ways in which the importance of the events described can be emphasized, including the use of counterfactuals (But for this, then . . .), comparatives, intensifiers, repetition, and so on. The result is what concludes the action and so the narrative. And the coda, if there is one, will shift the reader's point of view to the present. This structure admits of a variety of variations, such as flashbacks, reorderings, and monologues, but the basic structure holds. Clearly, these elements occur in liner order, except for the evaluation that may occur at any point in the narrative.

For historical narratives, the abstract and the coda are optional; some narratives will include one or both, and some will not. The orientation and the narrative itself, including the result, are obviously essential. The evaluation poses a more complex problem. It should be noted that, as Labov defines it, the purpose of the evaluation is to show why the narrative is "tellable" (i.e., why it is worth hearing or reading). This need not involve any moral judgments on the events described. In cases such as the French Revolution, the American Civil War, World War I, and World War II, the importance placed on these events by the culture makes no such argument necessary. But a historical account of the Leisler uprising or Bacon's Rebellion or the ministry of Lorenzo Dow may well require some evaluative comments to assure the reader that the narrative is worth his time.

This description of the narrative is largely syntactic and pragmatic; aside from the fact that Labov takes narratives to refer to sequences of events, the semantic question is left largely untouched. But I would add that just as temporality requires matching sequences of linguistic units to events, so also the order of causality is temporal. And it is a major part of the historian's endeavor to describe accurately not only what happened but why it happened. A historical narrative must refer to the causal structure of events and provide an explanation of why events turned out the way they did. This is a semantic requirement rather than a syntactic or pragmatic one, but it is a requirement for which the narrative linguistic structure usually provides a suitable vehicle. The justification for a historical narrative is that it tells the truth about what happened and why.

Throughout the writings of these thinkers, the terms *narrative*, *story*, and *plot* recur and very often are used to define each other. It is not much help to be told that a "narrative" is a "story" if a "story" is then defined as a "narrative." But there are certain terms and issues that seem to run through most of these writings: specifically, the chronicle-narrative distinction, explanation, significance, teleology, unity or coherence, and truth. These are large subjects, and a fully adequate analysis of all of them is daunting. Nevertheless, they require some discussion, however limited.

Before turning to the examination of these terms, several points need to be made. If a narrative is, as Labov said, an account that matches verbal units to a sequence of events, then historical accounts will usually be narratives. Other methods exist for giving such an account, but the narrative is an obvious method of describing such a series and is the one usually employed. But how are the events and characters in the narrative related? Historians do not simply describe events, they seek to explain them. If the temporality of experience requires the use of narratives, then so does the direction of causality, and historical narratives do contain causal models as a skeleton that is fleshed out in their accounts. They usually contain much more besides—descriptions of characters, situations, counterfactual arguments, and so on—but historians do seek to provide explanations of the events they describe, and this involves describing causal relations.

The word "interpretation" has so many meanings in current debates that one must at least try to specify which of these applies in history. Traditionally, historical "interpretations" were the narrative accounts given by historians which, as I have argued, are really theories. But there is a different use of "interpretation" currently invoked in debates about history. What seems to be the defining mark of such interpretation is that it ascribes "meaning" to events and objects. But one must be very careful here. Cultures have multiple semiotic systems, and these require different sorts of analyses. Thus in our present culture, if one wears a cross, then the cross denotes the cross of Christ and connotes Christianity, and the illocutionary force involved is the assertion of one's membership in the Christian community. If one drives a Ferrari, however, the car does not denote or connote anything; rather, it exemplifies the wealth and status of its owner. As Nelson Goodman showed,[25] various semiotic systems exist in any culture, and they must not be confused. "Meanings" of this sort are always meanings to someone; something cannot be a sign unless it is interpreted as a sign by someone, and even within a culture, different groups may have different sign systems. What a present-day historian thinks an action or an object meant may have no relation to what it meant in the culture in which it was used. Thus one might easily be puzzled by the variations in the forms of seventeenth-century New England Puritan meetinghouses and conclude that architectural design carried no meaning, but any seventeenth-century Puritan would know that what was important was that the building was *not* cruciform. To understand a culture, one must determine the semiotic codes it used, but there is no opposition between this sort of interpretative analysis and causal analysis. In fact, causal relations may give rise to semiotic relations too.

At the risk of being repetitious, it must be emphasized that to attribute a particular meaning to a past event or object is to propose a hypothesis. For that hypothesis to be true, the meaning has to be that which members of the culture involved attributed to the item referred to. Thus, for example, Wertenbaker "interpreted" Bacon's Rebellion as a prefiguration of the American Revolution. "The roar of their canon proclaimed to the world that Virginians would resist to the end all attempts to deprive them of their heritage of English liberty."[26] But is that how Bacon, or Virginians of his time, or the English saw the rebellion? Certainly not. Again, today we generally attribute King Philip's War to the incursion of the land-hungry Puritans upon the Indian lands. But the Puritans saw it in a very different light—as a punishment inflicted upon them by God for their failure to keep his covenant.[27] Put differently, what is the test of the truth of a hypothesis attributing "meaning" to a past event? If the test is not that the meaning attributed by the historian must match that attributed to it by the culture or cultures involved, then where is it to be found? If it is just what the historian thinks or imagines, then there is no standard at all, and everything is in the wind.[28]

Chronicle and Narrative

Classical historiography described the process of historical construction as consisting of two steps. First, by external and internal criticism of the evidence, the historian was to determine all of the "facts" relevant to his subject. Second, he was then to develop an interpretation, selecting those facts that were relevant to his purpose and creating a narrative of what happened. This description of how history should be done was adopted by Morton White, who formulated it as first the creation of a "chronicle" that listed all of the facts in chronological order, and then the "interpretation" that was to be given in narrative form.[29] This is the usage that most contemporary philosophers of history have adopted.

It is surprising that so Baconian a process should still be regarded as the proper method of doing history, particularly because in practice few historians actually follow it. The most obvious problem with it, as Charles Beard[30] and Carl Becker,[31] among others, pointed out long ago is that since the selection of "facts" is prior to the formulation of the interpretation, the criterion for selecting "facts" to be interpreted is subjective. This led both Beard and Becker to abandon any hope that historical interpretations could be true, since they would be shaped by the historian's bias. But this entire model of how history should be done is wrong. As I have argued before, it is the theory formulated by the historian (read "interpretation" if you like) that determines which facts are to be included. The so-called "facts" are part of the theory, and the whole structure rests on observations of the data. No working historian first selects some set of facts and *then* sets about interpreting them. What he does is study the data—the documents or artifacts or oral histories or whatever is being used—and then develops from them ideas about what happened. Those ideas form into a theory about the subject, and that theory in turn raises further questions that require searching for further evidence. The whole structure of fact and theory evolves together in the historian's mind as a model of what took place. And as the historian asks, over and over, "If that is what happened, then where is the proof?," he is led to search for other data that can support or refute the model. Very often a historian will become convinced that certain events must have occurred even though he lacks direct proof, just as Pagels concluded that the Gospel according to John was written as an answer to the Gospel according to Thomas. All Peirce scholars knew that Peirce had been guilty of some immoral indiscretion that led to his being fired at Johns Hopkins long before we knew what he had done. Fact and theory are parts of one conceptual structure accounting for the data. That conceptual structure guides the predictions that historians make as they search for further data. The chronicle-narrative distinction reflects an outdated concept of historical research that should be abandoned.[32]

Explanation and Teleology

As Dray pointed out, narratives are supposed to be explanatory. But just how do they explain? If we look first at a *fictional* narrative, then what seems to be meant is functional explanation. Thus if one asks why Herman Melville included Father Mapple's sermon in *Moby Dick*, the answer is provided by citing the function that that incident plays in the novel as a whole. As is well known, Jonah was often portrayed as a type of which Christ was the antitype. By situating the sermon early on in the story, Melville sets up a Christian paradigm against which Ahab's monomaniacal pursuit of the white whale is to be viewed. In more general terms, in a fictional narrative, every event included should contribute to the overall purpose and effect of the story. If the narrative is well constructed, then all of the events it describes should function to advance the story—that is, should help create the kind of story the author wants and augment its impact on the reader. Any incident in the story that is not thus functional diminishes the effectiveness of the story by diverting the reader's attention from the point of the tale.

Functional explanations acquired a bad name because of their use in biology. To say that the function of the kidneys is to remove impurities from the bloodstream is to imply that the kidneys were designed for that purpose, and so assumes a designer. But our eyes were not made so that we could see and our ears were not designed so that we could hear; rather, we see because we have eyes, and we hear because we have ears. But in discussing a novel, which is created by an author and is designed to produce certain effects on the reader, functional explanation is quite appropriate. Indeed, one may say that in a well-constructed novel, every incident should function to enhance the story and its impact on the reader. But to apply functional explanation to a *historical* narrative is a very different matter. There is no designer who determines the course of human history. It is true that individuals act purposefully (usually), but rarely do they have sufficient control over events to guarantee that all they do is functional for the achievement of their goals. And beyond the level of the single individual, people exhibit such variations in their desires, beliefs, goals, loves, and hates that nothing like the functional unity of a novel is possible. The real world is messy; human actions often contradict their stated goals and have unforeseen consequences that wreak havoc of the best-laid plans. To attempt to construct a historical narrative, the events of which can be functionally explained, would require such a selective use of the evidence that the result would be a serious distortion. What is required for the explanation of historical events is efficient causes, not final ones.

The "inevitability" that Scriven cites is one form of functional explanation, but it is not something that all narrative histories can exhibit. Scriven held that each incident of the narrative must surprise us as it occurs. Generally this is not possible in a historical narrative.

Readers usually know something about the subject, or they would not be reading this account, and so they already know at least some of the incidents leading up to the climax. Surprise, then, may be possible in fiction, but only to a very limited degree in history. And is there always a climax to which the narrative builds? That depends on what sort of history this is. If, like Sidney Fay, one is writing a history of the origins of World War I,[33] then the climax is clearly defined to be the outbreak of the war. But if one is writing a history of a period, then there may be no climax in Scriven's sense. Thus Schlesinger's *The Age of Jackson* is a history of a period that ends with a discussion of why the Jacksonians failed to develop an ideology; this is hardly a climactic state or event. And Schlesinger was one of the most accomplished writers in the American historical trade. Inevitability is perhaps something required by fictional narratives, but not a requirement for historical ones.

Unity

Leaving aside the question of inevitability, it is the case that historical narratives do strive for unity or coherence of some kind. What sort of unity this will be varies with the sort of subject dealt with. In a history of an era, usually the historian seeks to tie together the various incidents discussed by presenting them as expressions or illustrations of certain "themes" that characterize the period in question. These may be underlying causal factors or simply descriptive categories that run throughout the period. Thus, for example, Schlesinger sees class conflict as the basic theme of the Jacksonian period and seeks to show that the events of that time exemplify such a conflict. Such a structure is coherent, perhaps too much so, but it does not require a climactic event. It also involves certain dangers. We have a variety of histories of the United States in the 1960s. Some of these are written on the inevitability model, but they have a problem deciding what the climactic event is. Some stop in 1968, taking the chaos of that year and the Nixon election as the climax; others go to 1973 and see Watergate and the end of the war as the climax. But these histories usually are unified by the "theme" of social protest; they generally deal chiefly with the protest movements of the era. And here the dangers of this sort of unity are apparent. There were many social protest movements in the 1960s, but rarely are all of them dealt with. While the Civil Rights Movement, the AntiWar Movement and the Women's Movement are staples, others such as the Indian Rights Movement are often ignored. Furthermore, these social movements do not coincide with the 1960s. Civil Rights began well before that; in fact, it is not easy to say just when the Civil Rights Movement began. One can make a case that it started with Birmingham in the 1950s, with the *Brown* decision, with the Dixiecrat walkout, with the election of 1936, or even with the arrival of the first slaves in 1619. Similarly, the Gay Rights Movement and much of the Women's movement belong largely to the 1970s. But these historians ignore the Conservative Movement that grew dramatically in the 1960s, and that has had consequences at least as important as any of the others. Historians have selected the social protest movements that leaned to the Left; they have ignored the Conservative Movement, which was equally a social protest movement but leaned to the Right. Accordingly, such histories give a badly distorted picture even of the movements of the decade. The demand for unity can lead to a myopic focus that seriously misleads.

Historians find themselves facing a partially insolvable problem when it comes to unity, and one that is particularly well illustrated by period histories. The real world is chaotic; all sorts of things are going on all of the time. But historians have limited time and limited space; publishers will not publish books that run too long. If historians are to avoid "and then" histories (histories of the form "this happened, and then this, and then . . ."), they have to single out some aspect of the era as their focus. But this choice should not be purely arbitrary. If one is going to write about the social protest movements of the 1960s, then one ought to include those on the Right as well as those on the Left, especially because what happened in the Left movements provided a major stimulus to the movements on the Right. Indeed, if a right-wing leader had prayed for events and behavior that would arouse conservatives to action, then he could not have prayed for more than the Civil Rights, AntiWar, and Women's Movements and the CounterCulture provided.

The basic structure of a historical narrative is a series of temporally ordered linguistic units matched to a series of causally and temporally related events. The narrative provides a particularly useful structure for describing the temporal sequence of events, but this alone does not supply unity. What unifies the narrative is the causal dependencies among the events. Historians choose to investigate a particular subject. What is relevant for them are persons and events causally related to that subject, so that at the end they have not only a description of a temporal series of events but a causal account of why those events took place as they did. This basic causal theory need not be presented in narrative form, but the narrative is well suited for the purpose, and it is the form usually employed. But the unity of the historical narrative account is not produced by the narrative form; it is the product of the causal theory presented through the narrative.

It must be emphasized that the causal theory provides only the skeletal framework for the historical narrative. Usually historians will flesh out that structure with descriptions of scene and character, elaborations of points having particular interest, colorful anecdotes, comments designed to persuade the reader of the importance of the topic, and so on. It should never be forgotten that historical narratives are addressed not just to other historians but to layreaders as well. Usually there is nothing in a narrative history that any college graduate would have any difficulty understanding. And historical narratives are read by the laity. Some have made the best-seller list and won Pulitzer prizes. Few historians earn substantial sums from the sales of their works, but some do. The hope of doing so also helps explain why historians often choose to write on subjects of current popular interest. More than scholars in other fields, historians write for and are influenced by the popular culture.

Significance

Historians describe certain events as "significant," but what "significant" means when so used is less than clear. In ordinary speech, the term has multiple meanings, not all of which are relevant to history. As historians employ it, "significance" does not mean "meaning" in the linguistic sense. All historians agree that the Battle of the Nile was a significant event in the war between England and France, but the Battle of the Nile was not a linguistic entity, and linguistic concepts do not apply to it. This is not to deny that the Battle of the Nile may have had symbolic values, but not all symbols are linguistic. Rather, as used by historians, "significance" means "importance." But what makes an event important?

"Significance" is predicated of an event in at least two different senses. On the one hand, one can say that C is the most significant cause of E; on the other, one could say that event C is significant because of the consequences that it had. These are not the same. The first case arises only if E has multiple causes and the problem is to determine which one is the most important. Nagel proposed four different ways in which this might occur. First, suppose A and B are "contingently necessary conditions" for the occurrence of E, but A occurs much more frequently than B. One might then say that A is the more important or significant cause of E. Second, suppose A and B are again both necessary for E. If variation in A produces proportionally greater changes in E than do proportional changes in B, then A could be held to be the more significant cause of E. Third, let A be a contingently necessary cause of E; let B_1 be a member of a set of mutually independent factors

$B_1 \ldots B_n$ such that the occurrence of some B_i is a necessary condition for E. Even if the frequency of occurrence of the B_i is greater than that of A, E may occur when A is present but B_1 is not if some other B_j (i ≠ j) also occurs. Then, A could be said to be a more significant cause of E than B_1. For example, A might be what historians call an "underlying" cause, while the Bs are precipitating causes. Thus Sidney Fay sees the underlying cause of World War I as being the system of alliances that prevailed in Europe, whereas the assassination of Archduke Ferdinand was the precipitating cause. Fourth, suppose that the joint occurrence of A and B is not necessary for E, but the occurrence of each can cause E. If A occurs more frequently than B, then A might be said to be more significant as a cause of E than B.[34] These different uses of "significant" are all to be found in historical works, but they all involve causal sequences that are repeated—for example, migrations, wars, revolutions, and so on. Many historical events are not repeated, unless one classifies them under concepts so broad that most of their content is lost.

A more specific use of "significance" can be described as follows. Let A, B, and F be jointly necessary for the occurrence of E, but let it be the case that B and F do not operate unless A is present. If this were a contemporary problem, then one could easily imagine how the causal role of A could be demonstrated through the method of difference. But historians cannot vary the occurrence of past events, so in the historical case one would have to argue that had A not been present, even though B and F were, E would not have occurred—that is, one would have to argue counterfactually. A good example of this occurs in David Hackett Fischer's *Paul Revere's Ride*. Of course, multiple factors were responsible for the American victory at Lexington and Concord, but Fischer sees Revere's work as necessary for their effective combination. Says Fischer:

> In the flow of information [about the British] one may discover the importance of the preparations he [Revere] had made; the impact of his decisions along the way, and the role of his associations with other Whig leaders. Many of the links in that chain had been forged in advance. Others were improvised by Paul Revere and his friends who prudently prepared for the worst case.

Then comes the counterfactual:

> Had they acted otherwise, the outcome might well have been different. A few hours' delay in the alarm—perhaps less than

that—might have been enough for General Gage's troops to have completed their mission and returned safely to Boston before an effective force could muster against them.[35]

Here Fischer demonstrates the significance of Revere's activities by showing what the consequences would have been had those activities not occurred.

Asserting an event C to be the most significant cause of E is somewhat different from saying that C is significant because of the effects it has. In the former, one is trying to determine which among the various causes of E was the most important; in the latter, one is attributing significance to C, not as the most important among a set of causes but in terms of its consequences, which may be single or multiple. The problem here is quickly apparent. If C is significant because it has significant consequences, on what, then, will the significance of its consequences depend? If the answer is that it depends on the significance of their consequences, we are off on an endless series, and there seems to be no way to bring it to a close.

Here it is important to recognize that "significant" can be used either as a relative term or an absolute term. In the relative sense, to say "x is significant" is to say "x is significant to y," where the range of "y" can be a person, a group, a society, the human race, or any other set of human beings. Obviously, what is significant to one person may not be significant to another. Jones's being sent to prison may be the most significant event in his life yet be of little importance to his society. In this relative use of "significant," the question of whether or not event "x" is significant to "y" is an empirical one. In theory at least, one should be able to determine what the various people who are the values of "y" thought about "x." Practically, of course, this may be an extremely difficult thing to do, but the beliefs of the y's are matters of fact and therefore are, in theory at least, determinable. But "significant" is also used in historical writing in an absolute sense. Several different usages are involved here. As Labov noted, narratives often include evaluative statements the purpose of which is to show why the narrative is worth the telling.[36] Thus a history of the Manhattan Project will contain statements emphasizing the scientific achievement represented by the bomb and the subsequent effects of the bomb's invention. "Significant" also may be combined with other words such as "good," "bad," and "evil" used in a moral sense to praise or condemn actions, persons, or events. Thus "Hitler was evil" expresses a moral judgment on Hitler. Always implicit or explicit in such statements is some standard of value, often that of the author's culture or of some subgroup of his society, but sometimes simply that of the author. But whichever it is, the standard should be made explicit. Value judgments are not empirical statements and do not add to our factual knowledge. While they may express widely held beliefs, as in the case of Hitler, there is a danger that the work in which they occur may become propaganda designed to further some cause other than the pursuit of truth.

It has been claimed that the significance of a historical event varies over time, hence significance cannot be objectively determined. Historical events occur at particular times (or over specific time periods, which for our purposes can be taken as particular times). The consequences of an event extend indefinitely into the future. To use an analogy from physics, one may think of the consequences of the event E as a cone with E at the apex that expands steadily into the future. I know of no reason to believe that the cone ever ends. Who can say what the final consequence of a given event might be? But historians also live in time. If t_1 is the time of the occurrence of E and t_2 the time at which the historian writes, then the consequences of E available to the historian are those that occurred in the interval t_2—t_1. A later historian writing at t_3 ($t_3 > t_2$) will have a different body of consequences of E upon which to base his account. This may suggest that the greater the interval t_3—t_1, the better for the historian. But the amount of data concerning E that survives to t_x tends to vary inversely with the length of the interval t_x—t_1. For example, if the testimony of living witnesses regarding E is important for the historian, then the availability of such data is limited by the human life span. The combination of these two offsetting factors is perhaps responsible for the prevalence of the rule of thumb that one should not attempt a history of an event until thirty years after its occurrence.

Now it is obvious that the historian writing about event E at t_3 has a different set of causal consequences of E to consider than the one writing at t_2, and it would be remarkable if the two accounts did not differ. But such differences could hardly be called subjective. Since the data are different, the accounts will vary, but the change in the data is an objective fact owing to our temporality, not to subjective whim. To fix ideas, consider the following case. Consider two biographies of Winston Churchill, one written when he was thirty, the other when he was sixty-five. Would the causal consequences of the Boer War for Churchill be different in the two accounts? Let us first distinguish what Churchill considered the consequences of the war to be from what in fact they were. The first is a question of how Churchill's view of his youthful experience changed as he grew older. One would be surprised if there were no change. Increasing age usually does affect our view of our early experience, in part because of forgetting and in part because added experience leads us to reappraise our lives, but these are facts about Churchill; his changing views are subjective for him, but not for his biographers, for whom they are objective facts. But would the biographers' accounts of the significance of Churchill's Boer War experience vary from each other? In all probability, they would, since the later biographer would have thirty-five more years of Churchill's life as data and so a wider range of effects of his Boer War experience on Churchill to consider. But these differences in the historian's treatment of Churchill are not subjective for historians. Having access to different data at different times is an objective fact about the subject.

"Significance" gives us yet another case in which the shifting interests in the surrounding society influence history. After World War I, there was great interest in peacemaking and diplomacy, stimulated by the war itself and by what happened, and did not happen, at Versailles. Today, in an era when even the meaning of "war" is unclear, and the influence of diplomacy is in doubt, there is much less interest in the society and among historians in such questions. Historians' interests change over time in response to events in the world and in their society, and so of course do the subjects they study. It remains the case that the significance of events is relative to the interests of the historians, but in cases such as the shift away from the study of peacemaking, it is often possible to determine which events in the world caused this shift. That, however, is a question for the history of history—a field at present badly underdeveloped.

Roles

I discussed earlier the different senses of "explanation" that apply to fictional narratives and historical narratives, but clearly there are scholars who believe that historical narratives have further explanatory functions. What are those functions? Narratives are said to be stories. But stories are not just about events, they are also about characters, and these characters play certain sorts of roles in the story. Usually a story has a hero and a villain and seeks to create dramatic tension by the trials of the hero in overcoming a series of obstacles, generally created by or including the villain. The hero may triumph or may fail, but if he fails, it should be tragically. There is a strong tendency in historical narratives—stories—to portray the actors in the account as playing these roles. Thus for example Schlesinger portrays Andrew Jackson as the hero of the period, battling Nicholas Biddle (the villain) and the Bank of the United States. Similarly, Calhoun is given a villainous role in his contest with Jackson, though Schlesinger has too much respect for Calhoun to treat him as he does Biddle. Certainly this method of presentation adds drama to his account, but it is a drama that is notably lacking in Benson's account of Jackson. There are many examples of this sort of thing, but it is particularly common in biographies. One usually does not write a biography about someone for whom one's feelings are neutral, so the tendency to enrich the subject's life and character is very strong. In his biography of John Adams, David McCullough paints a portrait of Adams that makes him appear to be a paragon of virtue and downplays the elitism of his views, as evident, for example, in his *Thoughts on Government* and his plan for the constitution of Massachusetts.[37] The temptation to glorify one's subject is very strong, but it can be resisted, as, for example, in Robert Caro's biography of Lyndon Johnson.[38]

But there are problems here. It is not simply the appalling dearth of true heroes in the real world, but the fact that the procedure of casting characters in a narrative in such storybook roles as hero, villain, and so on imposes on the actual data a preconceived framework. One cannot make this point more clearly than Hayden White does in his discussion of Hillgruber's *Zweierlei Untergang.*

> Hillgruber's suggestion for the emplotment of the history of the eastern front during the winter of 1944–45 indicates the way in which a specific plot type (tragedy) can simultaneously determine the kinds of events to be featured in any story that can be told about them and provide a pattern for the assignment of the roles that can possibly be played by the agents and agencies inhabiting the scene thus constituted. At the same time, Hillgruber's suggestion also indicates how the choice of a mode of emplotment can justify ignoring certain kinds of events, agents, actions, agencies, and patients that may inhabit a given historical scene or its context. There is no place for any form of low or ignoble life in a tragedy; in tragedies even the villains are noble or, rather, villainy can be shown to have its noble incarnations.[39]

It is possible that the real actors who are the subjects of the historical narrative fit such preconceived roles, but the probability of this happening is vanishingly small. To force the data to fit some such preconceived schemes is virtually certain to distort the real picture. For example, in his six-volume history of World War II, Winston Churchill cast himself in the role of a hero. But as a recent book by David Reynolds makes clear, to do so Churchill often had to massage the data vigorously to make them fit the heroic image of himself that he wanted to project.[40] A second example is Richard Nixon. Certainly it is easy to cast Nixon as a villain, but to do so overlooks some of the accomplishments of Nixon that are almost universally approved in this country, and so distorts reality. If a historian is to write a narrative history, then his primary problem is to construct a causal model that accounts for the behavior of his characters. The model can usually be presented in the style of a narrative, but the narrative is simply a stylistic device for the presentation of the model. The narrative has no explanatory power of its own.

Truth

Can narrative accounts be true? This seems at first to be a relatively simple question. Take any narrative account regarded as true and substitute for all the proper names it includes fictitious names. Then the narrative becomes a fiction pure and simple. Take any fictional narrative—*Sister Carrie* or *The Great Gatsby* or *Winney the Pooh*—and for the fictional names substitute the names of real people. Then the narrative becomes a factual account that is either true or false. It would appear, then, that there is nothing about the narrative form per se that makes it either true or false. But this simple answer has been disputed.

How can a true theory be formulated in narrative form? A narrative is a particular literary device that is useful for dealing with temporal sequences of causally related events. Consider Sidney Fay's *The Origins of the World War*. Like many other scholars, Fay was puzzled that the war occurred despite the fact that none of the governments involved wanted it. As he examined the governmental records, press coverage, diplomatic correspondence, and so on, of the powers involved, what he found was a complex series of interactions extending over a long period of time. Each country was guided by its own interests, by its expectations concerning what the others would do, by the need to respond to the actions of the others, and by its alliances. For this temporally extended series of interactions, the narrative offered a viable means of presenting his account. The basic skeleton of the theory is a series of causal interactions among the powers, and these admit of narrative description. The truth of this account depends upon how well it accounts for the data employed. Fay could have used other methods of presentation; the truth of his account does not depend on its being a narrative but on the accuracy with which he characterized the causal relations that form the core of his theory and the extent to which that causal theory explains the data. The fact that he chose to give his theory a narrative presentation is irrelevant to its truth. There is, then, nothing about the narrative per se that makes a theory so expressed true or false.

So far, I have followed the usual meaning of "historical narrative" that is described by writers such as Dray and Cronin in the opening pages of this chapter. But as there remarked, I find this employment of the term confused and ambiguous. The problem seems to result from the conflation of a narrative with a story. As my colleague Bruce Kuklick has remarked, a story must have a point. But for a historical narrative, the "point," if I may call it that, is to tell the truth.

A historical narrative is a linguistic structure for describing and presenting an explanation of a sequence of past occurrences. The goal is accuracy of description and truth of description and explanation. Thus, for example, Peter Green's account of the career of Alexander the Great[41] is an objective account of what Alexander did and of why events took the course they did. It would be very hard to say that his account has a point beyond giving a true description and explanation of Alexander's career.

There is a difference between narratives and stories that is obscured in the comments of the authors cited at the beginning of this chapter. All stories may be narratives, but not all narratives are stories. Stories are teleological forms that exhibit functional unity and that present characters as heroes and villains. As many have pointed out, there are real problems about whether or not stories, so conceived, can be true. Historical narratives, however, are descriptions and explanations of past events, and their goal is the truth. They may or may not contain an abstract; if they do, it usually is presented as a preface or an introduction. They do contain an orientation telling the reader when and where the sequence of events occurred and what the situation was, but they need not contain evaluations or a coda. The danger of writing history in stories is that the literary form may require the making of a climax where there is none, or that the requirements of functional unity may constrain the selection and use of data, including only the events that fit the story line while ignoring other perhaps more important events, or it may impose roles upon historical actors that were not theirs.

There is, however, a more general issue about the determination of historical truth: To what extent are the accounts that historians write ideological? That depends on what one means by "ideology." If one takes this term in Karl Mannheim's general sense, then historical works are influenced by ideology. According to Mannheim:

When we attribute to one historical epoch one intellectual
world and to ourselves another one, or if a certain historically
determined social stratum thinks in categories other than our
own, we refer not to the isolated cases of thought-content, but
to fundamentally different thought-systems and to widely different modes of experience and interpretation. We touch upon
the theoretical or noological (*sic*; nomological?) whenever we
consider not merely the content but also the form, and even
the conceptual framework of a mode of thought as a function
of the life-situation of a thinker.[42]

On this view, there is no such thing as truth; every belief is the product of the social situation of the believer. It follows that our refusal to
grant witches the status of real entities is ideological. But there are well-
known difficulties with this position; it can be taken reflexively so that
Mannheim's theory of ideology becomes itself ideological and so can
only be relative to his life situation. As I shall use the term *ideology* it
will be in what Mannheim calls the "particular" sense—that one's ideas
"are regarded as more or less conscious disguises of the real nature of
the situation, the true recognition of which would not be in accord with
his [writer's] interests."[43] For example, Richard Bushman, a respected
historian, recently published a book on the history of Mormonism. As
a devout Mormon, Bushman's account of Joseph Smith's founding of
the Mormon religion accepts as true the Mormon Church's doctrine
that an angel delivered the golden tablets to Smith, the translation of
which yielded the Book of Mormon.[44] Much as I like Bushman, I do
not believe this account, and I doubt that anyone who is not a Mormon does either. But the fact that some historians are influenced by
particular ideologies does not prove that all of us are. The interest of
historians as a group is best secured by publishing historical works that
are so solidly researched that their colleagues will accept them as true.
It is not in the interest of historians to write ideological history, and
although some do, the imperative to discover and tell the truth is the
guiding principle of the trade.

Within the history profession itself, no one has opposed this view
more vigorously than Hayden White. Like a number of philosophers
and philosophers of history, White has made the "linguistic turn," and
evidence of the influence of "postmodern" French thinkers is plentiful
in his writings. This linguistic spell has led him to the construction of
an elaborate theory of the nature of history. But it is clearly stated in
his pages that his theory concerns only the writing of history; histori-

cal research is deliberately excluded. Historical research, he tells us, is no different from that of the journalist or the detective; what interests him is the writing of the historical work or, more precisely, how the results of historical research are transformed into a historical narrative.[45] When, therefore, he says that history is a verbal artifact,[46] it is written history to which he refers. White notes that there are non-narrative ways of writing history,[47] but he rightly says that the great majority of historical works are in narrative form, and it is this narrative history that he addresses.

In *Metahistory*, White sets out his theory. It will be best to see it in his own words here:

> Historical accounts purport to be verbal models, or icons, of specific segments of the historical process. But such models are needed because the documentary record does not figure forth an unambiguous image of the structure of events attested in them. In order to figure "what *really* happened" in the past, therefore, the historian must first *pre*figure as a possible object of knowledge the whole set of events reported in the documents. This prefigurative act is *poetic* in as much as it is precognitive and precritical in the economy of the historian's own consciousness. It is also poetic in so far as it is constitutive of the structure that will subsequently be imaged in the verbal model offered by the historian as a representation and explanation of "what *really* happened" in the past. But it is constitutive not only of a domain which the historian can treat as a possible object of (mental) perception. It is also constitutive of the *concepts* he will use *to identify the objects* that inhabit that domain and *to characterize the kinds of relationships* they can sustain with one another. In the poetic act which precedes the formal analysis of the field, the historian both creates his object of analysis and predetermines the modality of the conceptual strategies he will use to explain it.[48]

In view of this passage, it is obvious that historical research cannot be separated from historical writing. If the events and objects of the past, and the "facts," are constituted by tropical language, then there is nothing for the historian to research until the historical field has been constituted. What White really seems to be saying is that all historical conceptualization involves his tropes, and that therefore there cannot be any historical research until the field is constituted linguistically.

In *The Content of the Form*, White distinguishes between three "stages" in historical composition: annals, chronicle, and narrative.[49]

Usually he abbreviates this to chronicle and narrative. The point White wants to make is that the results of the historian's research must be conceptualized (as if they were not already) before they can be put into narrative form. Annals represent a low degree of conceptualization, chronicle a higher degree, and narrative the highest. But the data have to be organized in some form before composition is possible. Where does this conceptualization come from? It comes from what White calls in *Metahistory* the "deep structure," which is a set of linguistic categories ordering the data.[50] It is not entirely clear just where this deep structure lies in the human consciousness. White does not, as far as I know, use this term in his later works, but his analyses of the work of Piaget, Freud, and Durkheim he believes show the presence of these categories in the unconscious.[51] It is perhaps not incorrect to see them as functioning like Kant's categories to bring order out of chaos.

These basic categories are the four tropes of metaphor, metonymy, synecdoche, and irony. The typology, borrowed from Northrup Frye, is taken to afford fundamental ways of making sense of the data. As White says:

> The *shape* of the *relationships* which will appear to be inherent in the objects inhabiting the [historical] field will in reality have been imposed on the field by the investigator in the very *act of identifying and describing* the objects that he finds there. The implication is that historians *constitute* their subjects as possible objects of narrative representation by the very language they use to *describe* them.[52]

By the "historical field" White means "the unprocessed historical record." What this amounts to White makes clear as follows:

> History is the study, not of past events that are gone forever from perception, but rather of the "traces" of those events distilled into documents and monuments, on the one side, and the praxis of present social formations, on the other. These "traces" are the raw materials of the historian's discourse, rather than the events themselves. . . . [These discourses] are not reflections or mimetic reproductions of events but processings of these "traces" so as to endow them with "symbolic" significance.[53]

It is common doctrine among philosophers that observation terms are theory laden, but White means more than this. The point about historical events and objects is that they cannot be observed because they no longer exist. "How else," White asks, "can any past, which by definition comprises events, processes, structures, and so forth, considered to be no longer perceivable, be represented in either consciousness or discourse except in an 'imaginary' way?"[54] If these tropes are basic categories of the unconscious as well as the conscious mind, then White believes they must be involved in constituting the objects of the field. These objects cannot be the objects of the past, which no longer exist; they are linguistically constituted substitutes for past objects.

White is not perfectly clear regarding what is in the historical field. He says "events happen, whereas facts are constituted by linguistic description."[55] When he says that the field is "the past or the historical process,"[56] it seems that events are elements of the field. But facts are not; a "fact" must be regarded as "an event under a description,"[57] so it is clear that the historical facts are created by the historian on the basis of the evidence provided by the field. Nevertheless, as the passage last quoted shows, past events are not perceived but constituted from the evidence offered by the "traces" of the past. These events, which are linguistically constituted, are then organized into a chronicle that arranges them in temporal order.

The next step in the constitution of the historical narrative is what White calls "emplotment"—that is, the making of a story from the elements of the chronicle. White says that "the historian confronts a veritable chaos of events *already constituted*, out of which he must choose the elements of the story he would tell. He makes his story by including some events and excluding others, by stressing some and subordinating others. This process of exclusion, stress, and subordination is carried out in the interest of constituting *a story of a particular kind*. That is to say, he "emplots" his story."[58] Although White does at one point say that the plot "has to *appear* to emerge gradually and, as it were, naturally from the events,"[59] the use of "appear" shows that this is only an illusion. His general claim is that the historian's choice of plot type is free; in other words, the plot is imposed on the data by the historian.

How free is the historian in making his choice of plot? White generally holds that he is completely free. Nevertheless, White believes that virtually all plots fall into four categories: Romance, Comedy, Tragedy, and Satire.[60] (It should be noted that "comedy," as used here, does not mean "humorous" but a plot in which conflicts are reconciled.) The typology is of course traditional, but it is not taken to be exhaustive, since on various occasions he mentions "pastoral," "farce," and "epic" as plot types. But within the four plot categories, how free is the historian's choice? White wants to hold that it is entirely free; thus he says, "All the historian needs to do to transform a tragic into a comic situation is to shift his point of view or change the scope of his perceptions."[61] But there are two events that give him pause: the assassination of John Kennedy and the Holocaust. With respect to the first, he comments, "I do not suppose that anyone would accept the emplotment of the life of President Kennedy as comedy, but whether it ought to be emplotted romantically, tragically, or satirically is an open question."[62] As to the Holocaust, one can hardly imagine a comic treatment—a Broadway show entitled "Auschwitz, the Musical"? The idea is grotesque. White suggests that a new style is required.

> I do not think that the Holocaust, Final Solution, Shoah, Churban, or German genocide of the Jews is any more unrepresentable than any other event in human history. It is only that its representation, whether in history or in fiction, requires a kind of style, the modernist style, that was developed in order to represent the kind of experiences which social modernism makes possible.[63]

But just what this style is is a question to which I will return.

It is, according to White, emplotment that confers meaning on historical events. Thus, White says, "By plot we mean a structure of relationships by which the events contained in the account are endowed with a meaning by being identified as parts of an integrated whole,"[64] and "when the reader recognizes the story being told in a historical narrative as a specific kind of story—for example, as an epic, romance, tragedy, comedy, or farce—he can be said to have comprehended the meaning produced by the discourse. This comprehension is nothing other than the recognition of the form of the narrative."[65] What White intends here seems to be a very specific sort of meaning—that conferred upon an event by being shown to be an element of a larger unit. Thus to say "Jones shot Schmidt" leaves us with many questions, but to say "Jones shot Schmidt in the course of the Battle of the Bulge" makes the event intelligible—if we understand what the Battle of the Bulge was. This is not what is ordinarily meant by linguistic meaning.

The next step in the construction of the historical narrative is what White calls "argument," by which he means the strategy used to produce "explanatory affect": "explanation by formal argument, explanation by employment, and explanation by ideological implication."[66] Within these are four "modes of articulation," namely, Formism, Organicism, Mechanism, and Contextualism.[67] By "formal argument," White appears to mean covering law arguments and deductive arguments, and he denies the applicability of these to history because the required covering laws do not exist.[68] Explanation by ideological implication hinges on the meaning of "ideological." White says, "By the term 'ideology' I mean a set of prescriptions for taking a position in the present world of social praxis and acting upon it (either to change the world or to maintain it in its current state)."[69] White believes that all language is value laden, and that every historical narrative will present a picture of the past that has implications for the present. Thus he writes:

> In the world in which we daily live, anyone who studies the past as an end in itself must appear to be either an antiquarian, fleeing from the problems of the present into a purely personal past, or a kind of cultural necrophile, that is, one who finds in the dead and dying a value he can never find in the living. The contemporary historian has to establish the value of the study of the past, not as an end in itself, but as a way of providing perspectives on the present that contribute to the solution of problems peculiar to our own time.[70]

This is a startling statement for a professional historian, and not one that would be endorsed by most historians. It shows a degree of presentism in White's thought that gives his historical theory a clearly ideological cast. What justifies the study of history for White is the ideology that it supports. "I consider the ethical moment of a historical work to be reflected in the mode of ideological implication by which an *aesthetic* perception (the emplotment) and a *cognitive* operation (the argument) can be combined so as to derive prescriptive statements from what may appear to be purely descriptive or analytical ones."[71] Thus White apparently believes that all historical works provide historical justifications for an ideological position.

It is explanation by emplotment that White considers most critical to historical narratives. But "explanation" here does not mean causal explanation—it means understanding. This is provided "by endowing what originally appears to be problematical and mysterious with the aspect of a recognizable, because it is familiar, form."[72] For example, when the reader of the historical narrative recognizes the type of story he is reading (romance, tragedy, comedy, or satire), "he experiences the effect of having the events in the story explained to him,"[73] for White holds that "understanding is a process of rendering the unfamiliar . . . familiar."[74] This is of course a very special view of explanation, but it is the one White regards as relevant to narrative history.

Within explanation by emplotment, White lists four "modes of articulation"—Formism, Organicism, Mechanism, and Contextualism. These he describes as follows: Formism consists in identifying the elements of the field. "The Formist considers an explanation to be complete when a given set of objects has been properly identified, its class, generic, and specific attributes assigned and labels attesting to its particularity attached to it."[75] Organicism consists in showing that each object of study is part of an organic whole.[76] Mechanism is also an integrative view, but one that emphasizes causal relations falling under causal laws. The ideal here is the sort of explanation found in physics, and White cites Marxism as his example of such a position.[77] Finally, "The Contextualist insists that 'what happened' in the field can be accounted for by the specification of the functional interrelationships existing among the agents and agencies occupying the field at a given time."[78] But the term *functional* should not be read literally here. Contextualism for White is a "relative integration" that identifies trends or "threads" connecting the object of study to its origins, effects, and context generally; these are not functional relations in the strict sense.[79]

The last step in the constitution of the narrative is the choice of ideology. The issue of ideology points to the fact that White believes "there is no value-neutral mode of emplotment, explanation, or even description of any field of events, whether imaginary or real, and suggests that the very use of language itself implies or entails a specific posture before the world which is ethical, ideological, or more generally political: not only all interpretation, but also all language is politically contaminated."[80] White classifies the types of ideology as Anarchist, Conservative, Radical, and Liberal.[81]

In presenting White's theory, I have distinguished "steps." These are not always to be taken temporally, but analytically. How, then, are they related? White denies linguistic determinism, but he emphasizes that there is a certain "elective affinity"[82] among these components that he represents by the following:

Mode of Emplotment	Mode of Argument	Mode of Ideological Implication
Romantic	Formist	Anarchist
Tragic	Mechanist	Radical
Comic	Organicist	Conservative
Satirical	Contextualist	Liberal[83]

The particular combination of a given mode of emplotment, a mode of argument, and a mode of ideological implication constitutes a historian's *style.* These quadruples are related to the four types of tropes: Metaphor to Romanticism, Formism and Anarchism, Metonymy to Tragedy, Mechanism, and Radicalism, Synecdoche to Comedy, Organicismand Conservatism, and Irony to Satire and Contextualism and Liberalism. "In linguistic usage itself, thought is provided with possible alternative paradigms of explanation. Metaphor is representational in the way that Formism can be seen to be. Metonymy is reductive in a Mechanist manner, while Synecdoche is integrative in the way that Organicism is." Irony is rather obviously related to satire.[84]

White views the historical narrative as a linguistic artifact that is substituted for the actual referent. As he puts it, the discourse "substitutes another sign system for the putatively extralinguistic referent about which it pretends to speak"[85]; or, again, he emphasizes the "semiological apparatuses that produce meaning by the systematic substitution of signifieds (conceptual contents) for the extra-discursive entities that serve as their referents."[86] The actual historical events that the reader believes he is reading about are not capable of being experienced since they are gone; what the reader actually finds in the historical narrative is the historian's "interpretation" of those events.

I have tried to give here a fair presentation of the theory Hayden White has expounded in his books and articles. That the theory has considerable interest should be obvious. White has correctly seen that the objects and events of the past are unobservable, that the data of history consist of presently existing things, and that historical theories are constructions based on these presently existing data. So far we are in agreement. But from there on we part company. There are serious problems with the theory White develops. There is, first of all, the problem of truth. Can a historical narrative be true, and what does White mean by "truth"? He draws a distinction between the historical narrative as a whole and the singular existential statements contained in the narrative. According to White,

> This is not to say that a historical discourse is not properly assessed in terms of the truth value of its factual (singular existential) statements taken individually and the logical conjunction of the whole set of such statements taken distributively. For unless historical discourse acceded to assessment in these terms, it would lose all justification for its claim to represent and provide explanations of specifically real events. But such assent touches only that aspect of the historical discourse conventionally called its chronicle. It does not provide us with any way of assessing the content of the narrative itself.[87]

In what does the truth of singular existential statements consist? "Both the facts in their particularity and the narrative account in its generality must meet a correspondence, as well as a coherence, criterion of truth value."[88] Again, "Not only must the singular existential statements that make up the 'chronicle' of the historical account 'correspond' to the events of which they are predications, but the narrative as a whole must 'correspond' to the general configuration of the sequence of events of which it is an account. Which is to say that the sequence of 'facts' as they are emploted in order to make a 'story' out of what would otherwise be only a 'chronicle' must correspond to the general configuration of the 'events' of which the 'facts' are propositional indicators."[89] The "coherence" cited here is logical consistency. But what does White mean by "correspondence"? One might at first think he means correspondence to the real historical events, and he does say that events happen, whereas facts are events described. Recalling his description of how the historical field is constituted from historical traces, however, it is clear that "events" too are the products of interpretation. The statements of the chronicle—the singular existential statements—do not refer to the events of the real past but to the conceptualized versions of them in the field. Recalling that all interpretation is said to be governed by the basic tropes, it is not surprising that the statements of the chronicle correspond to events so constituted. These statements find in the events what the categories have put there. But this sort of correspondence is not that of the standard correspondence theory of truth.

White also says that narratives as wholes correspond to reality. But what he means by "correspondence" here is not at all what is usually meant in the correspondence theory of truth. Thus having identified historical narratives as stories, he writes, "Stories are told or written, not found. And as for the notion of a true story, this is virtually a contradiction in terms. All stories are fictions. Which means, of course, that they can be true only in a metaphorical sense and in the sense in which a figure of speech can be true."[90] Further, "the 'truth' of narrative form can display itself only indirectly, that is to say, by means of *allegoresis*."[91] Allegories do bear a "correspondence" of a sort to that of which they are allegories, but that relation has little to do with truth. Furthermore, according to White, the choice of plot for a historical narrative is arbitrary. The kind of "truth" that a historical narrative can have for White is the same kind of truth that a fictional narrative can have. "There has been a reluctance to consider historical narratives as what they most manifestly are: verbal fictions, the contents of which are as much *invented* as *found*, and the forms of which have more in common with their counterparts in literature than they have with those in the sciences."[92] And this of course means that narrative historical accounts cannot be disconfirmed.[93] Indeed, it is obvious that White's narratives cannot be true in any ordinary sense, since his plots are imposed on the "facts" by an arbitrary choice. White does occasionally speak of a "literal" use of language, so he does not regard all linguistic statements as figurative, but he does so regard narratives and apparently any text structured by figures of speech.

There are, however, cases in which White thinks historical facts can constrain the choice of plot. The crucial case here is the Holocaust. Some have argued that the Holocaust cannot be represented in language at all. White disagrees, but he admits that no comic or pastoral plot can be appropriate for such an event. Instead, he holds that what he calls the "modernist" style can do so. He quotes with approval Auerbach's characterization of "modernism."

1. The disappearance of the "writer or narrator of objective facts; almost everything stated appears by way of reflection in the consciousness of the *dramatis personae*";

2. The dissolution of any "viewpoint . . . outside the novel from which the people and events within it are observed . . .";

3. The predominance of a "tone of doubt and questioning" in the narrator's interpretation of those events seemingly described in an "objective" manner;

4. The employment of such devices as "*erlebte Rede,*" stream of consciousness, *monologue interieur* for "aesthetic purposes" that obscure and obliterate the impression of an objective reality completely known to the author . . . ;

5. The use of new techniques for the representation of the experience of time and temporality, e.g., the use of "chance occasion" to release "processes of consciousness" which remain unconnected to a "specific subject of thought," obliteration of the distinction between "exterior" and "interior" time, and representation of "events not as "successive episodes in [a] story" but as random occurrences.[94]

This, White tells us, "is as good a characterization as any we might find of what Barthes and Derrida might have called the style of "middle voicedness."

Attic Greek employed, in addition to the active and passive voices, a middle voice that expressed an action of a subject (1) on himself as direct object, for example, "I stop myself," "I persuade myself," and so on; (2) for or to with reference to himself, for example, "I take to myself a wife," "I plan for myself," and so on; (3) from himself, or from his own power or means, for example, "promise something to myself," "show forth my opinion," and so on. The point here is that if the Holocaust is to be described, it must be in a narrative in which the narrator is invisible and events are portrayed as experienced by the characters caught in the Holocaust. This provides a way of letting the past speak for itself as the characters describe their own experiences, with all of the apparent randomness and irrationality that characterized their fates. But one should also note what White does not say; he does not say that such a "modernist" story is true. Furthermore, as F. R. Ankersmit has noted, his position here is not consistent with his earlier position in *Metahistory*.[95]

The status of his tropological categories is also a problem that White does not meet satisfactorily. If these are innate categories of the human unconscious, as White appears to believe,[96] then it should be possible to demonstrate this by a psychological experiment. Arguing that these four types of figuration can be found in Piaget, Freud, Durkhein, and others is interesting if true, but it hardly establishes their "archetypal" status, and this is critical for White, because his plot forms, explanation forms, and ideological forms are all constructed to match his four basic types of tropes. The Kantian flavor of this construction is obvious, and White admits Kant's influence,[97] but if his four tropes are intended to generate a phenomenal field of experience in the way Kant's are, then an extended argument to this effect is needed.

White's presentism also poses a problem. Most historians that I know study the past because they are interested in finding out about the past, not because they imagine they can use their research to further an ideological agenda. There are, of course, some historians whose interest in history is primarily to support their ideological stance, but they are certainly a small minority. For most of us, the past is an exciting field for discovery itself, and our ideological views, such as they are, have little if anything to do with our research. I was a student of Perry Miller, who devoted most of his working life to the elucidation of the intellectual system of the New England Puritans, but Miller was an atheist and never pretended to be anything else. Those who study history for the purpose of advancing an ideological agenda are not likely to contribute much to our understanding of the field.

Writing history in order to produce certain ideological implications is sure to produce biased results. It is well accepted among historians that historical phenomena must be explained in terms of the historical culture in which they occurred. As noted earlier, attempts to impose ideas of our time upon actions in the past are very likely to distort "what really happened" in the past. The position White advocates comes very close to turning history into propaganda, and that is something that is roundly condemned by historians, and justly so.

White's view of what constitutes explanation in history is also inadequate. When a historian asks why something happened, he is not helped by being told it was part of a tragedy (or comedy, etc.) To "explain" has indeed multiple meanings in ordinary use. It can mean giving an account intended to clarify something, for example, the rules of chess, but when applied to events, it usually requests an account of why some event occurred. To say that John Kennedy's murder was a tragedy does neither of these and tells us nothing that either clarifies the event or accounts for its occurrence.

Yet White clearly has something in mind by his use of explanation that relates to narrative. I discussed earlier the use of functional explanation in fictional narratives, but this does not appear to be what White intends. Being told that *Moby Dick* is a tragedy or a comedy or a romance does not help us understand the specific incidents of the narrative. White's categories are too crude to provide such an understanding, and they cannot provide a functional explanation of the entire narrative unless it is related to some further objective to the realization of which it contributes. The only such objective that White has to offer is ideological implication, but it will require a more detailed argument than he has given to show that, for example, tragedy promotes Radicalism. Does *Macbeth* or *Hamlet* or *King Lear* promote a radical ideology? If so, I would be much obliged to have an explanation of how. And being told into what category the novel falls would not go very far in explaining why Melville constituted *Moby Dick* as he did.

Nor can it be held that the meaning of a narrative consists in the category type into which its plot falls. There is something to be said for White's point that understanding reduces the unfamiliar to the familiar, but the meaning or understanding of a narrative is not given by calling it a tragedy or a comedy, otherwise all tragedies would have the same meaning, which obviously they do not. And although part of understanding a narrative may be in recognizing its plot type, this can at most be only one element in the comprehension of the text.

What most disturbs me about White's theory is his view of historiography. To claim that historians first establish the facts and then arbitrarily choose a plot type for their description and explanation, selecting the facts that accord with their plot and rejecting those that do not, is to endorse the classical historiography that I have argued throughout is misguided. This is just the sort of procedure that led historians such as Beard and Becker to despair of the possibility of a historical work being true, and it misrepresents what historians do. Facts are parts of theories. Working historians are constantly trying out hypotheses as they perform their research. The search for data themselves is not blind but is guided by hypotheses about the subject of study. To suppose that a historian, having done his research, then ponders the question of whether to present his finding as a tragedy or a comedy, a satire or a romance, is to present a ludicrous portrait of what historians actually do. But White, like other so-called "postmodern" writers on history, insists on creating a gulf between historical research and historical writing and theorizing. There is no such gulf. The conceptualizations that the historian develops in the course of his research are those that structure his account, whether in narrative, exposition, analysis, or whatever the form. Fact and theory develop together from the analysis of the data. White's account of history is that of a novelist, not a historian.

White is quite right in saying that historical persons and events are gone forever and cannot be observed. He is also right that historical accounts are based on present data (traces) that are often fragmentary and incomplete. From these observations, he has correctly concluded that historical facts must be created by the historian through imaginative syntheses of what the data provide. Quite so. But what White has failed to recognize is that the imaginative constructions that historians create are theories in which the persons and events of the past occur as theoretical constructs. Instead, he has concluded that historical accounts substitute linguistic entities for the unobservable facts of the past. Hence, the reader who thinks that he is reading a history of the American Civil War is really reading a narrative about the linguistic entities created by the historian. But this view makes a mockery of history. An account of the fall of Vicksburg is not *about* a linguistic entity, it is *about* the fall of Vicksburg. If historical narratives were about linguistic entities, then they would have to be written in the metalanguage, which they clearly are not. Historical accounts are written in the object language, and they refer to the persons and events of the past—and these are not linguistic entities.

White is also right about the fragmentary nature of historical evidence. What he misunderstands is that what historians in fact do is create theories about the past in which events such as the fall of Vicksburg have the status of theoretical constructs, and that the whole theory of the past, and of all that has transpired, is well or ill confirmed by the evidence that remains. Theoretical entities are not linguistic entities.

Quarks are unobservable, but they are real entities, not linguistic entities; the same is true for Grant and Sherman. They may be referred to by linguistic means, but they are not themselves linguistic. Those who died fighting at Vicksburg did not die of linguistic bullets. The past as a whole is a theoretical construct to account for present data. The terms of historical accounts refer to the constructs in the theory, and the theory of the past and its contents is true only if it accounts for all of the presently existing relevant data.

Chapter 6

Confirmation 1

If historical accounts are theories, then the question of how these theories are tested and confirmed or disconfirmed must be answered. I deal first with the question of truth relativism. Then I discuss a number of examples of how hypotheses about past events and persons can be tested, and the problems involved in doing so.

❖

Historians are creatures of time who research and write their works at specific times. Let the subject one is studying be something E that occurred at time t_0. Then the consequences of the event E that are available to the historian working at t_x are those that lie in the interval t_x—t_0, whereas those available to a later historian writing at t_y will be those that lie in the interval t_y—t_0. It does not follow that the data available to the later historian will include all those available to the earlier one. The pool of eyewitness accounts of E may diminish between t_x and t_y, as, for example, the number of eyewitness accounts of the Nazi concentration camps is diminishing as the survivors age and die off. New data may also be discovered during the interval t_y—t_x; think, for example, of the Dead Sea Scrolls. All one can say here is that the data available to the two historians will probably differ. This is one reason no history is ever final, and why new histories of subjects that have been treated before are necessary. But it does not follow that theories formulated at t_x will be disconfirmed at t_y. The new data available at t_y may simply confirm what was propounded at t_x. And if it does, then that is stronger evidence for the original theory.

Worldviews also change over time, as do the cultures of which they are components. The worldview of Aristotle was very different than ours today. Science progresses; as we have seen, Kuhnian claims to the contrary are false. But science is only one part of the worldview. Other beliefs change as well. Our moral beliefs today are not Aristotle's; we condemn human slavery, but he did not. And technology has changed so radically, and so changed our environment, that much that Aristotle took for granted no longer holds. So too our view of what is possible has changed. The literature of the past contains many accounts of miracles, direct interventions in human affairs by a deity, magic, astrological influences, and so on that we now regard as not possible. How, then, can we understand this world?

The issue here is cultural relativism.[1] It is well known that beliefs, values, goals, and material cultures vary from one society to another. It is less often appreciated that cultures change over time, and where that change is sufficiently great, historians find themselves dealing with a different culture. The problem is whether or not members of one culture can understand members of another. In contemporary cultures, the answer is yes. All human languages are learnable by any human. Children are not born knowing a language; they have to learn it. And what children can do adults can do, though usually with more difficulty. As the existence of multilingual people shows, any language is learnable by speakers of any other. In the same way, one can learn another culture regardless of the one in which one was brought up. Again, the analogy to children holds. Children have to learn a culture; it is not innate. Then so can adults, given adequate opportunity and sufficient time. And time is important here, because there is so much to learn. One cannot hope to learn another culture in a year or even several; the immersion in the other culture must be for an extended period.

But can the outsider ever really learn an alien culture? Two different questions arise here: What must one learn? How must one learn it? The first is a question of what a culture is. The monolithic concept of culture that was popular in anthropology some time ago holds that all members of the society know "the culture." But it is also generally agreed upon that any culture involves more knowledge than any one person could learn in a lifetime. In response to this problem, many anthropologists have come to see culture as consisting not only of the overt behavior exhibited by members of a society but also of the ideational states and processes of its members. As Naomi Quinn and Claudia Strauss put it,

> How could something be ideational, but not in someone's head? Based on what people say they think, but not about what they think? It is time for us to confront the contradiction in the definition of culture as meaningful, symbolic, significant, conceptual, ideational, but not to anyone in particular, that has encumbered the analysis, and required circumlocutions in

the analytic language of so many anthropologists. It is time to say that culture is *both* public and individual, both in the world and in people's heads.[2]

Culture is a distributive phenomena. No one member of the society knows the entire corpus of cultural knowledge; different members know different segments of it. Some ideational elements are universally shared within the society, but others are not. Specialists exist in both thought and behavior in every society. Hunters know things that farmers do not, and vice versa. In our own society, doctors, lawyers, engineers, and painters all have not only some knowledge in common but special bodies of knowledge specific to their professions. An outsider does not need to learn all that everyone in the society knows but enough to be able to understand and operate in the society with sufficient understanding so that he can think and act in ways acceptable to the members.

The second question is whether or not an outsider can learn how at least some of the members of the society think and act. Over a century of ethnographic study has shown that the material technology and the overt behavior of the members of other societies can be accurately described; the problem has been to discover how members of other societies conceive their worlds and give them meaning. Writing in 1952, Robert Redfield described the "worldview" of a society as "the way the world looks to that people, looking out."[3] As Hallowell developed this concept, it includes how the members of a society conceive of time and space, of objects, of themselves, of their goals, and of their values and morality.[4] That goal of anthropological knowledge has been pursued vigorously ever since. Pike's introduction in 1952 of the emic-etic distinction helped clarify the debate; the etic perspective is said to be that of the outsider looking in, the emic of the insider looking out.[5] The debate over componential analysis that involved Ward Goodenough, Floyd Lounsbury, Anthony Wallace, Roy D'Andrade, and Kim Romney, among others, centered on this issue. In Wallace's phrase, given that different componential analyses of a set of terms are possible, which componential analysis is "psychologically real"? Romney and D'Andrade were able to show how the psychological reality of such a system could be tested.[6] Over the next several decades, "Cognitive Anthropology" emerged, drawing heavily on the cognitive revolution in psychology and becoming a recognized field within anthropology, and its scope broadened from taxonomies to the analysis of models, schemata, and cultural theories (i.e., explicit theories held by culture members about phenomena such as death, gods, morality, etc.). Anyone who has read Roger Schank's and Robert Abelson's famous restaurant script must be impressed with the range of cultural factors involved in the simple act of ordering a meal in a restaurant,[7] and anthropologists have long focused on cultural theories such as native religions. As D'Andrade's history of this movement shows,[8] its practitioners are now able to determine and describe much of the culture within the minds of individual members of a society. While controversy still exists over the issue of the extent to which outsiders can learn the inner workings of an alien culture, there is little doubt that much of it can be learned. As Ward Goodenough put it, what is required "is a model of what one needs to know to function acceptably as a member of that community."[9]

But what we are describing here is learning another culture where its living members are ready and willing to help the learner. The learning of past cultures is more difficult because interaction with members of past cultures is impossible. Ostensive definitions that aid scholars in learning from their contemporaries usually are not available in dealing with the past. Is it possible, then, for a historian to learn a past culture? The answer is a resounding maybe! The critical question is how much data are available and what sort of data they are. Perry Miller was shrewd when he began the study of New England because the body of data available was extensive and revealed most aspects of the culture, particularly its worldview. Historians of Colonial Virginia have had to make do with less data that are less comprehensive. There is a phrase that historians use to describe how one should approach a past society; it is "immersion in the period." The good historian lives with the data from one culture for an extended period of time. Miller devoted most of his working life to the study of Puritan New England; he read everything he could find and worked and reworked his material. The result was a description of the seventeenth-century Puritan worldview that set a standard yet to be equaled in the sixty-nine years since he published. Not only did Miller succeed in describing what the Puritans believed, he was also able to describe how they felt—what emotions drove them and gave life to their system of belief. There is no comparable work on Colonial Virginia, but this does not mean that we do not know a great deal about Colonial Virginia culture. From the study of the data we do have—laws, journals of the House of Burgesses, diaries, letters, and so on, scholars have been able to construct a model of that culture. Unlike most of the other colonies, Colonial Virginia had no urban center. There was no Boston or New York or Philadelphia or Baltimore or Charleston in Virginia. This was possible because the tidewater region had four major rivers—the James, the York, the Rappahannock, and the Potomac—that were navigable for the ocean-going ships of that day. Planters needed no major port city to handle imports and exports; trading ships could sail up to the planters' wharves. The closest thing Virginia had to an urban place was its capital, Williamsburg, but it was only when Burgesses was in session that the population of Williamsburg rose to that of a town, and Burgesses was not in session for very long. Although the colony had a royal governor (after 1624), the real power lay at the county level. The wealthy planters usually served on the Council that was the high court, and that, together with the House of Burgesses, formed the colony's legislative branch. Virginia was also a society that by the end of the seventeenth century had become firmly wedded to Negro slavery. As one would expect, the racial division between blacks and whites was very sharp, and racial mixing was condemned, though the application of this condemnation varied by sex. White woman were carefully protected from black men, and any crossing of this racial line was severely punished. But the chastity of white women also was protected by white men making sexual use of black women, despite the moral condemnation by the churches. Power in Virginia lay in the hands of the wealthy planters, who controlled their counties and modeled themselves on English country gentlemen. The large planters served as the justices of the county court, the vestrymen of the churches, and the members of Burgesses. Virginia was a highly stratified society, and the great planters were the elite that ruled it.

What was just described is a theory about Colonial Virginia society and culture. Is it true? To test it further, data must be used. Consider, for example, the visiting patterns of the planters. It is well known that there was extensive visiting among them, and that large sums were spent on entertaining guests. It is also part of the Southern tradition that Southern women were accomplished hostesses. Why should this have been so? Because Virginia had no urban center and planters lived scattered across the countryside, the only way they could coordinate action for economic and political purposes was by visiting, and such visits, requiring fairly extensive travel, meant that usually the visitors stayed overnight. But if the planters were to rule Virginia, and by and large they did, then such a visiting pattern was essential. The money spent on entertaining was not a sign of Southern extravagance but a necessary cost of maintaining control.

One of the difficulties facing historians is that they often find in the data evidence of events that were explicable to people in the past culture but are not explicable in the terms of ours. An obvious example of this is the witchcraft trials at Salem Village. For seventeenth-century Puritans, the existence and actions of witches were fully accepted. No one doubted that there really were witches, and that they could and did attack people. But historians writing today do not believe in witches.

How, then, should historians treat these past people and events? First, they must explain for readers what people of the past believed and how they accounted for such events. But second, historians still have to produce a causal explanation of what occurred. As noted earlier, in this case most historians have turned to psychodynamic theory to accomplish this, though Rosenthal's arguments present an alternative that has to be taken seriously. These cases can be extremely difficult; did God really part the waters of the Red Sea so that the fleeing Israelites could escape? Not only is there the problem of getting an accurate description of what actually occurred but finding a way to redescribe it in terms that we accept as possible is enough to tax the imagination of any scholar.

But there is a deeper issue raised by cultural relativism. It is held by some, especially the so-called postmodernists, that standards of truth are relative to cultures, so that to say " 'p' is true" means 'p' is true for us but not necessarily for members of other cultures, for whom it may well be false. It is sometimes held that this relativist position is incoherent, since it asserts its claim as something true of all cultures. But it is not incoherent. Rather, the relativity of truth to culture is put forward as a finding of our social science and therefore true in our science (i.e., our culture). It is asserted as true *of* other cultures according to our standards of truth, but that does not imply that it is asserted *by* other cultures. A statement about other cultures can be true for us, even if no other culture accepts it. But note that the doctrine of cultural relativism, so understood, is a scientific finding of our social science, and thus its truth must conform to our standards of truth. Hence the claim of relativity, if true, is true by our standards of truth and cannot be used to undermine them without destroying its own claim to truth.

There are problems with the claim that truth standards are relative to culture. First, there is no basis for holding that different cultures *must* hold different truth standards. It is sufficient to hold that some do. But second, one of the remarkable intellectual phenomena of our time is the rapid spread of science across cultural boundaries. Today, the Japanese, Chinese, Indians, Iranians, Koreans, North and South, all accept the same science we do. In recent history, the only case I know of where a culture adopted a different scientific theory from others was the Lysenko affair in the Soviet Union, because Lysenko's theories were held to be more compatible with Marxist-Leninism than Mendelian genetics,[10] but the adherence to Lysenko's theories ended even before the fall of the Soviet Union. Whatever standards of truth these other culture may hold in other domains, in science they appear to hold the same standards we do.

But one does not have to look to other cultures to find relativity of truth standards. In the United States, some people believe religious propositions are not only true but certain. Thus the coexistence of different standards is quite possible within a culture, or even within a particular person. This form of mild schizophrenia poses no real problems as long as the realms with different truth standards are disjoint, but trouble arises when they intersect. The current debates between scientists and creationists, and now between scientists and advocates of intelligent design, are examples of what happens when the two realms intersect. Rational argument in such cases is very difficult, because it is hard to find a basis for argument that both sides can accept. Scientists can point to the empirical evidence that supports their theories, but this is without effect upon those who hold the truth of Scripture as a matter of faith, since faith is independent of any empirical facts. It is astonishing, at least to me, how impervious religious doctrines are to empirical evidence. After a major calamity such as an airplane crash that kills 195 out of the 200 passengers aboard, the survival of the five is often cited as proof of the goodness of God. But what about the other 195 passengers? If this proves the goodness of God, then God must have a peculiar notion of goodness. Despite the fact that scholars agree that there is not a single sentence in the New Testament that we can be sure was spoken by Jesus, some continue to believe that the Bible is literally true.

The issue that has dominated the conflict between science and religion since 1859 is of course the theory of evolution. It is not a surprise that this issue is the focal point. If Darwinian evolution is true, then we are purely natural creatures with an animal ancestry. There is within this theory no reason to assume the existence of a soul, and without that assumption, there is no immortality and no postmortem reward or punishment. To abandon such beliefs means for many people abandoning religion. Yet the empirical evidence supporting Darwinian evolution is massive and constantly growing. The Christian religion has no scientific evidence to support it. To believe it is to accept it on faith, which requires no empirical evidence. The truth standards could hardly be more different. But rationality is on the side of evolution. Whether rationality will prevail has now become a political question, the answer to which is yet to be found.

Truth relativism applied to history holds, first, that the truth standards of past cultures stand on a par with ours, and, second, that even within our culture, different truth standards for historical truth are equally legitimate. The first point implies that there has been no progress in science. In support of this claim, Kuhn is the authority usually cited, but as we saw earlier, his argument against scientific progress is circular, since he assumes that statement as a premise. But that there has been progress in science, and also technology, is so obvious that it is hard to credit any denial of it. Our physics is better than Aristotle's, our medicine is better than Galen's, and our chemistry is better than Priestley's. Better how? Better in that it gives us greater control over nature and permits more extensive and accurate predictions. These are of course our criteria, but they are more than that; they are the criteria of science generally.

Second, are there different truth standards for history, either between cultures or within cultures? Certainly there have been in the past. The use of typology as a method of historical analysis is one such case in our own history.[11] The dispute in our culture involves several different issues. The Bible is a historical document. Fundamentalists who hold that it is literally true do so on the basis of faith. For them, the Higher Criticism that has analyzed the Bible as a historical document cannot be true, while for the rest of us the Bible is simply a fascinating evidence of early Jewish and Christian ways. Here again we have the conflict of empirical knowledge with faith. But this is not the only dispute over historical truth; there also is the conflict between those who hold that historical theories can be true, as I do, and those who deny that. This should be clear from the discussion of the theory of Hayden White. But these are issues that have been dealt with in chapter 5 and need not be rehearsed here.

Cultural relativity is a fact, but not one that poses insuperable problems. But the issue is often raised that each historian writes from a particular perspective that will color his work and make objectivity impossible. What particularly raises these problems is the issue of values. Can a historian coming to his subject with his own set of values be objective in his treatment? Several questions are mixed together here, and it will pay to separate them.[12] First, then, what of values? "Value" I take to be a relative term. To say that "x is valued" is to say that some person, z, values x. So seen, values enter historical accounts in at least two different ways. When describing historical actors and their actions, it is essential to describe *their* values, since these form part of the motivation for their actions. Whether or not one can do this is a question of what data one has. Clearly it is always preferable to have a statement by the actors themselves of what their values are, but lacking that it is often possible to infer their values from other data. It does not really matter here what the historian's values are, since the question is about the past subjects of his account, and to make their actions intelligible requires focusing on *their* actions, not the historians. Descriptive statements about what people believe or believed to be valuable are empirical statements like any other factual statements. But one may also find in the historian's writing seemingly absolute statements such as "Hitler was evil."

Secondly,[13] it is frequently said that all history is perspectival, and that it therefore lacks objectivity. Of course history is written from the point of view of the historian; who else's perspective could it have been written from? The term *objectivity* is more difficult. It seems to mean "disinterested," although not all writers use the term in this sense. It is apparently not required that the historian *be* disinterested but that he should treat his subject as if he were. It is entirely reasonable to hold that all historical accounts are perspectival, and even that few are objective; does that matter? It matters only if the methods by which the history is constructed are those of the classical historiography, and these are taken as determining its truth. The problem is that the classical historiography deals only with how the theory is created, not how it is tested after it is created. If historians select their facts from some antecedently created set of facts, then perspective and values may well influence the choice. But if the theory is subject to test after it is formulated, it really does not matter how it was formulated.

A comparison to science is useful here. I doubt that any scientist is ever disinterested in the outcome of his research. All scientists operate from a particular view that can, I suppose, be called "perspectival." But nobody cares, because the issue in science is not how the theory was born but whether or not it is true. And truth does not depend on where the theory comes from. Kekule's theory of the benzene ring was suggested to him by a dream of two snakes, each of which took hold of the other's tail. But all that matters in science is whether the theory, once formulated, is confirmed by tests of its predictive accuracy, by its ability to account for new data, and by its consistency with other theories.

Whether or not history is a science is not a question I consider worth arguing about. But whether they are scientists or not, the same question should be asked of historical theories as of scientific ones. Is the theory true? This is the question of the relation of theory to the data—a question that has to be examined *after* the theory is formulated, not before. Of course, issues of objectivity can still arise. Were the tests of the theory honestly carried out? Did someone fudge the data to make it appear that the theory was true when it was not? However important, these are not the sorts of considerations people have had in mind when they have said that history cannot be true because it is perspectival or not objective. If the theory is true, then nobody cares whose perspective it is formulated from, or whose subjective whim suggested it. In other words, the truth of a theory does not depend on how it was formulated, though some methods are better than others; it depends on how well the theory survives when it is tested.

But can historical theories be tested? Many issues exist here. Since there are so many different types of theories used by historians, there are many types of tests relevant to them. I will restrict this discussion here to two types: theories about a given past population, and theories about a small number of members of past societies. To answer the first question, let us take the population of interest to be all members of the U.S. Senate and House of Representatives in the 1850s, and suppose the theory says that the issue of foreign immigration was more important for how those people voted than the issue of slavery. "Important" here means important to the people who were senators and representatives. This is a very special case, because in the first place we have a record of how these men voted on the various bills that came before them, and second it is very likely that men who were elected to either the Senate or the House were prominent enough so that there is still extant considerable data about some of them and some data about all of them. That is, we have data for every member of that past population, and data of a sort that ought to reveal members' views on the question at issue. The choice here will be whether to try to use the entire population or whether to sample, since in this case probability sampling is possible. Either approach could be used, although the first will involve a lot more work and time than the second. Either way, we should be able to test the theory.

Now suppose we have a theory that claims that the percentage of Irish immigrants in Iowa declined from 1860 to 1870 because large numbers of the Irish left the state, moving west. That the percentage decline did take place is easily verified from the U.S. Census; the decline affected almost all of the counties in Iowa. But was the decline due to the Irish leaving the state, or was it due to an influx of non-Irish immigrants, such as Germans? We can find the answer to that. The U.S. Manuscript Censuses of 1860 and 1870 both give nativity. While probably neither Census is a complete enumeration of the Iowa population, it is close enough for our purposes. Then the question becomes one of tracing Irish immigrants from the one census to another. There are well-known problems in this sort of record linkage, but I will leave these aside. If names of the Irish appear in the 1860 census but not in the 1870 census, then either the persons in question died or moved, or, if female, they married. Sometimes we can tell which from the census itself (if Jones was sixty-five in 1860 and absent in 1870, although his wife is listed as living with her son, we can be reasonably sure Jones is dead). But the time required for this sort of person-by-person analysis would be very great, and the results would be inconclusive. If, however, we organize our Irish in the 1860 census by age cohorts, then we can estimate the number of deaths that should have occurred by 1870 from the cohort mortality rates calculated from information in the census. We can also estimate what the growth of that population should have been from the cohort nativity rates drawn from the Census, and similarly we can estimate the number of women married to non-Irish husbands. If we find that the number of Irish in 1870 is approximately what we would have expected as a result of births, deaths, and marriages among the Irish, and that it constitutes a much smaller percentage of the state population in 1870 than in 1860, then we can be quite certain that the percentage decline was due to non-Irish immigration. But if the number of Irish in Iowa in 1870 is much less than we should expect from the birth and death data, then we can be quite sure that a lot of them moved out of the state. But did they move west? To determine that would require tracing all of those names for every state west of Iowa. That is not something a single investigator could do. But if there was a large outmigration of the Irish in the 1860–1870 decade, then one would expect to find contemporary observations of that fact. Hence accounts in newspapers or other documents could be very useful here. In other words, the main question—the percentage decline question—can be answered from U.S. Census data. The question of where they went if they moved can only be answered from other documentary data, if at all. Should the day ever come when the entire U.S. Manuscript Census is made machine readable, that will be a different story.

A third type of question is yet more difficult. Suppose we have a theory that the population of prostitutes in Chicago rose from 1890 to 1900. Could we test that theory? The U.S. Census will not help here. The 1890 U.S. Census was destroyed by fire, and prostitutes, if included in the Census at all, rarely identified themselves as such. Nor will arrest records do the job; the number of arrests for prostitution varies from year to year, and often month to month, depending on how vigorous the enforcement is, and that in turn usually is the result of political pressure or public outcry. But there is a way to do this. Take all the ladies of the night arrested in each year in Chicago from 1890 to 1900. Arrest records give the age of persons arrested. We can therefore determine their average age of these charmers by year for each year of the decade. This is not of course a random sample of the population of prostitutes, but there is no reason to think it is biased in terms of age. Women who become professional prostitutes usually do so at a fairly young age, and once in their chosen profession usually stay in it as long as they can get an adequate number of customers. If, therefore, we find that from 1890 to 1900 the average age of the prostitutes arrested declined, then we have evidence that this population is growing—that is, more young women are entering the profession. If it rises, then fewer new girls are entering the trade; that indicates that the population is falling. And if it stays roughly constant, the population of ladies of delight is constant over the decade. Note, however, that this approach rests on certain hypotheses about the age at which girls enter their profession and how long they stay in it. These hypotheses must be independently verified. So too the population of pleasure damsels must be limited to full-time prostitutes rather than including the occasional prostitutes for whom the hypotheses probably would not hold.[14]

A final example of this type is a theory that holds that Wilson was reelected in 1916 because the voters he had in 1912 stayed with him, and he was able to pick up enough voters who had gone to Roosevelt in 1912 to obtain a majority. Here, as it happens, the necessary data are ready and waiting at the InterUniversity Consortium for Social and Political Research. The Consortium has on tape all of the county election returns for every presidential, congressional, and gubernatorial election in the United States from 1824 to the present. This enormous archive of machine-readable data is available, free of charge, to all scholars and students at all of the universities that belong to the Consortium. It is one of the great resources available to American historians. Using the county election returns and matching them to census information about those counties, one can determine quite accurately that this theory is false; Wilson's support in 1916 came from very different people than his backers in 1912.

These are of course merely examples of how some problems concerning past populations can be attacked. In a book I wrote over thirty years ago,[15] I discussed a variety of quantitative approaches to such problems that could be or have been used by historians. I am sorry to say that this is the chapter of the book that most historians skip. I will not try to repeat the description of those methods here; readers so inclined can find them in the last chapter of that book. Higher math is not required, so readers should not give up the moment they see an equation.

The second type of problem mentioned earlier is testing a theory about members of a small group in the past, or even an individual. There are so many variations of this sort of question that only some suggestive remarks are possible. In the account of Hart/O'Hart, I sketched the process of research used in that case to establish the identity of a single person. It may, however, be useful to consider several other types of problems. The first example I take from my own family's history. In a biographical sketch of my Great Uncle Ned—otherwise known as Red Ned, because of the color of his hair—my cousin, Thomas Murphy, claimed that Ned had been a scout for General Terry's forces at the Little Bighorn when the Custer massacre occurred. How would one verify this claim? First, there is an alternative family history written by my uncle that omits any mention of Ned's having been at the Little Bighorn. That itself is fairly strong evidence, because the Custer massacre was a major event for people in that part of the country, and if Ned had been there and my uncle knew about it, he certainly would have mentioned it. Second, the U.S. Army has no record of Ned ever having been employed as a scout. Third, there are a surprisingly large number of books written by people who were there, including some of the scouts, and in none of them is Ned mentioned. Fourth, people at the Custer Museum say they have no records of Ned's having been there. It seems clear, therefore, that the story is false; none of the confirming data that one would expect if the story was true can be found, and what can be found supports the conclusion that he was not there. Why, then, did Thomas Murphy think that he had been? During World War I, Murphy was stationed in Oklahoma, where he met Michael Casey, another relation of ours. From what Murphy says, I think it is clear that he got this story from Casey. Ned was the sort of man about whom stories develop. He was a hunter and trapper in Colorado and Wyoming in the 1860s and then a wagon master leading wagon trains to Oregon, California, and other points west. At the time of the Custer massacre, he and my grandfather were prospecting for gold in the Black Hills. Two years earlier an expedition under Custer's command had found gold in the Black Hills,[16] and Ned and my grandfather were among those who went looking for it. I regret to say they found none. Then the two of them bought a large rowboat and floated down Platte River to the Missouri, down the Missouri to the Mississippi, and down that to New Orleans. Having seen the sights of the big city, they then followed the harvests back home to Nebraska. Thus during the time when Ned was supposedly with General Terry's forces, he and my grandfather were together, and the family history mentioned earlier was written by my grandfather's oldest son, who certainly would have known if Ned had been on the Little Bighorn. I do not know where Casey got the story, but given the sort of adventurer Ned was, and the fact that he was in the general area at the time of the Custer massacre, it seems plausible that such a story should have grown up about him. Thus not merely is the story false, but there is a plausible explanation for why it might have been created. The strategy followed here was the same as in the

Hart/O'Hart case. Look first at the family information, then at the records of any institution with which he might have been involved, in this case, the U.S. Army.

As an example of a group hypothesis, consider the following: The claim is that in 1836 the Transcendentalists believed that it was possible for those who were truly redeemed to perform miracles, and that they would be able to do that themselves. The first problem is, who were the Transcendentalists? This is not a clearly defined group; there is no mark that distinguishes the Transcendentalists from others who were sympathetic to them but were not genuine Transcendentalists. The way to define such a group is by prototype; we can specify who the leading exemplars of the movement were and then define others as being more or less similar to them. The leaders were quite clearly Ralph Waldo Emerson, Amos Bronson Alcott, and George Ripley. All three wrote copiously, so there is plenty of available data. Of the three, Emerson was the most gifted writer; too gifted, in fact. One cannot always get behind his glittering prose to the man. But with Alcott, the question is simpler—his style is prosaic, and he says what he thinks. And Alcott's diary shows that he did believe that human beings, including himself, could reach a state of perfection in which they could work miracles.[17] With Emerson, it is harder to be certain, but the ending of *Nature* certainly appears to assert the same doctrine that Alcott held.[18] Ripley, as far as I can tell, did not go this far. While pushing likeness to God to a degree intolerable to Andrews Norton and the orthodox, he did not go as far as Alcott. So it appears that while some Transcendentalists did hold this doctrine, others did not. And as one looks at those in the next circle beyond this core group, I find no evidence for the claim.

This review should illustrate a number of points. Theories that contain generalizations about large numbers of people in the past require large numbers of cases for testing or aggregate data relevant to the generalization. The U.S. Census, both manuscript and published, is a prime source of such data, but it should be noted that there are surveys done by the federal government, state censuses and surveys, local directories, and many similar sources. There is never enough of this sort of data, but it is astonishing how much there actually is. In many of these cases, sampling designs offer ways to utilize such data that are less costly in time and money than examining every case. But it is more common to find partial data (i.e., data dealing with some but not all members of the population in question). Very often these data can be put to excellent use. Any sample that is not a probability sample must be regarded as biased, but if we know what the bias is, then we can correct for it. Sometimes the bias affects only variables independent of the ones that interest us. In other cases, the bias is related to the variables of interest. If one is sampling houses or letters or wills, then any historical sample will be biased toward the high-status members of the society, but by stratifying the sample by status, such a bias can be controlled. Or, it may be that the sample is biased in a given direction, although we do not know how much. Alex Inkeles and his coworkers wanted to determine what the attitudes of the Soviet people toward their government really were. At the time of this study, the chances of getting the Soviet government to allow such a survey were zero. But Inkeles had available a large number of Soviet citizens who were in DP camps in Europe. Some had been prisoners of war taken by the Germans; some were laborers the Germans had conscripted, and some were people who had fled the Soviet Union and had willingly accompanied the German army back to Germany. It was not possible to tell which individuals belonged to what group, because those who left the Soviet Union voluntarily lied about having done so, fearing accusations of being pro-German. Inkeles therefore knew that his sample was biased against the Soviet government, but he could not calculate how great the bias was. Accordingly, when he found that his sample gave answers to his questions that indicated a negative attitude toward the Soviet regime, he could not be sure that this was not due to bias. But when he found issues on which his sample held favorable attitudes toward the Soviet government, he could take their responses as representing the attitudes of the Soviet population generally, because the answers went against the known bias of the sample.[19] The point, of course, is that there are ways of putting such data to use if the historian is clever enough to figure them out. It also should be noted that there is a new research tool that is just beginning to be used—DNA. Already we have studies based on DNA evidence tracing migrations of peoples in antiquity, and the use of this sort of information certainly will increase in the future.

It must be emphasized that while in some cases the data may provide fairly conclusive tests of the hypotheses or theory in question, this is by no means always true. There is unfortunately no way to measure the degree of confirmation, or disconfirmation, that a given theory has. The most that one can say here is that if the theory accounts for new data as they are discovered, and holds for a wide range of different kinds of data, then it can be held as probably true. Certainty, of course, we can never have, but then no empirical theory ever can.

The data most serviceable for purposes of confirmation are new data—those not used in the formation of the theory. This may of course take the form of the discovery of hitherto unknown documents, and this does occur, but one should not bet the farm that one will be so lucky. Much more reasonable is the hope of extracting new information from data that already exist. Such dramatic strides have been made in the use of electronic machines to manipulate and analyze data since the arrival of the computer that a huge number of questions that could not be addressed before are now amenable to research. There is nothing new about voting statistics; people knew that the data existed for years before they were systematically used. For a political historian of the 1930s, the idea of analyzing all of the county election returns for, say, the presidential election of 1876 was only a fantasy; physically, the job could not be done by a single investigator. Today, with computers, it is a test easily accomplished. As Collingwood noted, advances in history often come from finding new ways to extract information from old data. Similarly, in recent decades, historians have come to realize what a treasure house of information is provided by material culture. Did Prohibition really stop the consumption of alcoholic wine? Then why did people continue to buy wine glasses? as Catherine Murdock has shown, they did.[20] And of course archaeology is constantly adding to our stock of material items from the past. Thus as I hope these few examples show, historians can test their theories. At least in many cases, the necessary data are known to exist, as are the necessary methods. But so far we have only discussed what historians could do to confirm their theories; it also is important to examine what they actually do.

Chapter 7

Confirmation 2

Historians do test historical theories by the processes of review and revision. In this chapter, I examine three famous examples of historical theories and how they fared at the hands of revisionists. The examples chosen are the explanation of the Great Depression, given by Milton Friedman and Anna Schwartz, the Frontier Thesis of Frederick Jackson Turner, and the economic "determinism" of Charles Beard.

⊶◇⊷

In science, when a new result is announced, the experiment or observation is replicated to see if other investigators can get the same result, and the finding is not accepted in the scientific community unless it can be replicated. But results in history are practically never replicated. No one repeats a historical investigation to see if they can get the same result. The reason is obvious. If all one finds is that what someone else found is the same as what you find, no one will publish your work. No publisher or journal editor wants the same thing over again; he wants something new. To replicate a serious historical investigation would require considerable time and work, and no one wants to put that kind of an effort into a project that may not be published. Publish or perish is still the rule in the profession. Accordingly, replications are not done in history.

But replications could be done. The whole point of footnotes is to allow other historians to find the data used by the author. Hence the location of the data should be easily determinable. It would in fact be an interesting and worthwhile teaching exercise to assign students the task of replicating a book's research. Students should be able to locate the data fairly quickly if the documentation of the book is adequate and then should be asked to evaluate the degree to which the data support, or fail to support, the theory presented in the book.

151

How do historians actually go about testing historical theories? The procedure used may be described as review and revision. When a historical work is published, the editors of historical journals make the decision as to whether or not to review it and how much space to allot for the review. Many works are not judged significant enough to merit reviews in the most prestigious journals, but probably the most important ones are. The reviewers are chosen for their knowledge of the subject treated in the book; sometimes they are people who have written on that subject, but often they are people who have published in that general area. Reviewing for the major journals is reserved for books only; articles—even important ones—are not reviewed. An important book usually will be reviewed by several journals, and the reviews have a major influence on a book's reception and sales. Good reviews will induce other historians to read the book; bad reviews can kill a book and lead to its being ignored. The review process is the initial test of the book, but such reviews are usually short and shallow—500 to 1,000 words—and are designed chiefly to tell prospective readers what the book contains. Reviews usually contain some evaluation of the book, praising its strengths and criticizing its weaknesses, but in very tempered terms. The politics of the profession will greatly influence the reviews scholars write. A bad review of a young scholar's book may cost him his job, and people are reluctant to do that. Furthermore, one never forgets the name of someone who writes a bad review of your book. Reviewers know that. And somewhere down the line the scholar whose book you slammed may be asked to review a book of yours or to serve on a panel making grants for which you are an applicant or may be asked to evaluate you as a candidate for a professorship you want. This is a situation where the need for tact trumps the need for rigor.

Once the book has passed the review process, it may or may not be judged an important book. But if the theory contained in the book is sufficiently attractive and exciting, then it draws attention, not only to itself but to the subject it treats. The subject may become what is called a "hot topic," and other historians may be drawn to its study. Some scholars—often the students of the original author—develop the implications of the theory and apply it to new topics. Think, for example, of the influence of Turner and Beard. Many historians built their work and their careers on the Frontier Thesis and on Beardian economic "determinism." But this work is not viewed as confirming the work of the master. The word "confirm" is rarely, if ever, used by historians. Rather, the application must be to a subject or an aspect of a subject sufficiently different from that treated by the original theory to constitute an independent piece of research, though the relation to the original theory may be explicit. If the application is successful, then it may enhance the standing of the original theory; if it is unsuccessful, then it may or may not diminish its standing, depending on whether the failure is attributed to the original theory or the ineptitude of the disciple. In neither case can one be said to have confirmed or disconfirmed the original theory.

But the higher the repute of the original theory, the better target it becomes. Other—usually younger—scholars who are out to make a name for themselves set out to show that the original theory is wrong. If they succeed in doing so, then they will get published, praised, and promoted. And they will find faults in the theory—some data the author "somehow managed to overlook," or a new methodological gadget he failed to use, or perhaps that he really is wrong. So appear the "revisionists," and—for a time—they will capture the attention of the trade. But if the original theory really was right, or if the revisionists fail to prove their case, then in due course the "rerevisionists" will appear and subject the work of the "revisionists" to the same sort of battering that they had inflicted upon the original theory.

What these processes do is not just advance people's careers, though that of course is the motive. They also lead to the discovery of new data, new methods of analyzing the data, and new ideas and new theories. In the end, we come out knowing a lot more about the subject than we did before the original theory was published, and often with a much better grounded theory about that subject. Thus historical theories are tested not by efforts to confirm them but, on the one hand, by their use and, on the other, by the effort to falsify them. Karl Popper would have been proud.

The aforementioned describes how the process is supposed to work, but it ignores the influence of several factors. First, any theory is better than no theory. Even when a theory has been severely criticized by revisionists, it will still persist, unless there is an alternative available to replace it. Second, factors external to the profession may greatly influence which works are seen as acceptable. Socialist and pro-Soviet writings of the 1930s were rejected in the 1950s because of the Cold War climate of opinion. Historians are not immune to such factors, nor are the universities in which they work. Success in a university environment requires not just that one publish but that what one publishes not arouse the hostility of the government or other institutions on which universities depend. Academic freedom is not always the protective shield it is supposed to be.

We have already seen one example of this process in Benson's revisionist book on Jacksonian democracy. But in the following pages I want to discuss three examples of this process. The first is Friedman and Schwartz's *A Monetary History of the United States.*[1] In this book, Friedman and Schwartz put forward an explanation of the Great Depression. As Peter Temin pointed out, there are really two quite separate questions concerning the Great Depression: (1) Why did a depression begin in 1929? (2) Why did that depression become an economic collapse far worse than any other in our history? The second question is really the important one. There is general agreement that in 1929 the economy entered a recession that appeared no different from other recessions it experienced—in the period 1920–1921, for example. The outstanding event in 1929 was of course the stock market crash, but the decline was evident some months earlier. Construction fell, agricultural prices fell, and so did industrial production, but economists have been unable to find anything in the data that can explain why what appeared in early 1930 to be a "normal" recession should have turned into an economic disaster without historical parallel.

The answer that Friedman and Schwartz give to this question is that the fall in the stock of money was the critical factor. And the stock of money did fall—33 percent from 1929 to 1933.[2] According to monetarist economic theory, this fall in the stock of money was the chief cause of the collapse of the economy. The fall in the stock of money was due, according to Friedman and Schwartz, mainly to two factors—bank failures and the Federal Reserve's failure to act. The Great Depression witnessed three waves of bank failures. The first began in October 1930[3] and continued into early 1931. The most dramatic event in this wave was the failure of the Bank of the United States—the largest commercial bank ever to have failed in American history up to that time.[4] The second and much more severe wave of failures began in March 1931 and ran until January 1932.[5] The third wave hit in January 1933 and lasted until the Bank Holiday in March.[6]

What was the cause of these failures? As far as the first wave of failures is concerned, Friedman and Schwartz think that it may have been due to poor-quality loans and investments made in the exuberance of the late 1920s. But this explanation does not hold for subsequent waves of failure. Thus Friedman and Schwartz argue:

> The banking system as a whole was in a position to meet the
> demands of depositors for currency only by a multiple contrac-
> tion of deposits, hence of assets. Under such circumstances,
> any runs on banks for whatever reason became to some extent
> self-justifying, whatever the quality of the assets held by banks.
> Banks had to dump their assets on the market, which inevitably

forced a decline in the market value of those assets and hence of the remaining assets they held. The impairment of the market value of the assets held by banks, particularly in their bond port-folios, was the most important source of impairment of capital leading to bank suspensions, rather than the default of specific loans or of specific bond issues.[7]

Events that shook the confidence of depositors, such as the failure of the Austrian Kreditanstadt, and the resulting financial crisis in Europe,[8] and the British departure from the gold standard, both of which occurred in 1931,[9] helped produce such runs on the banks, and once the panic began, it fed on itself. But as Friedman and Schwartz see the situation, it was not the fall in aggregate demand or the general deflation that produced the bank failures but the other way around. As they assert: "If the bank failures deserve special attention, it is clearly because they were the mechanism through which the drastic decline in the stock of money was produced, and because the stock of money plays an important role in economic developments."[10] For them, the stock of money was the key variable, the behavior of which brought on the general collapse.

But the collapse need not have occurred. Had the Federal Reserve intervened decisively by large-scale open market purchases, the fall in the stock of money would not have occurred, and the depression would never have become the Great Depression. Friedman and Schwartz describe the effects that open-market purchases of one billion dollars would have had if they had occurred at three different times during the contrac-tion: in "(1) the first ten months of 1930; (2) the first eight months of 1931; (3) the four months following Britain's departure from gold in September of 1931."[11] Had any one of these purchases occurred, the infusion of high-powered money by the Fed would have checked the fall of the money stock and halted the depression.[12] This counterfactual argument they regard as justified by their (monetarist) economic theory. The purchases did not occur. As Friedman and Schwartz remark:

> The leadership which an independent central banking system was supposed to give the market and the ability to withstand the pressures of politics and of profit alike and to act counter to the market as a whole, these—the justification for establish-ing a quasi-governmental institution with broad powers—were conspicuous by their absence.[13]

Why did the Fed fail to act? According to Friedman and Schwartz, it was because of the death in October 1928 of Benjamin Strong, governor of the New York Federal Reserve Bank. Thus according to Friedman and Schwartz:

> If Strong had still been alive and head of the New York Bank in the fall of 1930, he would very likely have recognized the oncoming liquidity crisis for what it was, would have been prepared by experience and conviction to take strenuous and appropriate measures to head it off, and would have had the standing to carry the System with him.[14]

Strong's death was followed by a shift in power within the System of which Friedman and Schwartz say, "The shift in the locus of power, which almost surely would not have occurred when it did if Strong had lived, had important and far-reaching consequences"[15] Chief among these were the increased difficulty of vigorous action by the Fed and the accession to positions of leadership of men lacking Strong's abilities.[16] This counterfactual argument thus leads to the conclusion that Strong's death caused the Great Depression.

In 1976, Temin published *Did Monetary Forces Cause the Great Depression?*,[17] in which he undertook to show that Friedman and Schwartz were wrong. As Temin emphasizes, there were by 1976 two competing theories of the causes of the Great Depression—the monetarist theory of Friedman and Schwartz, and what he called the "spending theory," that is, Keynesian theory. According to the latter theory, the depression was caused by a fall in autonomous spending, due chiefly to a fall in consumption, an excess of housing stock, and the crash of the market. The fall in spending produced a fall in real income and prices by the multiplier process. This led to a fall in the demand for money, which in turn led to a fall in the stock of money and in interest rates. The banking panics were the result of the fall in demand; by decreasing the stock of money, they actually helped "equilibrate the money market in the face of precipitously falling demand and increasing monetary base."[18]

> As the depression deepened, adverse expectations kept autonomous spending low. The international collapse intensified the Depression in the United States by further depressing expectations and by diminishing exports. In the face of a small aggregate demand, the economy settled down to an underemployment position.[19]

On this theory, then, the fall in the stock of money was not an independent phenomenon but was the result of the fall in demand. It cannot, therefore, be taken to have caused the Great Depression; it was a part of the Great Depression.

To discriminate between these two theories is not easy, given the state of the data, but Temin is able to do so. He argues that if the bank failures of the period 1929–1930 had the effects that Friedman and Schwartz claim, then the behavior of short-term interest rates would show it on the money hypothesis but not on the spending hypothesis.[20]

> At the time when the monetary pressure was applied to the economy, a temporary rise in these interest rates should have been visible. If the pressure was strong—strong enough to send the economy into its deepest depression, then the rise should have been dramatic and obvious. Yet there was no rise in short-term interest rates in this two-year period.[21]

While this test is fairly dramatic, Temin argues that other factors were important. Most striking is the very large drop in consumption in 1930—a drop that neither theory could explain in 1976. The fall in income and the deflation that marked the Depression are difficult to explain on the monetary theory. Particularly important is the fact that while nominal interest rates fell, real interest rates rose in 1930 and 1931. In fact, Temin writes:

> If the demand for money can be written in real terms, that is, if the demand for real balances is a stable function of the level of real income, then there does not seem to have been any contractionary pressure on real income from the supply of money. This, clearly, is inconsistent with the money [monetary] hypothesis.[22]

Temin concludes that the spending hypothesis fits the data better than the monetary hypothesis, though neither is entirely adequate.

Since Friedman and Schwartz are economists, and Temin is an economic historian, it may seem that the sort of revision just described is more a feature of economics than of history. But the same process operates in history generally, although it often operates more slowly. I want, therefore, to discuss two cases that are of particular interest because of the general acclaim that the profession gave to the works involved, the length of time that elapsed before they were seriously called into question, and the completeness with which they have been discredited. The first is the most remarkable example in American history of a hypothesis that gained wide acclaim and devoted adherents—Turner's Frontier Thesis.

In 1893, before an audience at the Chicago meeting of the American Historical Association, Frederick Jackson Turner read his famous paper, "The Significance of The Frontier in American History." A very young man at the time—he was only thirty-two—Turner's paper was to launch one of the most extraordinary careers in American academic history and for a time was the most influential single "interpretation" in the field. Until Turner's death in 1932, "The thesis was almost universally viewed as the sole valid interpretation of the nation's history."[23]

What was Turner's thesis? He led off with the claim, "The existence of an area of free land, its continuous recession, and the advance of American settlement westward, explain American development."[24] In Turner's view, as the frontier—that is, the line marking the Western edge of settlement—moved West, those at the frontier found themselves reduced to "primitive" conditions as they strove to deal with the wilderness and reverted to a primitive style of life. As the frontier line moved on, those who stayed in the area it swept out developed a civilized way of life, recapitulating as they did so the stages of human social evolution.[25] But in each area of new settlement, social evolution took a slightly different course, and traits characterizing the primitive frontier life continued to mark the developing civilization. Thus Turner wrote:

> The United States lies like a huge page in the history of society. Line by line as we read this continental page from West to East we find the record of social evolution. It begins with the Indian and the hunter; it goes on to tell of the disintegration of savagery by the entrance of the trader, the pathfinder of civilization; we read the annals of the pastoral stage in ranch life; the exploitation of the soil by the raising of unrotated crops of corn and wheat in sparsely settled farming communities; the intensive culture of the denser farm settlement; and finally the manufacturing organization with city and factory system.[26]

These recurring processes of social evolution in one area after another as the frontier marched westward produced a unique "American civilization." But by 1890, Turner held that the movement of the frontier line had ended. The 1890 U.S. Census Superintendent had announced that settlement of the country had reached the point where "there can hardly be said to be a frontier line."[27] The closing of the frontier marked in Turner's eyes the end of the first period of American history; what would happen without the frontier Turner did not say.

How did the successive social evolutions that followed the movement of the frontier line affect American civilization? First, "The frontier promoted the formation of a composite nationality for the American people."[28] Frontier life stripped away older customs, and the mixing of ethnic groups at the frontier produced a composite people. "In the crucible of the frontier the immigrants were Americanized, liberated, and fused into a mixed race."[29] Second, it decreased American dependence on England, and for that matter on all European nations.[30] Third, it promoted nationalism and the power of the federal government, as Western demands for better transportation, more land, liberal land policy, and tariffs came to dominate the federal agenda. It was the issue of the extension of slavery into the West that brought on the Civil War. Fourth, "The most important effect of the frontier has been on the promotion of democracy."[31] As frontier areas became states, they entered the union with wider suffrage, greater equality, and a more democratic cast of mind.[32] Fifth, the frontier promoted individualism. It broke down social controls over individuals and threw them on their own, ended artificial social distinctions and classes, and led each person to regard himself as the equal of any other.[33] Sixth, it promoted competition among religious groups, each trying to win more converts than the others.[34] Seventh, it emphasized practicality. The Westerner had little time for abstract notions being too busy dealing with the hard facts of existence. Eighth, it encouraged geographic mobility and made it a national characteristic.[35] Ninth, it encouraged "lax business honor, inflated paper currency and wild-cat banking,"[36] and even corruption in government. Finally,

> the result is that to the frontier the American intellect owes its striking characteristics. That coarseness and strength combined with acuteness and inquisitiveness; that practical, inventive turn of mind, quick to find expedients; that masterful grasp of material things, lacking in the artistic but powerful to effect great ends; that restless, nervous energy; that dominant individualism, working for good and for evil, and withal that buoyancy and exuberance which comes with freedom—these are the traits of the frontier.[37]

Americans found in Turner's thesis a portrait of themselves that they liked, and they came rapidly to accept his account of how they had become what they fancied they were.

The success of Turner's thesis was remarkable. It became for roughly forty years the dominant interpretation of American history.

It helped that Turner was a brilliant teacher, first at the University of Wisconsin and then at Harvard. Among his disciples were Carl Becker, Homer Hockett, Merle Curti, Frederick Merk, Frederick Paxson, and Ray Allen Billington. The essays by Becker and Hockett in the 1910 *Festschrift* for Turner show very well how his ideas could be applied.[38] Writing in 1930, Paxson adopted Turner's thesis entire and claimed that "the frontier affords a means of studying institutions while they are in the formative stage, and before they become inextricably involved in the complex of a going and sophisticated society."[39] But what happens when the frontier is gone? Will the United States become the scene of class warfare between industrial capital and the proletariat, as Paxson thinks Europe has? Paxson thought not. The heritage of the frontier, with its emphasis on democracy, equality, and individualism, would, he believed, guarantee that "class warfare is not to be an immanent American division."[40]

In 1949, Ray Allen Billington published *Westward Expansion*,[41]—an 873-page history of the settling of America written from a Turnerian point of view. Starting with the European settlements on the East Coast, which he labeled "Europe's First Frontier," Billington carried the story through to 1896 and then added a chapter on the Frontier heritage that not only reaffirmed the effects pointed out by Turner—democracy, nationalism, materialism, inventiveness, mobility, wastefulness, optimism, rugged individualism, and reliance on the federal government, when it was to their advantage, and resistance to government "interference" when it was not—but added American imperialism of the 1890s and the early twentieth century.[42] This was American history written according to the Frontier Thesis.

These are only two of the many volumes and articles published by Turner's followers. Turner's influence was astonishing. As George Pierson remarked in 1942, Turner's "brilliant papers have been the Bible, and today still constitute the central inspiration, of an extraordinary and widely held faith."[43] Louis Hacker, writing in 1933, put it more strongly:

> From that day [when Turner gave his paper], forty years ago, until now it may truly be said that he [Turner] has so completely dominated American historical writing that hardly a single production in all that time has failed to show the marks of his influence. Not only were Turner's own seminar students legion (he taught altogether for some thirty-four years) but his personal followers in turn scattered over the land to indoctrinate other vast numbers of eager scholars, thereby increasing the Turner host by geometric proportions.[44]

No other American historian has had such a broad influence. And the many works inspired by Turner's thesis seemed to show that indeed the thesis was the master key to understanding American history.

But by the 1930s, the revisionists were already at work. There was no one smashing attack but a number of small cuts. In 1934, political scientist Benjamin Wright pointed out that the new states formed in the West copied their constitutions and political institutions from the older states, and that the political structures so created were not noticeably more democratic than those from which they were copied.[45] This did not prove Turner wrong, but it was not what one would have expected on the basis of his thesis. But perhaps the most incisive critic of Turner's thesis in this period was George Pierson.[46] What exactly was the "frontier" of Turner's Thesis? Pierson pointed out that Turner used the term to refer to a place, a population, and a process, with resulting conceptual confusion. One aspect of Turner's frontier was the emphasis on migration, or mobility. But, Pierson asked, does migration always have these effects? Did the migrations in Europe, or South America, or Australia have these effects? Neither Turner nor his acolytes bothered with the comparative data necessary to substantiate their claims.[47] Just how did the frontier produce its effects? Turner talks like a geographical determinist,[48] but the determinism apparently operates through psychological intervening variables; the westward migration produced psychological characteristics in the migrants who then shaped their institutions accordingly.[49] These psychological characteristics—nationalism, individualism, and equalitarianism—are alleged to be determined by the frontier, though how is not explained. And the institutions—political and economic—that were created were generally copied from those of the Eastern states. How inventiveness and individualism square with copying is not explained. Pierson points out that Turner's idea of culture apparently included only government, business, education, and religion. He showed no great interest in other aspects of culture and cheerfully admitted that what he called the "highest arts and skills"[50] were abandoned on the frontier. Not only does Turner ignore the industrial revolution, the commercial revolution, and—worst of all—the agricultural revolution, but his theory is often self-contradictory.

> The nationalism of the frontier does violence to its sectional tendencies, innovations are derived from repetitions, the improvement of civilization is achieved *via* the abandonment of civilization, and materialism gives birth to idealism.[51]

Pierson does not charge Turner's thesis with being false, but he says it "needs painstaking revision." Further, "by what it fails to mention, the thesis today disqualifies itself as an adequate guide to American development."[52]

Revisionist attacks such as these called the frontier theory into question, but they did not bury it. In 1959, Merle Curti, a former student of Turner's who became a distinguished historian in his own right, published a remarkable book designed to test at least some portions of the Turner thesis. This is one of the few cases in American history where a study was carefully designed to test a theory. Curti stated the hypothesis to be tested as follows:

> In our opinion it is fair to summarize his [Turner's] views by saying that to him American democracy involved widespread participation in the making of decisions affecting the common life, the development of initiative and self-reliance, and equality of economic and cultural opportunity. It thus also involved Americanization of the immigrant.[53]

To test this hypothesis, Curti used Trempealau County in Wisconsin. The choice was dictated chiefly by the fact that it was a county that had been on the frontier and had extensive records that could serve as data. Curti did not claim that it was "typical" or "representative" of all frontier counties, but if the hypothesis held for this county, then that would suggest that similar studies of other counties might show the same thing.[54] Curti used both quantitative and qualitative data and studied the whole population, something he remarked that "would of course be out of the question were not modern calculating machines available."[55] The time period covered was the beginning of settlement to 1880.

What Curti and his coworkers found generally supported his interpretation of the Turner Thesis. As expected, he discovered the pioneer population to be young and chiefly single and the variety of occupations limited.[56] He further found that Trempealau County was ethnically diverse, with Scots, Irish, English, Germans, Poles, and Norwegians being the chief immigrant groups.[57] The distribution of property was badly skewed, with some people owning much more than others. The Poles and the Irish were particularly apt to be poor. But one of the most striking findings of the study was that among those who stayed in Trempealau County for multiple decades, there was a marked increase of wealth, and the rate of increase in wealth was considerably greater for those who started out poor than for those who started out with more; in 1860, the difference between the averages for these two groups was $563, whereas in 1870 it was $113. Everybody gained, but those who started with less gained faster. Thus over time, economic inequality decreased, and since many of those who started out poor were immigrants, it is clear that they became more equal to the wealthier group.[58] Social assimilation was not as rapid; intermarriage rates were low but increased slowly over time, as did rates of participation in other areas.[59] Curti also found democracy in Trempealau County. At first the typical American blueprint of government was imposed by the state of Wisconsin, but it was adopted without difficulty by all.[60] Within this general framework, "democracy flourished at the grass roots."[61] Immigrant participation in political decision making was low in the earliest period, but it increased over time,[62] and the percentage of foreign born in leadership positions also increased over time.[63] Assimilation took time, but it was clearly happening in Trempealau County. Finally, Curti found evidence that "frontier experiences in Trempealau promoted self-confidence, optimism, resourcefulness, perseverance, a quickening of "mental faculties," and, especially, neighborly cooperation as well as individual initiative and sense of responsibility."[64] Curti concluded:

> Our study, both in its quantitative and qualitative aspects, lends support to what we believe are the main implications of Turner's thesis about the frontier and democracy, so far as Trempealau County is concerned. It is indeed true that several important qualifications must be made—that for instance by some tests there was more democracy, as we defined it, in the 1870s than in the 1850s and early 1860s. But such qualifications are balanced by or findings which indicate that Turner's poetical vision of free land and of relatively equal opportunity was for a great many people being realized in Trempealau County. The story of the making of this American community is a story of progress toward democracy.[65]

While the revisionists chipped away at the Frontier Thesis, Turnerians continued to fight a rearguard action. A good example is Billington's *America's Frontier Heritage*.[66] Unlike his earlier *Westward Expansion*, which simply assumed the Turner thesis, this 1966 book is filled with qualifications, admissions of the importance of other factors, and defenses against revisionist attacks. For example, Billington admits that the direct safety valve did not operate in nineteenth-century America—that is, laborers suffering from low wages and poor working conditions did not flock to the frontier—but he holds that indirectly the frontier did act as a safety valve, since westward expansion drew away from the East immigrants and workers, thereby creating upward pressure on wages.[67] Again, he admits that social stratification existed on the frontier to a greater extent than Turner recognized but argues that economic mobility and opportunities offered by the frontier created a more open status system than could be found in the Old World.[68] After reviewing one by one the characteristics Turner attributed to the frontier and admitting in each case that qualifications are required and that other factors operated besides the frontier, he still holds that "to deny that three centuries of frontiering endowed the people with some of their most distinctive traits is to neglect a basic molding force that has been the source of the nation's greatest strength—and some of its most regrettable weaknesses."[69]

Nevertheless, the revisionists won. By the 1980s, an accumulating body of work that refuted the Turner Thesis in one area after another was sufficient to lead to the widespread rejection of the Thesis. Patricia Limerick's *The Legacy of Conquest*[70] synthesized the revisionist arguments in a way that left little of the Turner Thesis still standing. Turner had claimed that the frontier "closed" in 1890, thereby dividing American history into two periods which, if his thesis was correct, must be very different. Limerick countered that the history of the West was continuous—that there is no evidence of any dramatic change caused by the vanishing of the frontier line. Further, she denied Turner's claim that the frontier closed in 1890, since there were many areas with a population density less than two persons per square mile (the Census definition of "frontier") that were still unsettled after 1893.[71] This criticism actually misses the mark. What Turner referred to when he spoke of "the closing of the frontier" was the disappearance of a continuous line marking the Western edge of settlement. He never said that there were no low-density pockets of population left. Further, what Turner had called "free land" was in fact inhabited by Indians; the history of the West was in large part a history of conquest, and its legacy of Indian problems after 1890 was a continuation of the problems before 1890.[72] The same was true for most aspects of Western history. Far from the West being an area of independent and self-sufficient heroes, Limerick pointed out that the West had been a perpetual supplicant at the federal trough. Western farmers, struggling with the waywardness of nature and the fluctuation of the markets, had repeatedly turned to the federal government for help. No section of the United States received more aid from the federal government during the 1930s than the West, and no section was more churlish in its ingratitude. Water, which in the arid West is the lifeblood of agriculture, was and is a constant problem in the West, and repeatedly the federal government was called upon to provide damns for irrigation and power.[73] These arguments exposed a contradiction in Turner's Thesis. He had indeed said that the "frontier" would turn to the federal government for aid, but he also emphasized the traits of individualism and autonomy that were supposedly produced by the frontier. It is not easy to reconcile these. Further, Western economic development, like all economic development, required capital and labor, and the capital came from the East.[74] The West, before and after 1890, has been ethnocentric and racist, not only in its treatment of blacks and of Indians, but also of Chinese, Japanese, and Mexicans.[75] Perhaps European immigrants were assimilated with relative ease, though there is considerable evidence that they were not, but immigrants from Asia, Africa, and south of the border had a different experience. Corporations came to the West early and have grown ever more powerful, not just in mining but in cattle raising and agriculture.[76] Today, less than 3 percent of the population are farmers. By the time Limerick is through, not only is the Turner Thesis devastated, but it is clear that adherence to it has been fundamentally misleading to the students of American history.

It was not only scholarly evidence that made Limerick's book the success it was. From the Indian Rights movement of the 1960s on, Indians (Native Americans) became increasingly important both politically and socially. Recognition of the injustices done to them was widespread, and there was a growing body of scholarship about them. In Turner's time, no one had had any doubts that the whites had conquered the West. That fact was not then considered important, but by Limerick's time, it was. Similarly, in 1900, only 40 percent of the U.S. population was urban, and idealization of the family farm was widespread. By Limerick's time, only 3 percent of the population was in farming, and the rural ideal had faded. Historians, like other people, respond to the changes in the culture. Further, the conceptual flaws in the Turner Thesis have become obvious. Even by the 1950s, geographic determinism was a dead doctrine. Theories of phylogenetic and ontogenetic recapitulation were discredited in the social sciences, thus rendering Turner's use of recapitulation theory and his claims that the United States recapitulated the stages of social evolution untenable.

Lastly, Turner's Thesis is, as far as I know, unique in American history in having been advanced as a theoretical claim without supporting evidence. Of course Turner expected the evidence to be filled in and provided some of it himself in his subsequent work, but the original 1893 paper simply announced the Thesis. And, by any standard, it presented Americans with an explanation of how they had become the marvelous people they thought they were. In ringing and poetic terms, Turner attributed to the frontier's influence all of those traits about which Americans boasted—individualism, democracy, equality, absence of class, ingenuity, and on and on. The ability of the Turner

Thesis to withstand a withering fire of criticism was in considerable part due to the fact that people wanted to believe it, not because the data supporting it were overwhelming, which they were not, but because people thought it showed that they were the embodiment of the virtues Turner claimed for them.

My third example of the revision process is Charles Beard's *An Economic Interpretation of the Constitution of the United States*.[77] Few books in American history have ever enjoyed the influence this one had. First published in 1913, at a time when the Founding Fathers and the U.S. Constitution they wrote were sacrosanct, Beard was widely accused of having "muckraked" the Constitution. He claimed that the Constitution was an economic document, written by men who were personally interested in serving their own economic interests and ratified through a skillfully conducted campaign that allowed a minority with particular economic interests to outmaneuver the majority who did not share those interests. Beard's book was bitterly contested at the time of its publication and thereafter, but nothing draws attention to a book like a roaring controversy. Beard won the battle; by the 1930s, he was "*the* American historian," and his interpretation of the Constitution was incorporated into college textbooks as a new orthodoxy.[78]

Although the relation of Beard's book to the Progressive Movement, in which he was an active participant, was obvious, Beard claimed in his 1935 introduction to the second edition that "this volume is, strictly speaking, impartial."[79] In one sense, it was; Beard did not explicitly praise or condemn the people he discussed. But in another sense, the book was anything but impartial. His objective was to show that the U.S. Constitution was not the product of the whole people, as previous authors had claimed, but of a relatively small group of self-interested men, and that it was drawn to serve their economic interests. To have shown that, in the Progressive Era, was to condemn the authors of the document.

Beard was explicit in saying that his interpretation was based on "economic determinism," though just what he meant by "determinism" was never clear. Disavowing the influence of Marx, he claimed to have derived his theory from Madison's famous Number Ten of the *The Federalist*, which Beard called "a masterly statement of the theory of economic determinism in politics."[80] The point was to clear himself of any charge that his theory represented a European import, and specifically of the influence of Marx. Who, after all, could be more American than James Madison? But Beard did not really advance a theory of strict economic determinism; rather, what he presented was a theory that economic factors were of greater importance than others in determining people's actions, though others factors were also important. Accordingly, just what Beard meant by an "economic interpretation" was left ambiguous.

In the second chapter of the book, Beard surveyed the economic interest of the country in 1787. He first enumerated what data would be required to determine what those interests were. Having done so, he said:

> Pending the enormous and laborious researches here enumerated, the following pages are offered merely as an indication of the way in which the superficial aspects of the subject may be treated. In fact, they sketch the broad outlines of the study which must be filled in and corrected by detailed investigations.[81]

Leaving aside the legally disenfranchised, Beard divided the property owners into two groups: holders of real property (i.e., land) and holders of personalty (i.e., personal property). The real property owners he divided into the "small farmers," the "manorial lords of the Hudson Valley region,"[82] and the Southern slaveholders. The personal property owners consisted of owners of money capital, owners of public securities,[83] those with capital invested in manufacturing and shipping,[84] and those with capital invested in Western lands.[85] The owners of personalty were "the dynamic element in the movement for the new Constitution."[86]

Beard then describes the movement for the Constitution. In a pattern that runs through many of his chapters, he first describes what data would have to be at hand to prove his thesis, admits that the data have not been collected and analyzed, and then proceeds to offer "a superficial commentary on some of the outward aspects of the movement for the Constitution which are described in the conventional works on the subject,"[87]—that is, in secondary sources. Having done so, he concludes that the personalty interests were suffering under the Articles of Confederation, and that finding themselves unable to amend the Articles they launched the movement for a convention to revise them, in what Beard calls a "revolutionary programme."[88]

Beard then turns to the selection of the delegates to the Constitutional Convention. The selection was made by the state legislatures, as required by the U.S. Congress. But Beard holds that the property qualifications for voting in all of the states limited the franchise to only a fraction of the adult males.[89] The point, of course, is to show that the delegates cannot be regarded as having been chosen by the people for this task. Then, in Chapter 5, the most famous chapter in the book, Beard reviews the property holdings of the delegates one by one. The result of this tallying is that most of them were lawyers, most came from towns or areas "near the coasts,"[90] none were small farmers or "mechanics," and that "at least five sixths, were immediately, directly, and personally interested in the outcome of their labors at Philadelphia, and were to a greater or less extent economic beneficiaries from the adoption of the Constitution."[91] Specifically, of the fifty-five delegates, forty at least held public securities, fourteen were involved in land speculation, twenty-four had money loaned at interest, eleven had capital in mercantile, manufacturing, and shipping lines, and fifteen had property in the form of slaves.[92] Hence, Beard concludes, "We are forced to accept the profoundly significant conclusion that they knew through their personal experiences in economic affairs the precise results which the new government that they were setting up was designed to attain."[93]

To bolster his case, Beard then seeks to show that the leading men of the time saw the Constitution as an economic document. Rather than trying to survey public opinion in 1787, Beard claims that the "true inwardness" of the Constitution is revealed in *The Federalist*.[94] In that famous work, Beard says, "Every fundamental appeal in it is to some material and substantial interest."[95] He then reviews the political doctrines of the Convention delegates, one by one.[96] His conclusion is "that the authors of *The Federalist* generalized the political doctrines of the members of the convention with a high degree of precision, in spite of the great diversity of opinion which prevailed on many matters."[97] This Beard takes as showing that *The Federalist* expresses the views of the leading men of that time.

In Chapter 8, Beard deals with the process of ratification. He views the decision to demand ratification by conventions elected for that purpose in each state as a revolutionary departure from prior practices and one that served the interests of the personalty group. He then briefly reviews the ratification in each state, starting with New Hampshire and ending with Georgia—that is, in geographical order. Beard stressed the difficulty of obtaining ratification, with particular emphasis on Virginia and New York. To what extent ratification can be regarded as an expression of the will of the people depends, as Beard sees it, on who voted for the members of the state conventions. Beard's conclusion is that about 5 percent (160,000 people) of the population voted in these elections. That the figure was so low Beard attributes to the extensive disenfranchisement; thus, he wrote,

> The disenfranchisement of the masses through property qualifications and ignorance and apathy contributed largely to the facility with which the personalty-interest representatives carried the day.[98]

Even so, in some states, the AntiFederalists had the majority in the conventions and had to be won over. But superior organization, combined with the fact that "talent, wealth, and professional abilities were, generally speaking, on the side of the Constitutionalists,"[99] carried the day.

Then, relying on Libby's *The Geographical Distribution of the Vote of the Thirteen States on the Federal Constitution*,[100] he tries to establish a correlation between the economic characteristics of the different geographical regions of each state and their votes for or against the Constitution. Again, he goes state by state, from the North to the South, and he finds that support for the Constitution came chiefly from those areas in which the personalty interests were strongest, while opposition was centered in regions that were agricultural, and where paper money and other depreciatory schemes had flourished. This conclusion is supported by a review of what various leading men said at the time. Beard claims:

> No one can pore for weeks over the letters, newspapers, and pamphlets of the years 1787–1789 without coming to the conclusion that there was a deep-seated conflict between a popular party based on paper money and agrarian interests, and a conservative party centered in the towns and resting on financial, mercantile, and personal property interests generally.[101]

All of this, Beard holds, supports the conclusion that the Constitution was an economic document designed to protect and profit the interests of personalty.[102]

Beard's analysis of the Constitution became the generally accepted view in the historical profession until the 1950s. There were, of course, historians who disagreed with Beard, but no successful attack on his economic interpretation was mounted until Robert Brown published *Middle-Class Democracy and the Revolution in Massachusetts 1691–1780*[103] in 1955 and *Charles Beard and the Constitution*[104] in 1956. In the former, Brown presented a well-documented study that showed that at the time of the Revolution and the making of the Constitution, Massachusetts was a "relatively equalitarian, middle-class society in which there was a great deal of economic opportunity."[105] Furthermore, Brown argued that the property requirements for voting in Massachusetts were low enough and the general level of wealth was high enough so that most adult males in the state could vote.[106] Further, Brown's analysis showed that the system of representation in Massachusetts gave control of the Colonial assembly to the agricultural towns, not to the personalty interest of Boston and Salem.[107] Such restrictions on democracy in Massachusetts as there were during the Colonial period were imposed by England, and these were largely unsuccessful and of course ended with the Revolution. Massachusetts had no significant class conflict before the Revolution.[108] The Revolutionm in fact preserved the democratic order that already existed in the state rather than overturned it.

That Brown's description of Massachusetts contradicted Beard's economic interpretation was obvious, and in 1956 Brown published a full-scale attack on Beard's thesis. Proceeding chapter by chapter through Beard's book, Brown attacked not only his findings but his use of historical method. The question Brown asked was, "Did the actual evidence which Beard presented really justify the Beard interpretation of the Constitution?"[109] His answer was no. Repeatedly Beard described what evidence would be needed to substantiate his thesis, admitted that the evidence was not available, and then went right ahead on the basis of secondary works.[110]

Brown then takes up Beard's claim regarding disenfranchisement. If the Constitution was "put over undemocratically," then the majority of men must not have been able to vote.[111] Brown notes that in some states even those without property could vote, and he argues that, as he had found in Massachusetts, the distribution of property was so broad that most adult white males could vote. He also emphasized that Beard's own data contradict his assertion, and that some of his claims were unsupported by any evidence—for example, "without any proof, he assumed that the farmers were 'a large debtor class' who were dependent on the towns for capital to develop their resources."[112] At one point, Beard cited as proof of disenfranchisement the fact that in New York City, with a population of 30,000, only 5,091 voted. But 30,000 was the total population, including women and children. Estimating adult men as one out of five or six, it is clear that almost all men of age in New York City did vote.[113] Moreover, Beard confounded the question of who *could* not vote with the question who *did* not vote, claiming that many were "disenfranchised through apathy and lack of understanding."[114] But those who could have voted but chose not to cannot be said to be disenfranchised.

Brown's analysis of Beard's famous Chapter 5 is equally unsparing. The real issue, Brown argues, is not whether a delegate had personal property but whether the value of his personal property exceeded the value of his real property. On Beard's own evidence, "Only six delegates had personal property in excess of their reality."[115] Brown's answer is:

> To say that the Constitution was designed in part to protect property is true; to say that it was designed only to protect

property is false; and to say that it was designed only to protect *personalty* is preposterous.[116]

Beard also misinterpreted Madison's argument in *The Federalist*; Madison saw the economic divisions in American society as vertical, not horizontal, and as yielding three sectors: the landed, commercial, and manufacturing, with the landed (realty) interest far greater than the other two.[117] Moreover, Beard misused the whole *Federalist*, which contains many arguments for the Constitution that are not economic, contrary to what Beard claimed.[118]

Beard presented the process of ratification as a close contest in which the personalty interests outmaneuvered the reality interests. But, as Brown notes, Beard discussed the states in geographical order, from the North to the South. If instead they are ordered by the dates on which they ratified, the picture is quite different. Three of the first four states to ratify did so unanimously, and in none of the first five is the vote less than two to one for the Constitution. In Massachusetts, the vote was closer, but the margin of victory for the Constitutionalists was substantial. Maryland and South Carolina, which came next, voted at least two to one for ratification, and only in the last three—New Hampshire, Virginia, and New York, was the vote really close.[119] Beard failed to explain why some agricultural states ratified unanimously and why the conventions, taken as a whole, favored ratification by two to one. As Brown put it, "Why was the Constitution ratified by the landed interests if it was designed to protect personalty? Beard never answered this question."

Brown's conclusion was that Beard violated the canons of historical method repeatedly, that "the conclusions which he drew were not justified even by the kind of evidence which he used,"[120] and that Beard's thesis was false. Indeed, the question one is left with after reading Brown's attack is, why was Beard's thesis ever accepted in the first place?

In 1958, Forrest McDonald completed the destruction of Beard's economic interpretation in his *We the People*.[121] Beard had repeatedly outlined the research that was needed to test his thesis but then went ahead to propound his thesis without doing the necessary research. McDonald set himself to do the research "to fill in the details, on his [Beard's] own terms, in the framework of his own assumptions, methodology, and questions,"[122] to see if the research Beard had called for would, if done, support his thesis. If not, McDonald hoped to determine whether any economic interpretation could be done, or failing that, what alternatives were available.

McDonald reviewed in detail the holdings of the members of the Constitutional Convention. He found a variety of different economic interests, with many delegates having multiple interests. Beard's claim that the members of the Constitutional Convention were a consolidated group of personalty interests therefore required substantial qualification.[123] The personalty interests did dominate the Convention, thirty-one to twenty-four,[124] but the voting patterns in the convention did not coincide with the personalty/realty division.[125] In fact, McDonald says, "So far as can be ascertained from the votes of individual delegates, no alignment of *personalty interests* versus *realty interests* existed in the Convention."[126]

Beard does not fare better when it comes to ratification. In Delaware, New Jersey, Georgia, Connecticut, and Maryland, where ratification was rapid and nearly unanimous, Beard's thesis breaks down. In Georgia, New Jersey, and Delaware, most of the support came from farmers (realty) and in Maryland from the planters (realty); in Connecticut, Beard's thesis holds to some degree, but not completely. In two states, New Jersey and Connecticut, economic factors were the chief reasons for ratification; in Georgia, Delaware, and Maryland, noneconomic factors dominated.[127] In Pennsylvania, New Hampshire, Massachusetts, and South Carolina, the contests over ratification were closer, but Beard's thesis fails for all of them. In Pennsylvania, for example, the paper-money party opposed ratification; in South Carolina, it supported it, and in New Hampshire it was divided equally.[128] In Massachusetts, the personalty interests favored ratification, but so did the farmers and the lower urban class. In New Hampshire, the farmers split, some on each side. In Pennsylvania and South Carolina, occupations and personalty holdings were similar on both sides, but holders of public securities generally opposed ratification.[129] In Virginia,

> Public security holders were almost equally divided and the majority of the small farmers supported ratification. The wealthy planters were almost equally divided on the question of ratification, but planter-debtors, and particularly the planters who had brought about the passage of laws preventing the collection of British debts, favored ratification by a substantial margin.[130]

In New York, holders of personalty were divided about equally; artisans, mechanics, and small farmers near New York City supported ratification while upstate farmers did not.[131] Rhode Island and North Carolina did not ratify until after the new government went into effect. McDonald concludes, "On all counts, then, Beard's thesis is entirely incompatible with the facts."[132] Furthermore, after reviewing the economic interests of the country in 1787, McDonald concludes that they were so diverse and so often in conflict that

> it is therefore not even theoretically possible to devise a single set of alignments on the issue of ratification that would explain the contest as one in which economic self-interest was the principal motivating force.[133]

The rerevisionists were not far behind. Lee Benson's *Turner and Beard*[134] provides one of the better examples. Benson is not a defender of Beard; he is critical of Beard's conceptual analysis, his methodology, and his findings. But he also is critical of both Brown and McDonald, both of whom fare worse on his pages than Beard. Benson holds that Beard was confused over the difference between *economic determinism* and *economic interpretation*; he treated the terms interchangeabley, and the confusion permeates his work. Economic determinism holds that all aspects of social life, in this case, particularly politics, are completely determined by economic self-interest. An economic interpretation holds that although many factors enter into the determination of behavior, economic factors are often the most important and economic conditions provide the conditions within which the other factors operate.[135] What Beard actually provided was an economic interpretation, though he repeatedly said that his theory was one of economic determinism. But, according to Benson, both Brown and McDonald were just as confused on this score as Beard was, with the result that their criticisms often miss the point.[136]

Benson is also highly critical of the methodology of all three. As he points out, Beard confused "interest group" with "social class."[137] He failed to see that he was really talking about coalitions of interest groups.[138] But Brown and McDonald made the same mistake. Moreover, Beard formulated his interpretation in terms of a two-variable relationship between social class and political behavior.[139] But any viable economic interpretation of political behavior would have to include other variables—ethnicity, religion, region, and so on. Only if Beard were a strict economic determinist would the two-variable design be justified. Since, in fact, he provided an economic interpretation, even if he found the two-variable relation he was looking for, it would not have proven his thesis. Brown and McDonald are equally guilty of this mistake. McDonald's criticism of Beard for having begun with a theory that he then claimed to test and his call for a return to Baconian induction[140] bring sharp criticism from Benson as a worse error than Beard's.[141] Similarly, Benson faults

Beard's assumption that from "group divisions among the delegates to the Constitutional Convention, we can infer the group divisions among voters," a fault he finds especially in McDonald.[142]

I will not prolong this recital, but I think enough has been said to make clear how the process of revision works. The Turner Thesis was in the forty years after Turner propounded it an astonishingly popular, well-received hypothesis. Under Turner's flag, a great many books and articles were written that substantially contributed to our knowledge of American history, particularly the history of the West. Curti's study of Trempealau County is a good example of the contributions to Western history inspired by Turner. But by the 1940s, research results were accumulating that were not consistent with the thesis, and criticism of it grew. Limerick's book was the summation of a rising chorus of disagreements with Turner's claims. Today the Turner Thesis is remembered as an interesting chapter in American historiography, but few accept it. Similarly, Beard's book received a great amount of attention, both positive and negative, but by the 1950s it had become generally accepted. The revisionists not only undertook to discredit Beard's work by direct criticism of it but amassed research to produce findings that contradicted his. Brown's work on Massachusetts and McDonald's research covering all of the states brought into play important data that had not hitherto been used. This was particularly true of McDonald, whose research was prodigious. These were genuine contributions to an understanding of the period and of the process by which the U.S. Constitution was created. But as their books gained recognition and acceptance, they in turn became targets for criticism. Benson's critique was one of the most perceptive, faulting Beard and his critics on their conceptual analysis, their methods, and their conclusions. At the same time, Benson made a strong case for his own methodological approach, particularly for multivariate analysis, which also constituted an important contribution to historical study.

Does the process of revision and rerevision constitute a viable method of confirming or disconfirming historical theories? It does not. While obviously better than nothing, the process is haphazard and unbalanced. If a historical work gets through the reviewing process intact, then it is generally assumed to be correct in its use of data and their interpretation. Only when findings appear that contradict some of its major claims is it called into question, and rarely is it the object of specific revision. Friedman and Schwartz's work was called into question in large part because Monetarist economic theory and Keynesian economic theory disagree, and Friedman and Schwartz's work was used in contemporary arguments to bolster the Monetarist position. Turner's

Frontier Thesis came under attack in part because of the accumulation of research findings that contradicted it, but also because the vagueness of its formulation invited attack and because it too obviously told Americans what they wanted to hear. Beard's work came under attack in the 1950s, when theories of economic determinism were no longer popular, in large part because of the Cold War and in part because the growing sophistication of the social sciences made such theories implausible. But there is no systematic program for testing and evaluating historical theories. The research in published historical works is not replicated to see if the same results would be obtained the second time. The closest approximation to this in the cases cited earlier is McDonald's work, but McDonald did not replicate Beard's work; instead, he did the research Beard said should be done but did not do. Only a few historical works ever receive the kind of critical analysis given to Turner and Beard, because few historical works have the influence that theirs had. And even in those cases, it took roughly forty years after their publication before they were subjected to serious revision. Revisionist works usually present a new theory of some phenomenon and attack all of the earlier accounts inconsistent with their own. Benson's *The Concept of Jacksonian Democracy* and Gabriel Kolko's *The Triumph of Conservatism*[143] are examples of this, since they involve the rejection of what many prior scholars had said. The revisionist process usually does involve the correction of, or at least an attack on, earlier works, but there is no systematic effort to test the truth of historical accounts. The general rule is that if a book survives the review process or an article is published in a refereed journal, they remain an accepted part of the literature of the subject until they are forgotten or shouldered aside by later works that ignore them. There is thus no systematic effort to confirm or disconfirm historical theories.

It must also be emphasized that history, far more than science, even the social sciences, is affected by the changing political and cultural climate of the time. In the days before the automobile, the radio, and the TV, when the majority of Americans did not live in cities, Turner's theory had a plausibility that it lacks in present-day urban America. Beard's economic "determinism" was an acceptable theory in the 1930s, but one who espoused it in the 1950s was apt to be called a Communist. This responsiveness to the "climate of opinion" is no accident. Historians write not only for other historians but for the general public (or at least that part of the general public that reads), and there are a number of examples of historical works that have been best sellers. Like other authors, historians keep a wary eye on popular taste and cater to it. Far from living in ivory towers, historians live if not in the marketplace then at least close enough to it to keep track of what happens there. Under such circumstances, it is surprising how much good work does get done.

History is a cumulative study in the sense that historians build on each other's work. Dissertations in history invariably begin with a survey of the literature on the subject in question. As noted earlier, one of the peculiarities of the Hart/O'Hart case was the complete lack of prior scholarship about the man. And there is "progress" in history in the sense that we come to know more and more about the history of particular subjects as one study succeeds another. But this progress is not the result of any systematic process of testing historical hypotheses. It is a haphazard process that lurches forward by fits and starts. Nevertheless, knowledge does increase over time, in spite of the unsystematic character of the process of testing historical theories.

Conclusion

The Logic of History

History, as all historians agree, is a form of empirical knowledge. Accordingly, the logic of history is similar to that of other forms of empirical knowledge. The basis of historical work is evidence, which as every philosopher of history, from Collingwood on, has agreed, consists of observations made on artifacts from the past. Historical theories rest upon, and explain, these observations of artifacts—usually documentary but also including many other types of evidence. It follows that the historian's basic task is the finding and interpretation of such artifacts. A fortunate historian may find that all of the evidence he needs is neatly collected in a single place, such as the National Archives, but this is rare—usually the evidence must be found. I recall one eminent historian remarking, with respect to a work on South American slavery, on the fact that its author had found much of his best evidence in the Vatican Archives in Rome. "How did he know to look there?" my distinguished historian asked. That is precisely the question that every historian has to ask: Where is the evidence, and how can I get it? This is why I have emphasized the fact that historians predict, and what they predict is what they can find and where they can find it. I used the Hart/O'Hart case as an example of a problem where there was no secondary literature and no archived material, so the evidence had to be assembled from scratch. The search for evidence is rarely, if ever, blind; one is guided by hypotheses concerning what the relevant evidence might be. One may be wrong, as one will discover in the course of one's research, but one is often right. And how else could one proceed? Searching all of the databases of the world is not a viable option for one who will grow old. Prediction and test are the only way one can proceed.

Given the emphasis on hypotheses and theories in this book, the question of where these hypotheses and theories come from is inescapable. Finding the right hypothesis or theory is the process Peirce called "abduction," and what more recent writers have called "inference to the best explanation." But as Peirce and later writers have made clear, there is no formal abductive logic that will lead an investigator from a given set of data to the best explanatory hypothesis. What can be said is that when an investigator has mastered his data thoroughly, then he will be in a position to recognize an explanatory hypothesis when he meets it. Just how this will occur cannot be predicted. Kekule had worked long and hard on the problem of the molecular structure of benzene, so that when in a dream he saw two snakes take hold of each others' tails, he recognized that a ring structure would solve his problem. But if he had not worked so hard for so long on that problem, then he would not have recognized the solution when he saw it. Once one has thoroughly mastered the data, one is in a position to recognize a likely hypothesis, if it is suggested. But it may not be suggested. Many investigations lead to dead ends, because the investigator is never able to find an adequate explanatory hypothesis. This is the risk we all take when we invest years of work in a given problem. We may not find an answer, there may not *be* an answer, or there may be one that eludes us. This is why luck and imagination are ineliminable features of our work.

There is, however, a general principle that can serve as a useful guide and goal here. In statistics, the preferred method of estimating a parameter is the maximum likelihood method. In history, we rarely, if ever, have a likelihood function to maximize, but the general idea is applicable. Given some set of data, what we want is that hypothesis or theory that maximizes the probability of our having just this set of data. That is, we want that hypothesis or theory that gives us the maximum probability of our having the data we have. Since we do not have a likelihood function to maximize, we cannot say that the hypothesis or theory we have is the best, but we can compare it to alternative hypotheses or theories and choose that which does the best job in accounting for our data. But to "account" for the data also means to explain why we have the data we have. Thus a hypothesis about the Russian Revolution would not only have to make the surviving data probable but would have to compensate for the fact that the Stalinist regime sought to change the history of that event by, for example, destroying evidence concerning the significance of the role played by Trotsky. Thus if we have two hypotheses or theories—call them A and B—both of which account for our set of data—then we will prefer that one on the basis of which the occurrence of this data is most probable. Of course, in the historical case, the probability spoken of must be subjective probability, since we almost never have frequency-based probability functions, but subjective probabilities can usually do the job. Or, one can ask oneself, given that

A is true, what are the odds we would have just this set of data, and are the odds if A is true, greater, or less than those if B is true?

As this suggests, historians working on a particular subject are well advised to try to formulate alternative hypotheses or theories that will account for their data. It does happen, more often than one might think, that the first hypothesis or theory that one comes up with in the course of research will not prove as satisfactory as a subsequent hypothesis or theory created after further reflection. Furthermore, if one is writing about a subject upon which other historians have written, there will be no lack of alternative hypotheses or theories for comparison. Suppose that you are researching the election of 1896, and you want to determine the most significant cause of Bryan's defeat. One hypothesis might be that his advocacy of free silver frightened the business classes who thought a Bryan victory would take the United States off the gold standard. Certainly there is considerable support for this hypothesis in the campaign literature of the time. But knowing that Bryan was a fervent evangelical Protestant, one might also hypothesize that his religious beliefs and statements cost him the election. Which cause was the more important? Since we have the actual voting statistics for 1896, we can tell that many normally Democratic urban workers—particularly those who were Catholic—went for McKinley. This would be probable on the second hypothesis, but not on the first. Certainly the silver issue was *an* important factor in the election, but the business classes would normally have been Republican anyway, although they were especially so in 1896. Bryan hoped to create an alliance of farmers and workers, but the voting statistics show that he failed.

Historians see themselves as dealing with facts. But it should be obvious that most historians have not observed the facts they describe—certainly this is true for all facts of the deep past, and even in dealing with the recent past, no historian relies on his own memory alone. If history is an empirical discipline, and if it deals with facts not observed by the historian or—usually—by anyone now alive, then what is the status of the "facts"? I think it is clear that what are called "the facts" are hypothetical constructs postulated by the historian, because by doing so he can account for the evidence he has. "Evidence" is a relative term, relating something observed now to a hypothesis or theory. A document by itself is just something with writing on it. It becomes historical evidence only when it contains information relevant to hypotheses about persons or events in the past.

Historical accounts are theories in the simple and obvious sense that they are sets of statements about persons and events in the past that explain and account for the presently existing evidence. To say, for example, that Nathaniel Bacon led a revolt in Virginia in 1676 is to assert the existence of events and persons that no one now alive has witnessed. Of course, the support for that statement must be indirect; it is the simplest and most likely explanation of a fairly large body of data that we now have. Because the data are what would be expected to have been created by those past persons who witnessed the revolt or heard about it, they support the hypothesis.

Skeptics who claim that historical accounts cannot be true seem to me to have missed the point. Of course, it is important to examine how the theory was constructed, how the research was done, how extensive the body of evidence was, and so on. We know enough about theory construction to know that the better the research, the better the theory will likely be. But the fundamental question is whether or not the theory is true. That question can only be answered by testing the theory *after it has been created.* How could we know which one of several competing accounts of the American Revolution (if any) is true? Clearly we should have to test them by asking, if this account is true, then what evidence should we be able to find? As I stressed earlier, this question involves the further questions of which data could have been created, of which data once created were preserved, and given that the data were created and preserved, where are they? Because various answers to these questions are possible, failure to find data one would expect to find does not disconfirm the theory, although finding data that contradict the theory does. But finding data of the expected sort does go to confirm the theory, particularly if they are data that were not known to the theory's author when he published.

But one should note here that the finding of relevant data is sometimes a matter of sheer luck. No scholar predicted the finding of the Dead Sea Scrolls; had a Bedouin shepherd boy not pitched a rock into a cave and heard something break, they might well be undiscovered yet. Morgan pointed out that the only record we have of what happened in the House of Burgesses when Patrick Henry gave his speech that bordered on treason was found in the diary of an anonymous French traveler who just happened to visit the House on that day.[1] No one could have predicted that. There is an old saying that it takes luck to find something and genius to know what one has found. This is as true in history as it is in science. To recognize what one has found requires that one be so thoroughly familiar with the problem in question that one *can* recognize its relevance. Bone hunters such as the Leakeys had to be lucky to find the hominid bones they found, but it was not just luck; they knew their field so well that they knew where to look and could recognize what they found.

I do not wish to give the impression that matters such as the historian's process of selecting and classifying data are not important. Of course, they are important. There is surely a positive relation between the careful and systematic construction of a theory and its truth. But the processes of theory construction and theory testing are not the same, and the failure to distinguish between them has been the cause of much of the skepticism about history. I have belabored the cases of Friedman and Schwartz, Turner, and Beard precisely to make that point. When I was a young graduate student, we voted in my historiography class on who was the greatest American historian. The winner, almost unanimously, was Charles Beard. Had that vote come a decade later, after Brown, McDonald, and Benson had published, the outcome would have been very different. But it is worth bearing in mind how completely Turner and Beard dominated American history in their time. In hindsight, one is surprised by this. Why, one wonders, were the errors pointed out by Brown, McDonald, and Benson not caught for forty years after Beard published? Why was Turner's thesis so uncritically accepted, when fifty years later his thesis was under scholarly attack? Those who followed in the footsteps of Turner and Beard were not stupid or ignorant; many of them, such as Merle Curti, were distinguished historians in their own right. But the fact that Turner and Beard dominated the field for so long is a demonstration of how inadequate the procedures for testing historical theories were, and, I regret to say, still are.

None of the matters discussed here have anything to do with the question of whether or not history is a science. That is, I believe, an unfortunate question; it presupposes a precise definition of "science" that I doubt can be given. There are many sciences, and they answer to different criteria. But since this issue has been raised by not a few writers, some comment is required. First, there are sciences that investigate the past: Cosmology is one, the Big Bang was a historical event, and Geology, Paleontology, and evolutionary Biology are other examples. But if the definition of "history" is narrowed to involve only the study of the past of Homo sapiens, or even Homo sapiens' history since the invention of writing, then if history is a science, it must be a social science—indeed, it must include all of the social sciences, since we have political history, economic history, social history, and so on. But there are significant differences between history and the social sciences, most of which are due to the differences in the kinds of data used in the two fields. While there are probably no questions asked in the social sciences that are not asked in history, the difference in the data means that different methods are usually employed. It is characteristic of historical data that they are fragmentary and incomplete, and that new data cannot be generated at will. The social scientist can talk to his subjects, provoke them to respond, question them and get answers, and observe them under conditions fixed by the investigator. The historian can do none of these things. Many of the techniques of the social sciences require complete populations or complete response sets—complete enough so that nonresponse is not a problem. Questionnaires and interviews present stimuli to their subjects and record their responses. Such data are very rarely available to the historian. Social scientists can sample the populations that are of interest to them. Usually, historians cannot, and so much of the statistical apparatus used in the social sciences cannot be applied in history, except in very special cases. Does this mean that history is not a science? I do not know, and I think the question itself is too ill defined to permit an answer, nor do I think the question is important. What is important is that, as most historians agree, history is an empirical discipline the goal of which is truth. What I have presented in this book is merely the working out of the consequences of that claim. History is also an empirical discipline that could, and should, do better in developing its methodology, in the construction and, above all, in the testing of its theories. If that is granted, then I shall be quite content.

Notes

Preface

    1. Charles Langlois and M. J. C. Seignobos, *Introduction to the Study of History*, trans. G. G. Berry (London: Duckworth, 1912).
    2. Paul de Man, *Allegories of Reading* (New Haven, CT: Yale University Press, 1979), ch. 3.

Chapter 1   Metaphysics and Epistemology

    1. A. P. Elkin, *The Australian Aborigines: How to Understand Them* (Sydney: Angus and Robertson, 1959); W. E. H. Stanner, *On Aboriginal Religion* (Sydney: Australian National Research Council, 1963).
    2. C. I. Lewis, *An Analysis of Knowledge and Valuation* (LaSalle, IL: Open Court Press, 1971), ch. 11, sect. 11.
    3. Ibid., 332–62.
    4. R. G. Collingwood, *The Idea of History* (Oxford: Oxford University Press, 1961), 246–47.
    5. Patti Block, *Weeping Water Legend* (Lincoln: Nebraska State Historical Society, 1995).
    6. W. V. Quine, "Reply to Chomsky," in *Words and Objections*, ed. Donald Davidson and Jaakko Hintikka, 309 (Dordrecht: D. Reidel, 1969).
    7. Moritz Schlick, "Meaning and Verification," in *Philosophical Papers*, vol. 2, ed. Henk Mulder and Barbara van de Velde-Schlick, 456–81 (Dordrecht: D. Reidel, 1979).
    8. A. J. Ayer, *The Problem of Knowledge* (Baltimore, MD: Penguin Books, 1962), 157–58.
    9. Ibid., 158.
    10. Ibid., 176.
    11. Murray G. Murphey, *Our Knowledge of the Historical Past* (Indianapolis, IN: Bobbs-Merrill, 1973), ch. 1.
    12. Bas van Fraassen, *The Scientific Image* (Oxford: Clarendon Press, 1980).

13. Michael Dummett, "The Reality of the Past," in *Truth and Other Enigmas* (Cambridge, MA: Harvard University Press, 1978).

14. Michael Dummett, "Statements about the Past," *Journal of Philosophy* 100 (2002): 28, 36; Dummett, *Truth and the Past* (New York: Columbia University Press, 2004), 44.

15. Dummett, *Truth and the Past*, 44–45, 65–66.

16. Dummett, "Statements about the Past," 32–36; "The Metaphysics of Time," 39; *Truth*, 62–70.

17. Dummett, "The Metaphysics of Time"; *Truth*, 62–70.

18. Joachim Fest, *Inside Hitler's Bunker* (New York: Farrar, Strauss and Giroux, 2004).

19. Dummett, "The Metaphysics," 42–43; *Truth*, 62–68.

20. Dummett, "The Metaphysics," 39; *Truth*, 68–70.

21. Hilary Putnam, "The Meaning of Meaning," in *Mind Language and Reality*, 227–29 (Cambridge: Cambridge University Press, 1975).

22. Ibid., 66–67.

23. Frank Anderson, *The Mystery of "A Public Man"* (Minneapolis: University of Minnesota Press, 1948).

24. Dummett, "The Metaphysics," 42–43; *Truth*, 68.

25. Fest, *Inside Hitler's Bunker*.

26. Dummett, *Truth*, 73–86.

27. Ibid., 74.

28. Ibid., 75.

29. Ibid., 92.

Chapter 2   Evidence

1. Collingwood, *The Idea of History*, 246–47.

2. Murray G. Murphey, *Philosophical Foundations of Historical Knowledge* (Albany: State Univesity of New York Press, 1994), chs. 1, 6.

3. Sam Jaffe, "Scientists Puzzle over Ancient Ossuary," *The Scientist* (April 12, 2004): 48–49.

4. Thomas Marston, "Recent History and Acquisition," in *The Vinland Map and the Tarter Relation*, 2d ed., ed. R. A. Skelton, Thomas Marston and George Painter, 4 (New Haven, CT: Yale University Press, 1995).

5. George Painter, "The Tarter Relation," in *The Vinland Map*, 21–23.

6. Marston, "Recent History," in *The Vinland Map*, 6–11.

7. Ibid., 10, emphasis in original.

8. Lawrence Witten, "Vinland's Saga Recalled," in *The Vinland Map*, xli–lviii.

9. Painter, "Introduction," in *The Vinland Map*, ix–xii.

10. Thomas Cahill and Bruce Kusko, "Compositional and Structural Studies of the Vinland Map and the Tarter Relation," in *The Vinland Map*, xxix–xxxviii.

11. Katherine Brown and Robin Clark, "Analysis of Pigmentary Materials on the Vinland Map and the Tarter Relation by Raman Microprobe Spectroscopy," *Analytical Chemistry* 74 (2002): 3659, 3661.

12. Brown and Clark, "Analysis," 3661.

13. Cf. W. Washburn, ed., *Proceedings of the Vinland Map Conference*, (Chicago: University of Chicago Press, 1971).

14. Murphey, *Our Knowledge*, ch. 2.

15. Marston, "Recent History," in *The Vinland Map*, 6–9.

16. Stanley Fish, *Is There a Text in This Class?* (Cambridge, MA: Harvard University Press, 1980), 322 ff.

17. Murphey, *Philosophical Foundations*, chs. 1, 2, 6.

18. Eve V. Clark, "Meaning and Concepts," in *Cognitive Development*, ed. John M. Flavell and Ellen Markman, 788, vol. 3, *Handbook of Child Psychology*, gen. ed. Paul Mussen (New York: Wiley, 1983).

19. John L. Austin, *How to Do Things with Words* (New York: Oxford University Press, 1965).

20. Collingwood, *The Idea of History*, 275.

21. Edward E. Hale, *Letter on Irish Immigration* (Boston, MA: Phillips, Sampson, and Co., 1850), 53.

22. Thomas Shepard, "A Defense of the Answer" in *The Puritans*, ed. Perry Miller and Thomas Johnson, 118 (New York: American Book Co., 1938).

23. Jonathan Edwards, *Freedom of the Will*, ed. Paul Ramsey, 147 (New Haven, CT: Yale University Press, 1957).

24. *The Book of the General Laws and Liberties Concerning the Inhabitants of the Massachusetts* (Cambridge, MA: Hezekiah Usher, 1648), 51, emphasis in original.

25. Anderson, *The Mystery of "A Public Man,"* 3.

26. Ibid., 68–69.

27. Ibid., 36–41.

28. Ibid., 65.

29. Ibid., 135.

30. Ibid., 93–102.

31. Ibid., 97–102.

32. Ibid., 124.

33. Ibid., 141–44.

34. Ibid., 146–78.

35. Ibid., 170.

36. Roy Lokken, "Has the Mystery of "A Public Man" Been Solved?," *Mississippi Valley Historical Review* 40 (1953): 419–40.

37. Frank Anderson, "Has the Mystery of "A Public Man" Been Solved— A Rejoinder," *Mississippi Valley Historical Review* 42 (1955): 101–107. Roy Lokken, "Has the Mystery of "A Public Man" Been Solved—A Rejoinder: Reply," *Mississippi Valley Historical Review* 42 (1955): 107–109.

38. Frederick Mosteller and David Wallace, *Applied Bayesian and Classical Inference: The Case of the Federalist Papers* (New York: Springer-Verlag, 1984).

39. Jonathan Edwards, *Religious Affections*, ed. John Smith, 75–77 (New Haven, CT: Yale University Press, 1959).

40. Leon Goldstein, *Historical Knowing* (Austin: University of Texas Press, 1976).

41. Murphey, *Our Knowledge*, 144.

Chapter 3   Explanation

1. Michael Scriven, "Truisms as the Grounds for Historical Explanations," in *Theories of History*, ed. Patrick Gardiner, 452 (Glencoe, IL: Free Press, 1962).

2. Carl Hempel and Paul Oppenheim, "Studies in the Logic of Explanation," *Philosophy of Science* 15 (1948): 135–75. Reprinted in Carl Hempel, *Aspects of Scientific Explanation* (New York: Free Press, 1965), 245–90.

3. Carl Hempel, "The Function of General Laws in History," in *Aspects*, 231–41; Carl Hempel, "Inductive Statistical Explanation," in *Aspects*, 381–410.

4. Donald Davidson, *Essays on Actions and Events* (Oxford: Clarendon Press, 1980), 160.

5. David Hume, *A Treatise of Human Nature* (Oxford: Clarendon Press, 1949), 155–72; David Hume, "An Abstract of a Treatise of Human Nature," in *An Inquiry Concerning Human Understanding and an Abstract of a Treatise of Human Nature*, ed. Charles Hendel (Indianapolis, IN: Bobbs-Merrill, 1955).

6. David Hume, *Enquiry Concerning the Human Understanding and Concerning the Principles of Morals* (Oxford: Clarendon Press, 1946), 76, emphasis in original.

7. Hume, *A Treatise*, 155–56.

8. Patrick Suppes, *A Probabilistic Theory of Causality* (Amsterdam: North Holland Press, 1970), 30–33.

9. Nelson Goodman, *Fact, Fiction, and Forecast* (Cambridge, MA: Harvard University Press, 1955), 24–25.

10. Hume, *Enquiry*, 70–71.

11. J. L. Mackie, *The Cement of the Universe* (Oxford: Clarendon Press, 1986), 37.

12. Ibid., 55.

13. Ibid., 53–54.

14. Saul Kripke, "A Completeness Theorem for Modal Logic," *Journal of Symbolic Logic* 24 (1959): 1–14.

15. David Lewis, *Counterfactuals* (Cambridge, MA: Harvard University Press, 1973), 4–8.

16. David Lewis, *On the Plurality of Worlds* (New York: Basil Blackwell, 1982).

17. Lewis, *Counterfactuals*, 16–20.

18. Ibid., 20.

19. Allen Tate, *Stonewall Jackson* (Ann Arbor: University of Michigan Press, 1965), 320.

20. Nancy Cartwright, *How the Laws of Physics Lie* (Oxford: Clarendon Press, 1983).
21. Ibid., 3.
22. Nancy Cartwright, *Nature's Capacities and Their Measurement* (Oxford: Clarendon Press, 1989).
23. Ibid., 2.
24. Ibid., 2, 95.
25. Ibid., 226.
26. Ibid., 163, 181.
27. Ibid., 181.
28. Ibid., 144.
29. Ibid., 228.
30. Ibid.
31. David Armstrong, *A Combinatorial Theory of Possibility* (Cambridge: Cambridge University Press, 1989), 40–43.
32. David Armstrong, *A World of States of Affairs* (Cambridge: Cambridge University Press, 1997), 202.
33. Ibid., 217.
34. Ibid., 225.
35. Ibid., 227.
36. Richard W. Miller, *Fact and Method* (Princeton, NJ: Princeton University Press, 1987), 78.
37. H. L. A. Hart and A. N. Honore, *Causation in the Law* (Oxford: Clarendon Press, 1859), 26.
38. Ibid., 27.
39. Ibid., 48–55.
40. Ibid., 55–57.
41. Ibid., 52.
42. Hume, "An Abstract," 186–87.
43. A. Michotte, *The Perception of Causality* (New York: Basic Books, 1963).
44. Ibid., 28–32.
45. Ibid., ch. 3.
46. Ibid., 103.
47. Ibid., 85–86.
48. Alan Leslie and Stephanie Keeble, "Do Six-Month Old Infants Perceive Causality?," *Cognition* 25 (1987): 265–88; Alan Leslie, "The Perception of Causality in *Infants*," *Perception* 11 (1982): 173–86; "Spatiotemporal Causality and the Perception of Causality in Infants," *Perception* 13 (1984): 287–305; "Getting Development Off the Ground: Modularity and the Infant's Perception of Causality," in *Theory Building in Development*, ed. Paul van Geert, 405–37 (Amsterdam: North Holland, 1986).
49. Noam Chomsky, *Cartesian Linguistics* (New York: Harper and Row, 1966).
50. Armstrong, *A World*, 213; Evan Fales, *Causation and Universals* (London: Routledge, 1990), ch. 1.

51. Albert Bandura, "Exercise of Personal and Collective Efficacy in Changing Societies," in *Self-Efficacy in Changing Societies,* ed. Albert Bandura, 1–45 (Cambridge: Cambridge University Press, 1995); Albert Bandura, *Self-Efficacy: The Exercise of Control* (New York: W. H. Freeman, 1997).

52. W. V. Quine, *The Roots of Reference* (LaSalle, IL: Open Court Press, 1973), 4–8.

53. Charles S. Peirce, *The Collected Papers of Charles Sanders Peirce,* edited by Charles Hartshorne and Paul Weiss (Cambridge, MA: Harvard University Press, 1935), 6.12.

54. C. I. Lewis, *Mind and the World Order* (New York: Dover, 1929), 334.

55. James Woodward, *Making Things Happen* (Oxford: Oxford University Press, 2003).

56. Suppes, *A Probabilistic Theory.*

57. Armstrong, *A World,* 238.

58. John Stuart Mill, *System of Logic* (London: Longmans, Green and Co., 1886), 253–99.

59. Mackie, *The Cement of the Universe,* 62.

60. Armstrong, *A World,* 242–48.

61. Isek Ajzen, *Attitudes, Personality, and Behavior* (Chicago: Dorsey, 1988).

62. Murphey, *Philosophical Foundations,* ch. 5. Any discussion of rules and rule following must deal with the problems raised by Wittgenstein and Kripke. I have done this in the book just cited; see pages 188–98.

63. Karin Calvert, *Children in the House* (Boston, MA: Northeastern University Press, 1992).

64. John Kasson, *Rudeness and Civility* (New York: Hill and Wang,1990), 189.

65. Ibid., 143.

66. Robert Fogel and Stanley Engermann, *Time on the Cross* (Boston, MA: Little, Brown and Co., 1974), 2 vols.

67. Paul David, Herbert Gutman, Richard Sutch, Peter Temin, and Gavin Wright, *Reckoning with Slavery* (New York: Oxford University Press, 1976).

Chapter 4   Theory

1. Quine, "Reply to Chomsky," in *Words and Objections,* ed. Donald Davidson and Jaakko Hintikka, 309 (Dordrecht: D. Reidel, 1969).

2. Arthur M. Schlesinger Jr., *The Age of Jackson* (Boston, MA: Little Brown and Co., 1946).

3. Herbert Croly, *The Promise of American Life* (New York: Macmillan, 1912).

4. Lee Benson, *The Concept of Jacksonian Democracy* (Princeton, NJ: Princeton University Press, 1961).

5. Ibid., 329.

6. Elaine Pagels, *Beyond Belief* (New York: Random House, 2004).

7. Ibid., 31–38, 42–44.

8. Ibid., 34–35.

9. Burnett Streeter, *The Four Gospels* (London: Macmillan, 1964), 10–15.

10. Pagels, *Beyond Belief*, 227–42.

11. Risto Uro, *Thomas at the Crossroads* (Edinburgh: T&T Clark, 1998), 1.

12. Ibid., 13–31.

13. Ibid., 33, 60–66.

14. Ibid., 40.

15. Gregory Riley, *Resurrection Reconsidered* (Minneapolis, MN: Fortress Press, 1995), 178.

16. Ibid., 178.

17. Pagels, *Beyond Belief*, 54, emphasis in original.

18. Ibid., 53.

19. Ibid., 57.

20. Ibid., 58.

21. Ibid., 80.

22. Ibid., 128.

23. Ibid., 134–50.

24. Ibid., 111–12.

25. Ibid., 171–73,

26. Ibid., 172–78.

27. Ibid., 168.

28. *The New English Bible*, edited by Samuel Sandmel et al. (New York: Oxford University Press, 1972), Mark 1:9.

29. Ibid., Luke 3:21.

30. Ibid., Matthew 3: 13–16.

31. Benson, *The Concept*, 276.

32. Richard Jensen, *The Winning of the Midwest* (Chicago: University of Chicago Press, 1971).

33. Paul Kleppner, *The Third Electoral System 1853–1892* (Chapel Hill: University of North Carolina Press, 1979).

34. V. O. Key, "A Theory of Critical Elections," *Journal of Politics* 17 (1955): 16.

35. Benson, *The Concept*, 121–31.

36. Angus Campbell, Philip Converse, Warren Miller, and Donald Stokes, *The American Voter* (New York: Wiley, 1964).

37. John Demos, *Entertaining Satan* (New York: Oxford University Press, 1982), 131–33.

38. Paul Boyer and Stephen Nissenbaum, *Salem Possessed* (Cambridge, MA: Harvard University Press, 1974).

39. Ibid., 213.

40. Demos, *Entertaining Satan*.

41. Ibid., 371–77.
42. Ibid., 337–79.
43. Ibid., 380–86.
44. Ibid., 181–82.
45. Ibid., 380–86.
46. Ibid., 370.
47. Ibid., 309.
48. Ibid., 310.
49. Ibid., 206.
50. Carol Karlsen, *The Devil in the Shape of a Woman* (New York: Random House, 1987).
51. Ibid., 47.
52. Ibid., 71–72.
53. Ibid., 67.
54. Ibid., 71.
55. Ibid., 128.
56. Ibid., 140.
57. Ibid., 142–44.
58. Ibid., 217.
59. Ibid.
60. Ibid.
61. Ibid.
62. Ibid., 223.
63. Ibid., 166, emphasis in original.
64. Bernard Rosenthal, *Salem Story* (Cambridge: Cambridge University Press, 1993).
65. Ibid., 185.
66. Ibid., 53, 121.
67. Ibid., 61.
68. Ibid., 50.
69. Ibid., 49.
70. Ibid., 55, 60–61, 110.
71. Ibid., 197–201.
72. Ibid., 60.
73. Samuel Stouffer, et al., *The American Soldier* (New York: John Wiley and Sons, 1965), 2 vols.
74. Robert K. Merton, *Social Theory and Social Structure*, rev. ed. (Glencoe, IL: Free Press, 1957), chs. 8, 9.
75. Anthony F. C. Wallace, "Paradigmatic Processes in Culture Change," *American Anthropologist* 74 (1972): 467–78.
76. Thomas S. Kuhn, *The Structure of Scientific Revolutions*, rev. ed. (Chicago: University of Chicago Press, [1962] 1970), 10, 70.
77. Ibid. Kuhn's theory is detailed in *The Structure*.
78. Paul Hoyningen-Huene, *Reconstructing Scientific Revolutions: Thomas S. Kuhn's Philosophy of Science* (Chicago: University of Chicago Press, 1993), 26; Kuhn, *The Structure*, 100–101, 109–10, 172–73.

79. Kuhn, *The Structure*, 206–207.

80. Thomas S. Kuhn, *The Copernican Revolution* (Cambridge, MA: Harvard University Press,1957), 59, 64 ff, 80.

81. Kuhn, *The Structure*, 148, 150–62; Kuhn, *The Road since Structure* (Chicago: University of Chicago Press, 2000), 35–36.

82. Kuhn, *The Structure*, 150, ch. 10.

83. Kuhn, *The Road*, 15–17.

84. Ibid., 44, 65–75.

85. Kuhn, *The Structure*, 167–70; Kuhn, *The Essential Tension* (Chicago: University of Chicago Press, 1977), 211–12.

86. Kuhn, *The Structure*, 104–106.

87. Ibid., 170–73.

88. Ibid., 155 ff.

89. Ibid., 168 ff; Kuhn, *The Road*, 109–10.

90. Kuhn, *The Essential Tension*, 291.

91. Kuhn, *The Road*, 96–100.

Chapter 5   Narrative

1. Miller Perry, *The New England Mind: The Seventeenth Century* (New York: Macmillan, 1939).

2. Peter Temin, *Did Monetary Forces Cause the Great Depression?* (New York: Norton, 1976).

3. Fogel and Engermann, *Time on the Cross*.

4. Peter Temin, *Lessons from the Great Depression* (Cambridge, MA: MIT Press, 1989).

5. W. H. Dray, "Narrative and Historical Realism" in *The History and Narrative Reader*, ed. Geoffrey Roberts, 157–80 (London: Routledge, 2001).

6. Noel Carroll, "Interpretation, History, and Narrative," in *The History and Narrative Reader*, 261.

7. Francois Furet, "From Narrative History to Problem Oriented History," in *The History and Narrative Reader*, 270.

8. Lawrence Stone, "The Revival of Narrative: Reflections on a New Old History," in *The History and Narrative Reader*, 281.

9. Edgar Kiser, "The Revival of Narrative in Historical Sociology," in *The History and Narrative Reader*, 323.

10. Margaret Somers, "Narrativity, Narrative History, and Social Action," in *The History and Narrative Reader*, 360.

11. William Cronin, "A Place for Stories: Nature, History, and Narrative," in *The History and Narrative Reader*, 411.

12. Ibid., 426.

13. Donald Spence, *Narrative Truth and Historical Truth* (New York: W. W. Norton, 1982), 180.

14. Seymour Chatman, *Story and Discourse* (Ithaca, NY: Cornell University Press, 1978), 19–20.

15. Jean-Francois Lyotard, *The Postmodern Condition* (Minneapolis: University of Minnesota Press, 1993), 19.

16. Ibid., 2.

17. Michael Scriven, "Truisms as the Grounds for Historical Explanations," in *Theories of History*, ed. Patrick Gardiner, 470 (Glencoe, IL: Free Press, 1959).

18. William Labov, "The Transformation of Experience in Narrative Syntax," in *Language of the Inner City*, ed. William Labov, 359–60 (Philadelphia: University of Pennsylvania Press, 1972).

19. Ibid., 363.

20. Ibid., 370.

21. Ibid., 364.

22. Ibid., 366.

23. Ibid., 369.

24. Ibid., 368.

25. Nelson Goodman, *Languages of Art* (New York: Bobbs-Merrill, 1968), 52 ff.

26. Thomas Jefferson Wertenbaker, *Bacon's Rebellion 1676* (Williamsburg: Virginia 350th Anniversary Corporation, 1957), 58.

27. Perry Miller, *The New England Mind: From Colony to Province* (Cambridge, MA: Harvard University Press, 1953), 20–33.

28. Murray G. Murphey, "Signs, Acts, and Objects," *Social Science History* 11 (1987): 211–32.

29. Morton White, *Foundations of Historical Knowledge* (New York: Harper and Row, 1965).

30. Charles Beard, "Written History as an Act of Faith," *American Historical Review* 39 (1934): 219–29.

31. Carl Becker, *Everyman His Own Historian* (New York: Appleton-Century-Crofts, 1935).

32. Murphey, *Our Knowledge*, ch. 2.

33. Sidney Fay, *The Origins of the World War* (New York: Macmillan, 1929), 2 vols.

34. Ernest Nagel, *The Structure of Science* (New York: Harcourt, Brace and World, 1961), 583–85.

35. David Hackett Fischer, *Paul Revere's Ride* (New York: Oxford Univeristy Press, 1984), 148.

36. Labov, *Language of the Inner City*, 366–78.

37. David McCullough, *John Adams* (New York: Simon and Schuster, 2002).

38. Robert Caro, *The Path to Power* (New York: Knopf, 1982); *Means of Ascent* (New York: Knopf, 1990); *Master of the Senate* (New York: Knopf, 2002).

39. Hayden White, *Figural Realism* (Baltimore, MD: Johns Hopkins University Press, 1999), 32–33.

40. David Reynolds, *In Command of History* (New York: Random House, 2005).

41. Peter Green, *Alexander of Macedon* (Berkeley: University of California Press, 1991).

42. Karl Mannhein, *Ideology and Utopia* (New York: Harcourt, Brace and World, 1936), 57.

43. Ibid., 55.

44. Richard Bushman, *Believing History* (New York: Columbia University Press, 2005).

45. White, *Figural Realism*, 7–8.

46. Hayden White, *Tropics of Discourse* (Baltimore, MD: Johns Hopkins University Press, 1978), 81.

47. Hayden White, *The Content of the Form* (Baltimore, MD: Johns Hopkins University Press, 1977), 2.

48. Hayden White, *Metahistory* (Baltimore, MD: Johns Hopkins University Press, 1973), 30–31, emphasis in the original.

49. White, *The Content*, 6–21.

50. White, *Metahistory*, ix.

51. White, *Tropics*, 7–13, 20–22; *Figural Realism*, 102 ff.

52. White, *Tropics*, 95, emphasis in the original.

53. White, *The Content*, 102.

54. Ibid., 57.

55. White, *Figural Realism*, 18.

56. White, *The Content*, 65.

57. Ibid., 66.

58. White, *Metahistory*, 6. n5, emphasis in original.

59. White, *Figural Realism*, 143, emphasis added.

60. White, *Tropics*, 70.

61. Ibid., 85.

62. Ibid., 84.

63. White, *Figural Realism*, 42.

64. White, *The Content*, 9.

65. Ibid., 43.

66. White, *Metahistory*, x.

67. Ibid.

68. Ibid., 11–12.

69. Ibid., 22.

70. White, *Tropics*, 41.

71. White, *Metahistory*, 27, emphasis in original.

72. White, *Tropics*, 98.

73. Ibid., 86.

74. Ibid., 5.

75. White, *Metahistory*, 14.

76. Ibid., 15.

77. Ibid., 16–17.

78. Ibid., 18.

79. Ibid., 18–19.

80. White, *Tropics*, 129.

81. Ibid., 70.
82. Ibid., 36–38; *Tropics,* 70–74.
83. White, *Metahistory,* 29.
84. Ibid., 36–38.
85. White, *The Content,* 192.
86. Ibid., x.
87. Ibid., 45–46.
88. Ibid., 40.
89. Ibid., 40–41.
90. White, *Figural Realism,* 9.
91. White, *The Content,* 46.
92. White, *Tropics,* 82, emphasis in original.
93. White, *Metahistory,* 4; *Tropics,* 89, 97.
94. Hayden White, "Historical Emplotment and the Problem of Truth," in *Probing the Limits of Representation,* ed. Saul Friedlander, 50–51 (Cambridge, MA: Harvard University Press, 1992).
95. F. R. Ankersmit, "Interview," in *Encounters,* ed. Eva Domanska, 83 (Charlottesville: University of Virginia Press, 1998).
96. White, *Tropics,* 5–22.
97. Ibid., 22.

Chapter 6   Confirmation 1

1. Keith Windschuttle, *The Killing of History* (Paddington: Macleay, 1996), 270–81.
2. Naomi Quinn and Claudia Strauss, "A Cognitive Cultural Anthropology," in *Human Motives and Cultural Models,* ed. Roy D'Andrade and Claudia Strauss, 229 (Cambridge: Cambridge University Press, 1992), emphasis in original.
3. Robert Redfield, in A. I. Hallowell, *Culture and Experience,* 76 (Philadelphia: University of Pennsylvania Press, 1955).
4. Ibid., 75–110.
5. *Emics and Etics: The Insider/Outsider Debate,* edited by Norman Headland, Kenneth Pike, and Marvin Harris (Newbury Park, CA: Sage Publications, 1990).
6. Murphey, *Our Knowledge,* ch. 2.
7. Roger Schank and Robert Abelson, *Scripts, Plans, Goals, and Understanding* (Hillsdale, NJ: Lawrence Erlbaum, 1977), 45 ff.
8. D'Andrade, *Development.*
9. Ward Goodenough, "In Pursuit of Culture," *Annual Review of Anthropology* 32:1–12 (2004): 7.
10. Conway Zirkle, ed., *The Death of a Science in Russia* (Philadelphia: University of Pennsylvania Press, 1949).
11. Sacvan Bercovitch, ed., *Typology and Early American Literature* (Boston, MA: University of Massachusetts Press, 1972).

12. Windschuttle, *The Killing*, 230–31.

13. Ibid., 137–38; Keith Jenkins, *On "What Is History?"* (New York: Routledge, 1995), 13.

14. This method was suggested to me by Robert Olson.

15. Murphey, *Our Knowledge*, ch. 6.

16. *Custer and His Times*, ed. Gregory Urwin (University of Central Arkansas Press, 1987), 13.

17. Elizabeth Flower and Murray G. Murphey, *A History of Philosophy in America* (New York: Putnam's Sons, 1977), 1, 416.

18. Ralph Waldo Emerson, "Nature," in *Nature, Addresses, and Lectures* (Boston, MA: Houghton Mifflin and Co., 1885), 79–80.

19. Alex Inkeles and Raymond Bauer, *The Soviet Citizen* (Cambridge, MA: Harvard University Press, 1959).

20. Catherine Murdock, *Domesticating Drink* (Baltimore, MD: Johns Hopkins University Press, 1998).

Chapter 7 Confirmation 2

1. Milton Friedman and Anna Schwartz, *A Monetary History of the United States 1867–1960.* (Princeton, NJ: Princeton University Press, 1964).

2. Ibid., 301–302.

3. Ibid., 308.

4. Ibid., 310.

5. Ibid., 315–22, 342–49.

6. Ibid., 349–50.

7. Ibid., 355.

8. Ibid., 314.

9. Ibid., 314–22.

10. Ibid., 352.

11. Ibid., 391.

12. Ibid., 391–406.

13. Ibid., 391.

14. Ibid., 412–13.

15. Ibid., 414.

16. Ibid., 414–19.

17. Peter Temin, *Did Monetary Forces Cause the Great Depression?* (New York: Norton, 1976).

18. Ibid., 9–10.

19. Ibid., 10.

20. Ibid., 102.

21. Ibid., 169.

22. Ibid., 166.

23. Ray Allen Billington, *America's Frontier Heritage* (New York: Holt, Rinehart, and Winston, 1966), xii.

24. Frederick Jackson Turner, *The Frontier in American History* (New York: Henry Holt and Co., 1966), 1.

25. Ibid., 11.

26. Ibid.

27. Ibid., 1.

28. Ibid., 22.

29. Ibid., 23.

30. Ibid., 23–24.

31. Ibid., 30.

32. Ibid., 30–32.

33. Ibid., 32.

34. Ibid., 36.

35. Ibid., 21.

36. Ibid., 32.

37. Ibid., 37.

38. *Essays in American History, Dedicated to Frederick Jackson Turner* (New York: Peter Smith, [1910] 1951).

39. Frederick Paxson, *When the West Is Gone* (New York: Henry Holt and Co., 1939), 27.

40. Ibid., 124.

41. Ray Allen Billington, *Westward Expansion* (New York: Macmillan, 1949).

42. Ibid., 743–56.

43. George Pierson, "The Frontier and American Institutions," in *The Turner Thesis*, ed. George R. Taylor, 66 (Boston, MA: D. C. Heath, 1949).

44. Louis Hacker, "Sections—and Classes," in *The Turner Thesis*, 61–64.

45. Benjamin Wright, "Political Institutions and the Frontier," in *The Turner Thesis*, 42–50.

46. Pierson, "The Frontier."

47. Ibid., 68–81.

48. Ibid., 81.

49. Ibid., 68.

50. Ibid., 70.

51. Ibid., 83.

52. Ibid.

53. Merle Curti, *The Making of an American Community* (Stanford, CA: Stanford University Press, 1959), 1.

54. Ibid., 5.

55. Ibid., 7.

56. Ibid., 55.

57. Ibid., 91–96.

58. Ibid., 176–209.

59. Ibid., 105–108.

60. Ibid., 261.

61. Ibid., 295.

62. Ibid., 444.

63. Ibid., 424.

64. Ibid., 447.

65. Ibid., 448.

66. Billington, *America's Frontier Heritage*.

67. Ibid., 32–38.

68. Ibid., 105.

69. Ibid., 235.

70. Patricia Limerick, *The Legacy of Conquest* (New York: Norton, 1987).

71. Ibid., 23.

72. Ibid., ch. 6.

73. Ibid., 87–88, 135–39.

74. Ibid., 135–40.

75. Ibid., 235–58, ch. 8.

76. Ibid., 99–133.

77. Charles Beard, *An Economic Interpretation of the Constitution of the United States* (New York: Macmillan, 1949).

78. Peter Novick, *That Noble Dream* (Cambridge: Cambridge University Press, 1988), 96–98, 240. Robert Brown, *Charles Beard and the Constitution* (Princeton, NJ: Princeton University Press, 1956), 9.

79. Beard, *An Economic Interpretation*, x.

80. Ibid., 15.

81. Ibid., 24.

82. Ibid., 28.

83. Ibid., 32.

84. Ibid., 40.

85. Ibid., 49.

86. Ibid., 51.

87. Ibid., 54.

88. Ibid., 63.

89. Ibid., 64–65.

90. Ibid., 149.

91. Ibid., 149–51.

92. Ibid.

93. Ibid., 150–51.

94. Ibid., 152.

95. Ibid., 154.

96. Ibid., ch. 7.

97. Ibid., 216.

98. Ibid., 251.

99. Ibid.

100. Orin Libby, *The Geographical Distribution of the Vote of the Thirteen States on the Federal Constitution 1787–1788* (New York: B. Franklin, 1969).

101. Beard, *An Economic Interpretation*, 292.

102. Ibid., 292, 324–25.

103. Robert Brown, *Middle-Class Democracy and the Revolution in Massachusetts 1691–1780*. (Ithaca, NY: Cornell University Press, 1955).

104. Robert Brown, *Charles Beard and the Constitution*.

105. Brown, *Middle-Class Democracy*, 19.

106. Ibid., 24, 37, 60.

107. Ibid., 66.

108. Ibid., 401–404

109. Brown, *Charles Beard*, 22.

110. Ibid., 33–34.

111. Ibid., 34.

112. Ibid., 46.

113. Ibid., 63–64.

114. Ibid., 159.

115. Ibid., 89.

116. Ibid., 111, emphasis in original.

117. Ibid., 95.

118. Ibid., 136–37.

119. Ibid., 142–43.

120. Ibid., 195.

121. Forrest McDonald, *We the People* (Chicago: University of Chicago Press, 1958).

122. Ibid., 16–17.

123. Ibid., 92.

124. Ibid., 95.

125. Ibid., 97.

126. Ibid., 100–101, emphasis in original.

127. Ibid., 113–72.

128. Ibid., 225–346.

129. Ibid., 350–55.

130. Ibid., 283.

131. Ibid., 283, 310.

132. Ibid., 357.

133. Ibid., 398.

134. Lee Benson, *Turner and Beard* (New York: Free Press, 1960).

135. Ibid., 153, n1.

136. Ibid., 137–50.

137. Ibid., 153.

138. Ibid., 123, 153.

139. Ibid., 152–62.

140. Ibid., 172–73.

141. Ibid., 173–74.

142. Ibid., 161.

143. Gabriel Kolko, *The Triumph of Conservatism* (Glencoe, IL: Free Press, 1963).

Conclusion

1. Edmund Morgan and Helen Morgan, *The Stamp Act Crisis* (New York: Macmillan, 1963), 122.

Index

Abolitionists, historians interest in, 70

Abraham, evidence for, 8; and Bible, 76

Aggregate demand, in Great Depression, 156

Ajzen, Isek, theory of planned behavior, 65–66

Albany Regency, attacks on, 80

Alcott, Amos Bronson, 148

American Republican Party, electoral support, 87

American Soldier study, and reference groups, 97

American System, and Whigs, 82

Anderson, Frank, and "Diary of a Public Man," 34–35

Ankersmit, F. R., on consistency of Hayden White, 131

Anomalies, definition of, 95

Anthropologists, knowledge of the past, 2

Antimasonic movement, and New York politics, 78–80, Schlesinger on, 82

AntiRealism and history, 1, 5; and van Fraassen, 13; problems of, 14

Antislavery movement, and Jacksonians, 78; and Whigs, 82

Antiwar movement, 111

Application of Historical theories, 152

Archaeology, and new data, 150; of Jews in Egypt, 8; new data; of prehistoric persons, 19; of Sumer, 7

Armstrong, David, and perception of causes, 58–59; and probabilistic cause, 62; theory of cause, 55

Aristotle, beliefs of, 135; and narrative form, 103; physics, 99, 142; Kuhn's discovery of, 100; theory of four elements, 75

Aspirations, economic, in Jacksonian era, 89

Athanasius, and Gospel of John, 86; and Irenaens, 87; and New Testament canon

Austin, John, speech acts, 31

Authorship, determination of, 33

Ayer, A. J., and time travel, 10–11

Bacon, Nathaniel, last words, 38; meaning or rebellion, 108

Bank holiday, 154; failures, causes of, 154; fall in the stock of money, 155; notes, and Jackson, 77; of the United States, 77, 89, 154; runs, 155; war, and Jackson, 77; three waves of, 154

Battle of the Nile, 113

Beard, Charles, and Progressive Movement, 166–167; conflict of personalty and realty, 169; delegate selection and franchise, 167; economic determinism, 151, 166; economic holdings of delegates, 168; economic interpretation, 167; his research, 167; Madison, not Marx, 166–167; misinterpretation of Madison's #10 *Federalist*, 171;

Hart, James O., case, 45; research on, 40–46

Hegelian theory, 97, 99

Hempel, Carl, ix, explanation in history, 47–48

Henry, Patrick, 45

Higher criticism of the Bible, 142

Historical, accounts and ideology, 120; and lay readers, 113; as empirical discipline, 182; as fictions, 120; alternative hypotheses, 179; data of, 72; explanation, 70, 73; events in, 1223; field of, 123; functional explanation, 110; interpretations as theories, 75; knowledge of, 6; narratives, 120

Historical prediction, 177; research, 40–46; societies, 38

Historical theories, account for evidence, 180; as accounts of particular subjects, 26; and coherence, 76; and the data, 75; and evidence, 177; as explanations of data, 75; as grand theory, 76; as selective, 75; confirmation of, 135; consistency of, 75; constructs in, 133; testing of

Historians, and their audience, 176; choice of subjects, 70, 113; models of the past, 109; work of, 24

History, and social science, 182; and present problems, 126; as cumulative study, 176; as empirical knowledge, 177; as interpretative discipline, 1031 as perspectival, 143; correcting by history, 25; as science, 143, 181; meaning of, 1; objectivity of, 143; of history, 117; of the 1960s, 112

Hitler, Adolph, suicide of, 16, 19, 20, 32; judgments on, 115

Hoew, William, 6

Hoyningan-Huene, Paul, Kuhn's theory of science, 99

Hubble, Edwin, 4

Human action, explanation of by desire and belief, 65

Humean position, on cause, 49, 67

Hume, David, and counterfactual conditional, 59; on cause, 49; on innate ideas, 58; on perception of cause, 56; on regularity, 55; paradigm case of cause, 56–57; regularity as evidence of cause, 60

Hutchinson, Thomas, on witchcraft, 95

Hutton, James, and age of the earth, 3

Hypotheses, classificatory, 25, 29; explanatory, 5

Incommensurability of paradigms, 99–109

Idealism, linguistic and skepticism, 12–13

Idealists, and history, 5

Identifying single individuals, Hart/O'Hart, 136

Ideology, and history, 131; and truth, 120–121, 126.; of Jacksonians, 78; types of, 127

Illocutionary act, 31

Immersion in the period, 135

Impossibility, physical and logical, 9

Indians, Northeast Woodland, 8

Indian Rights Movement, 60, 111; influence on Frontier Thesis, 165

Inductive logic, 178

Indus Valley Civilization, script of, 19

Inevitability, in historical narrative, 110

Inference to the best explanation, 177

Influence of society on historical works, 175

Ink, and dating manuscripts, 27

Inkeles, Alex, *The Soviet Citizen*, 149

Innate ideas, 58

Interest rates, in Great Depression, 157

Linguistic, substitution for past
events, 128; turn, and history, 121
Locke, John, on innate ideas, 58
Locofocos, 78
Logic, modal, 51; of history, 177
Lokken, Roy, on "Public Man," 36
Lounsbury, Floyd, componential
analysis, 137
Luck, in historical research, 180
Luke, on the baptism of Jesus,
87–88
Lysenko affair, in Soviet Union, 140

Mackie J. L., causal field, 63; causal
selection, 62; on cause, 50; on
possible worlds, 51
Madison, James, 13; and *Federalist,*
36
Mannheim,Karl, and ideology, 120–
121
Mark, Gospel of, 83, 87–88
Marx, Karl, as social thinker, 102;
grand theory of, 97–99
Masons, as conspiracy, 80
Masssachusetts, as equalitarian, 169;
church members, 33
Material culture, and historical data,
157; and rules, 69
Mather, Increase, on witchcraft, 91
Matthew, and baptism of Jesus,
87–88
Maximum likelihood method, application to history, 178
Maya, deciphering glyphs, 19, 24
Maysville veto, 77, 90
McCrone, Walter, and Vinland Map,
27
McDonald, Forrest, Beard on ratifica-
tion, 172; economic divisions, 173;
economic holdings of delegates,
171;economic divisions, 173; falsity of Beard's thesis, 172; no
Personalty-Realty division in Convention, 172; research, 171

Meaning, and emplotment, 125;
change over time, 29; differences in different cultures, 108;
hypotheses, tests of, 108; in present culture, 108; intuitionism of
Dummett, 15; nature of, 29; of
documents, 28; problems of interpretation, 30; truth conditions of,
14
Melville, Herman, functional explanation in *Moby Dick*, 110
Memory, and evidence, 5; and history, 1–2; and knowledge, 3; credibility of, 2
Merton, Robert K., reference group
theory, 97
Metaphysics, and history, 3, 5; Chapter 1; questions in history, 1
Method of difference, 61
Michotte, A., perception of causality,
57–60
Middle voice, definition of, 131
Mill, John Stuart, methods of, 71;
on causes and conditions, 63; on
innate ideas, 58; on regularity, 62
Miller, Perry, 131, 138; character of
his work, 131
Miller, Richard, on cause, 56
Minoan Linear A, 24, 28
Modernist style, 125, 130–131
Module, and cause, 58
Money supply, instability, 77
Monetarist economic theory and
cause of the Great Depression,
154; versus Keynesian theory, 152
Moral beliefs, changes over time, 135
Mormon, book of, 121; photograph-
ing of records, 45
Morgan, Edmund, and evidence
regarding Henry's speech, 180
Morgan, William, disappearance of,
80
Moses, evidence for, 8–9
Mosteller, Frederick, authorship of
Federalist papers, 36

16154207R00121

Printed in Great Britain
by Amazon